40-00

*Hardy's Fables
of Integrity*

HARDY'S FABLES OF INTEGRITY

Woman, Body, Text

MARJORIE GARSON

CLARENDON PRESS · OXFORD
1991

Oxford University Press, Walton Street, Oxford OX2 6DP

Oxford New York Toronto
Delhi Bombay Calcutta Madras Karachi
Petaling Jaya Singapore Hong Kong Tokyo
Nairobi Dar es Salaam Cape Town
Melbourne Auckland
and associated companies in
Berlin Ibadan

Oxford is a trade mark of Oxford University Press

Published in the United States
by Oxford University Press, New York

British Library Cataloguing in Publication Data
Data available
ISBN 0-19-812223-3

Library of Congress Cataloging in Publication Data
Garson, Marjorie.
Hardy's Fables of Integrity
Woman, Body, Text / Marjorie Garson
Includes bibliographical references and index.
1. Hardy, Thomas, 1840–1928—Criticism and interpretation.
2. Body, Human, in literature. I. Title
PR4757.B57G37   1991
823'.8—dc20   90-49130
ISBN 0-19-812223-3

Typeset by Downdell Limited, Oxford
Printed and bound in
Great Britain by Bookcraft Ltd
Midsomer Norton, Bath

For Sara

Acknowledgements

It is a pleasure to thank those who have assisted me, advised me, and put up with me during the writing of this book. Financial support came from the Social Sciences and Humanities Research Council of Canada in the form of a Postgraduate Fellowship—other kinds of support from individuals whose names I am happy to have this opportunity to record.

My greatest personal debt is to Jane Millgate and Michael Millgate, my teachers and colleagues at the University of Toronto. It was in Michael Millgate's graduate seminar that I first began thinking seriously about Hardy, and it has been his patient and percipient attention to this manuscript in each of the many forms it has taken which persuaded me that a book was indeed emerging. I have relied upon Jane Millgate's friendship and encouragement throughout all the stages of this project and on her practical support throughout my academic career. Without Jane's and Michael's affection, counsel, and scholarly example, this book would certainly not have been written.

I also want to thank Geoffrey Rockwell, at the University of Toronto Computing Services, and Ian Brodie, for computer help at critical moments; Richard Dellamora, whose interest in this study in its early stages gave me confidence in what I was doing; Judith Williams, who listened patiently as many of the arguments unfolded and made a number of helpful specific suggestions; and Charles Lock, who read the manuscript punctually, intensely, and creatively, and whose detailed suggestions and criticisms helped me refine a number of the points in the argument. Many lively discussions with Sara Beam, whose engagement both with Hardy's novels and with the theoretical issues of this study made her a most valuable confidante and critic, helped me clarify my ideas; I was also able to rely on her scrupulous attention to detail in the preparation of the manuscript. I am grateful to Tim Richards, Penny Forrest, Jordan Richards, and Matthew Beam, for taking for granted that I had to do this—particularly to Matt and Jord, who were living at home when I did it. And, for his love, tolerance, and optimism, I thank Paul Richards, whose eagerness to see this book completed has been equalled only by his faith that it was worth writing.

Contents

Introduction

The study which follows is a reading of seven of Hardy's novels as fables about the constitution of the self and about its inevitable dissolution. It is an attempt to demonstrate how concern about integrity and wholeness—both psychic and bodily—inform and distort Hardy's fictional material. It begins with the human body: both with the bodies of actual human characters and with figurative language which may make the earth, the sky, the heath, the town, the college, the barn, or the house into bodies as well.

Hardy's writing seems to express, albeit somewhat obliquely, what might be called 'somatic anxiety'—anxiety about bodily integrity, fear of corporeal dissolution. Nature in his novels may manifest itself as a fragmented human body, often in rhetorically heightened episodes which demand critical attention: the description of the sticky garden through which Tess walks towards Angel, for example, or the 'Unfulfilled Intentions' passage in *The Woodlanders*, or Bathsheba's experience in the swamp in *Far from the Madding Crowd*.[1] Nature however is not the only vehicle for such concerns, which are also reflected in other images—in certain 'humanoid' figures (like the gargoyle and the quarter-jack in *Far from the Madding Crowd*), in imagery of clothing, and even in some very odd descriptions of clocks and watches. They are also reflected, I shall argue, in plot and in characterization. Many of the instabilities, contradictions, and grotesqueries in the fiction—the 'flaws' to which realistically minded readers have always drawn attention—make considerable sense in the light of this pervasive anxiety.[2]

---

[1] Carpenter (1960) calls such imagery 'grotesque'; Winfield (1973, 37) 'anthropomorphic'; Sumner (1985) 'surrealistic'. Jacobus observes that 'Instead of endowing Nature with everlasting life, the mind endows it with its own threatened death' (1982, 266).

[2] It has recently been argued (Widdowson 1989, Wotton 1985) that 'Hardy', the realist novelist of 'character and environment', is himself a construction—a construction which has led both to the dismissal of the so-called 'minor' novels and to the condemnation of non-realistic features of the 'major' novels. Boumelha (1982),

I have come to the conclusion that there is a mythic subtext in many of Hardy's novels: that beneath and behind the obvious patterns which carry his moral (for the novels always express strong and quite readable moral positions) there is always another story, and that this story may intersect with or turn against the moral fable in interesting and often quite complicated ways. Its plot takes shape around a number of figures who return, again and again, in more or less visible form, to subvert the canny patterns established on the surface of the narrative. To identify some of them here may clarify the specific readings which follow.

There is the Son—sometimes explicitly a Christ-figure— whose filial position is important in his construction. There is the Son's Father: a figure whose absence, weakness, or eclipse exposes the son to woman and to disintegration. There is the Son's Mother, a figure who, when she is presented symbolically (as, for example, the Great Mother Nature in *Far from the Madding Crowd*) may be perceived in positive terms, but who in the form of a person is usually destructive. She often doubles with or aligns with the Other Woman—my phrase is intended to suggest both woman as rival to the Mother and woman as Other—whose own wholeness, however problematical its constitution, exposes male fragmentation. There are the Other Men, who rival or parody the male protagonist, and whose virility is usually an issue: as main characters they tend to be flashily phallic, as 'minor' rustic characters, comically impotent. Behind these human figures, there is Nature the Great Mirror, the Other whose support or confirmation is crucial to the characters' identity and survival, and who often appears either as a splendidly integral or (as in the episodes cited above) as a weirdly fragmented body.

As these remarks will have suggested, I have found some of Lacan's paradigms particularly useful in approaching Hardy,

---

Widdowson (1989), and Goode (1988) call attention both to the socially disruptive dimension of Hardy's fiction and to the way it subverts the assumptions of realism and the liberal-bourgeois ideology from which these assumptions emerge: that is, they construct a 'Hardy' who is both more destructive and more deconstructive than criticism has been able to admit. Wotton (1985), with a somewhat different emphasis, reads the fiction as the site of the production of ideology, analysing the bourgeois and idealist assumptions which shape the texts and generate their contradictions.

especially his analyses of mirror-stage identifications, of the *corps morcelé*, and of the constitution of Woman as Other.[3] Certain of Hardy's texts—*The Woodlanders*, for example—lend themselves almost uncannily to a Lacanian reading, which alone seems to make sense of their otherwise anomalous details; and some of Hardy's most celebrated individual scenes have a power which Lacan's theories can help to explain. To see the Great Barn in *Far from the Madding Crowd*, for example, as the fortress or stadium which Lacan identifies as often expressing, in dream and fantasy, the illusion of wholeness[4] is not only to clarify the position of Gabriel Oak (who reigns in the Great Barn and who also aligns himself with the Great Mother) but also to relate the barn itself—as an implicitly maternal image, an enduring and capacious female *body*—to other mothers and mother-figures in the novels.[5]

I am suggesting, then, that Hardy's fiction expresses certain anxieties about wholeness, about maleness, and particularly about woman, in ways which are fairly consistent, though never simple or predictable. There are also anxieties about social class. For Hardy—a man who moved between architecture and literature, Dorset and London, family and fairly high society, and whose frustrated aspirations to a university education have seemed to be reflected in his last novel—the Other always has a class aspect. While Hardy can be read as especially sympathetic to women and to working people, his sympathy is by no means unambiguous, and to see him simply as politically correct is to miss the anxieties, ambivalences, and ambiguities, the defensiveness and self-consciousness, which often get expressed in the novels both in the structure of the fables and in nervously figurative language.[6]

[3] See bibliographical entries for Lacan; also commentaries of Rose (1982), Benvenuto and Kennedy (1986), Gallop (1982), Muller and Richardson (1978), and MacCannell (1986). Wright (1984) has discussed the application of Lacan's theories to criticism. References to specific concepts are given below. Goode (1988), 171 n. 7, has noted the relevance of Lacan to Hardy. On woman as Other in Hardy, see Wotton (1985), 127–31.

[4] Lacan (1977a), 4–5.

[5] Among those who have discussed the Great Barn are Carpenter (1963–4), 339–40; Eastman (1978), 24–5; Johnson (1983), 29–31; Bullen (1986), 64–5; Beegel (1987), 219–21; Wotton (1985), 48–50; Goode (1988), 16–32.

[6] Goode (1988), Jacobus (1975), Boumelha (1982), and Morgan (1988) emphasize Hardy's sympathy with women, Childers (1981), Rogers (1975), Freeman (1982), and

This study, then, is about texts and subtexts, and deals both with the larger structures of plot and character on the one hand and on the other with the details of imagery and rhetoric—particularly with the narrator's evasive but revealing formulations and with the ways in which his words implicate him in the very processes and attitudes he is anxious to disavow. It looks at characters in terms of their function in the structure of the underlying fable, sometimes discovering that individuals who seem to oppose one another are covertly working together and that apparently 'minor' characters are the focus of central concerns. In discussing *Tess of the d'Urbervilles* I have drawn specifically on the methodology of Fredric Jameson, who sees fictional characters as constructed to resolve contradictions in ideology; and in general I deal with Hardy's characters not as if they were real people, with an inner life which is amenable to analysis, but rather as nodes or pressure points in the mythic structure—as generated by Hardy to solve certain personal as well, in some cases, as fictional and professional problems.[7]

Indeed I treat Hardy himself less as a real person than as a text. By Hardy I always mean 'Hardy', the larger text woven by the writer's or speaker's words in all of the discrete texts assembled under that name. The status of the narrative voice in Hardy is a peculiar one. While it would be naïve to attribute to the individual who lived at Max Gate a philosophy extrapolated from the narrator's generalizations in the novels, it has also been observed that the 'voice' in the non-fiction texts often seems to overlap with this narrative voice in significant ways—

Silverman (1984) his misogyny or negative stereotyping of women. Eagleton (1978, 1987) and Goode (1979*a*, 1988) see Hardy as sympathetic to working people; others point out his condescending, even derisory treatment of them (Snell 1985), his nostalgic mythologizing of their putative point of view (Barrell 1982), his eagerness to suppress his own class affiliation (Widdowson 1989), and his unreliability as a social historian (Snell 1985). Wotton (1985) insists on the ideological nature both of Hardy's production of the workfolk (42–8) and of critical readings of Hardy's women which repress the contradictions in the writing (172–3). For Hardy's feelings about his own social class, see Eagleton (1978); Collins (1980); Winter (1980); Williams and Williams (1980); Millgate (1982); Snell (1985); Widdowson (1989).

[7] Deleuze (Deleuze and Parnet 1977, 51) has pointed out that Hardy's characters are merely 'collections de sensations intensives', and that the intense concern with the individual in Hardy is the paradoxical result of his conception of individuals as 'autant de "chances uniques"'. Spector (1988) discusses Fancy Day as a knot or trope, who foregrounds the tropological nature of the text's methods of characterization.

and that the *Life* is perhaps the most devious and slippery fiction of all.[8] There are in this study, then, two parallel discourses, one about the individual novels, in the chapters, and the other about 'Hardy', the wider text, in the footnotes. It would be simpler to say that the footnotes often supply biographical and autobiographical details (details from the *Life*, or from the life) which can interestingly intersect with the novels— were it not that such a formulation might imply that these 'lives' possess some kind of extra-textual status.

Although I am impressed by recent arguments about the construction of the Hardy canon and understand what is seen to be at stake when that canon is uncritically endorsed, my choice of texts has in fact been thoroughly canonical. Other novels and stories might seem even more obviously relevant to a study which deals with Hardy's feelings about the body— *Desperate Remedies* and *The Well-Beloved*, for example, 'The Withered Arm' or 'Barbara of the House of Grebe'. There is a reason, however, for not including them. What I am interested in is how private myth and private obsessions get themselves expressed within narratives which have been read as more or less decorous, more or less controlled—novels which defer sufficiently even to the expectations of 'realistic' readers to be seen as 'central' or 'great'. Texts which are less canny in masking their concerns do not invite an exploration of how the masking takes place. It is that exploration which is the purpose of the analyses which follow.

---

[8] Millgate (1971*a*), 231. For a summary of the evasions and contradictions in the *Life*, see Widdowson (1989), 129–54.

1

Under the Greenwood Tree: 'United 'ooman'

Hardy's comments in the Author's Preface to *Under the Greenwood Tree* about the titles of this novel point to a fundamental dualism in its conception. The final title and the subtitle ('A Rural Painting of the Dutch School') both identify the novel as pastoral; the original title (*The Mellstock Choir*) suggests the limits of that pastoralism, for we learn that the subject of the narrative is the choir's extinction.

The world of Mellstock is a green but not a golden one: time and death are found here, along with courtship and marriage. Hardy deliberately qualifies the ideals of traditional pastoral by setting them against the real, though now extinct, world of Dorset in the 1840s.[1] The dream of a classical golden age, when no one killed for food and no one used money, is explicitly undermined in the syllogistic discussion about honey-taking:[2] no honey without killing bees; no honey, no money; 'without money man is a shadder' (156).[3] The pastoral, seasonal sequence of the novel's five sections, which might imply an idyllic life attuned to the rhythms of nature, is

---

[1] Hardy said the novel was based on 'the impressions which all unconsciously I had been gathering of rural life during my youth in Dorsetshire': see Millgate (1982), 135. The frontispiece to the Wessex Edition of *Under the Greenwood Tree* is a photograph of Stinsford church.

[2] Millgate (1971*b*), 50, notes the 'importance of honey in the rural economy when sugar was an imported luxury'. In the Hardy household, honey sometimes functioned as money: in 1873, the music teacher of Thomas Hardy's younger sister Katharine was paid partly in honey (27). Millgate (1971*b*), 44–7, discusses Hardy's interest in *As You Like It* and the ways in which the allusion to the play illuminates the novel. I take the discussion of honey-taking as another facet of this allusion, analogous to the issue of killing deer in Shakespeare's play.

[3] *Under the Greenwood Tree or The Mellstock Quire: A Rural Painting of the Dutch School* (London: Macmillan, 1912), Wessex Edition, vol. vii, 156. All subsequent quotations from the novel are from the same edition.

qualified by the rhythm of the Christian calendar, which marks death ('Remember Adam's fall', 27) as well as rebirth ('Remember God's goodnesse'): there is premonitory irony in the sound of 'the fall of an apple' as Fancy confesses to Dick her flirtation with Mr Shiner (137), and the cry of a bird being killed by an owl as Dick asks her father for her hand (162). Indeed, the contrast between the golden world and the fallen one is dramatized on the very first page of the novel where, in the midst of a toughly individualized English winter landscape, Dick Dewy sings of generalized summer and roses, identifying himself as the pastoral lover and suggesting at the same time both his own innocence and the limits of the pastoral vision.

Set against Dick's 'pastoral' romanticism is the older generation's accommodation to an imperfect world. Hardy feels affection and respect for those individuals who endure life's exigencies with generosity, compassion, and good humour, accept their fellow men unjudgementally, and embrace the community at large with an inclusive kindliness. *Under the Greenwood Tree* is based on Hardy's memories of his own father and grandfather; it is about fathers, and about various kinds of fatherhood.[4] The three fathers in the novel—William Dewy, Reuben Dewy, and Geoffrey Day—are alike in ways which reflect the novel's moral values. All three embody an unselfconscious, untheoretical Christianity which takes life as it comes and people as they are.

Fancy's and Dick's fathers are big, solid men physically, built on a grand (Ann Dewy would say coarse) scale, and their largeness of body is emblematic of a corresponding largeness of spirit. Though very different in personality, they respect one another and align easily with one another when the young people's engagement brings them together. They display similar virtues in parallel situations: both agree to include Thomas Leaf in events or rituals from which he expects to be excluded; both act as hosts, presiding over the hospitality offered in their households, and as providers of food and drink—Reuben

---

[4] Hardy's grandfather, who had become the 'leading spirit' of the Stinsford choir from the early years of the century, played the bass viol; his uncle James and his father Thomas played violins. The choir disbanded in the early 1840s, after the grandfather's death and the arrival of a new and less supportive vicar: see Millgate (1982), 14. See Widdowson (1989), 142, on the way the *Life* deals with the father and grandfather.

dispensing the cider, Geoffrey entertaining Dick at dinner and conferring with the butcher over Fancy's bill. Both are contrasted to their snobbish or exclusive wives, and, although consistently and, the context implies, understandably somewhat misogynistic and sceptical about romance and marriage, both men exhibit a kind of monumental imperturbability in the face of these difficult women.

Indeed, Reuben and Geoffrey are surprisingly objective towards anyone who has trespassed against them, their tolerance rooted in compassion for fellow 'mortals', Reuben's sympathy for the man who cheated him ('poor heart', 11) and Geoffrey's for the bees that are stinging him and who are doomed to die ('little mortals . . . poor things', 158–9) linking the two men thematically in a rather striking way. Reuben's fairness to Parson Maybold, whom he defends in the face of universal condemnation and even though Maybold's decision means 'death' (85) for the choir, is in line with his characteristic generosity. His equability is rooted in a certain fatalism— 'Your parson comes by fate', he observes (71); Maybold is a 'good enough' preacher, and his sermons, 'good or bad', will not make 'a penneth o' difference to we poor martels here or hereafter' (70)—and he accepts the parson's grudging compromise with the same fatalism ('mortal men mustn't expect their own way entirely', 89).

It is this sense of the limits of the mortal state which unites the two fathers with the grandfather, William Dewy. As Reuben Dewy, who calls everyone 'my sonnies', is a kind of father not only to the choir but to the community as a whole, so Grandfather William has the status of a kind of universal grandfather. A mild-mannered, gentle man, he nevertheless has a strong moral authority over the other men, and when he opposes whispering in church or dancing on Christmas Day, his strictures are accepted without question. Grandfather William does not, however, so much proscribe activities as put them in their proper place and time. He does not prevent the dancing, which begins at midnight, nor stifle the men's resentment at Fancy, which gets aired later on. His moral position is rather characterized by the sense that 'for everything there is a time'.

This attitude to time is presented as an exemplary one. The

wisdom of Ecclesiastes is especially congenial to the choir—one of its members responding to the criticism of Maybold's sermon in terms of a comparison with Ecclesiastes—and Grandfather William's outlook is of the same stamp. Its benevolence is made clear at the wedding. When Grandfather James rather sourly wonders whether Fancy is thinking more about Dick or about her wedding dress, Grandfather William defends her in biblical terms: 'Well, 'tis their nature. Remember the words of the prophet Jeremiah: "Can a maid forget her ornaments, or a bride her attire?"' (204). Youth is a time for vanity, the wedding-day a time for the bride to be thinking about her appearance: Grandfather William's uncompromising but generous framework of belief puts Fancy's frivolity into charitable perspective and undermines the narrator's own ironies at her expense.

The three father-figures in the novel, then, share not so much specific character traits as an inclusive and expansive orientation to those around them. They contain and include rather than define and exclude. In different ways, they stand for fellowship, connectedness, even nurture, usurping indeed certain roles usually reserved for women. In a novel where the bonds of community are important, the fathers represent consolidation, continuity, and connection. The patriarchal order they embody seems not only resilient but positive. Yet it is easily shaken by Fancy Day, who defeats her own father directly, by playing her anorexic trick on him, and the Dewys indirectly but even more decisively, by disrupting the choir of which they are the centre.

How seriously, then, are we to take their defeat and her victory?

A fine balance is maintained throughout the narrative between pathos and comedy, irony and sentiment, 'extinction' and rebirth. Although the choir themselves describe their disbanding as a kind of death (85), the very inflation of their language may tend to undercut the seriousness of their complaint, while at the same time their philosophical acceptance of their demise encourages us, too, to accept it as inevitable. While the choir is disbanded, the union of the young couple is consolidated; as in Frye's archetypal comic plot, the older generation and its institutions move into the background to 'make room for the next generation' (90).[5] This, the genial tone implies, is how things must be: Grandfather William's sense of time is projected as it were on to the very structure of the narrative which records his 'extinction'.

In pursuit of this balanced if elegiac vision, the novel develops a kind of rhythm based on coming apart and coming together. It opens with the men of the choir assembling at Reuben Dewy's for what turns out to be their last Christmas Eve circuit round the parish; it closes with the whole community assembling for the procession to celebrate the wedding of Dick and Fancy. The pattern is compensatory: something has been lost, but a fundamental unity remains; the choir has split up, but the community has not—indeed it celebrates its consolidation once again in the union of the young lovers, whom it will absorb into itself. The Noah's-ark imagery which is humorously linked with the nuptials of Dick and Fancy seems to point not only to couples pairing off two by two, as the wedding guests and the bride and groom do in the wedding procession, but also to a new little world forming after the extinction of the old. Fancy in marriage becomes aligned, willy-nilly, with the generations who have gone before; Dick, who has already laid in enough food for 'a grown-up family' (198), is designated as the father of the future. The tone of the beautifully handled 'Conclusion' seems essentially optimistic, as the whole community gathers under the Yggdrasil-like greenwood tree, emblem of continuity and connection.

Yet it is worth looking more closely at this balance of two tendencies, this rhythm of fragmentation and consolidation, dismemberment and re-embodying, a rhythm which, I would argue, has deeply suggestive ramifications, not all of them as positive as the overall comic tone of the novel seems to imply.[6]

The counterpoint is finely and subtly established in the opening three chapters, which deal with the gathering together of the members of the choir in preparation for the Christmas carolling. Around Dick, alone in the darkness, assemble, one by

---

[5] Frye (1957), 163–71.

[6] Hardy suggested that his narrative suppressed a darker one which could not be told as long as members of his family were alive: see Millgate (1982), 34–5. On the dark possibilities of the novel see Brown (1961), 45–8, Danby (1959), and Draffan (1973).

one, the other members of the Mellstock choir, who then move
off as a body to the warmth, light, and good cheer of his
father's cottage. The fellowship of men is treated as a very
positive thing in this novel: although Hardy introduces each of
the individuals with some irony, he presents their association as
something to be celebrated. The choir, in the heart of the Dewy
family, is itself a kind of family, with shared traditions, shared
memories, and a fund of gossip and good talk. The men speak
warmly of and to their fellow men, characteristically either
referring to a man by his vocation ('pedlar', 'shoemaker',
'dance-maker', 'auctioneering feller', 'seller', 'hedger-and-
ditcher', 'brass-man', 'reed-man', 'drum-man', 'man of
strings') or by nouns suggesting relationship: 'fellow-craters',
'neighbours', 'chap', 'lad', 'my friends'—their host's characteristic 'my sonnies' suggesting his fatherly role in relation to
all of them. The heart of the choir is the patriarchal line of
Dewy males, and the suggestion is that they are also the heart
of the community.

Yet while the men's fellowship exemplifies community,
conviviality, and continuity, their conversation strikes—however casually and humorously—a consistent note of dissolution, imperfection, and decay. They are drinking cider made
from apples ('Remember Adam's fall'); the body of the cask
from which Dewy draws it is rotten; Sam Lawson, the man from
whom he bought it, cheated him (as an auctioneer cheated
Michael Mail), and has himself subsequently died (11).
Reuben has made many repairs to the cask; and the motif of
continual repair is echoed in the next chapter when Robert
Penny displays the last for Geoffrey Day's boots and mentions
'doctoring' (18) it to reflect the wear and tear of time and 'crass
casualty' on Day's feet (it is a nice point that 'doctoring' the
last means making Day's bunion bigger). Things and people
fall apart, the men acknowledge, even as they celebrate their
own social unity.

It is significant that the way Fancy Day is introduced into the
conversation, as Robert Penny produces her boot alongside the
last of her father's foot, strikes a humorous and yet poignant
note of mortality.[7] To everyone but the shoemaker himself, who

[7] This scene is discussed by Spector (1988), 479–84.

can see the family resemblance between Fancy's foot and her father's, the most striking aspect of the juxtaposition is the contrast between her delicate little foot and her father's battered and deformed one. Yet the boot has value, especially for Dick—who feels that it is so intimate a reflection of her that he ought not to look at it without her permission—because it, like her father's last, is a record of her body's past history: 'A character, in fact—the flexible bend at the instep, the rounded localities of the small nestling toes, scratches from careless scampers now forgotten—all . . . repeated in the telltale leather' (19). Erotic appeal depends on the vision of pristine perfection which is nevertheless subject to, if not yet marked by, the ravages of time.[8] The effect is funny, sexy, and slightly disturbing all at once. The focus on Fancy's disembodied foot suggests the delicately fetishistic dimension of Dick's attraction to her—and to her handkerchief, her clothing, her hair, her hat, the very wine she leaves in her glass and her crumbs on the plate. At the same time the comparison of Fancy's foot with her father's reminds us of the continuity between the generations, the strength of family ties (as opposed to sexual attraction), the vulnerability of Fancy herself to that time which has marked him. The little boot casts an erotic spell while poignantly making us aware of the limits and the ironical context of that spell.

The motif of a disembodied foot is picked up a page later, and in a way which associates it even more clearly with mortality, when Penny tells an unconsciously grisly anecdote about identifying the foot of a drowned man by its family resemblance. The tale is funny in the same way as the remarks of the gravediggers in *Hamlet*, expressing for the speaker primarily his own professional expertise, but echoing for the reader the concerns of the work as a whole.[9] It is ironical that

[8] Hardy often comments on the poignancy of the marks of time, observing for example that the 'beauty of association is entirely superior to the beauty of aspect, and a beloved relative's old battered tankard to the finest Greek vase' (Hardy 1928, 158). Also relevant is Hardy's interest in the story of a young woman who jilted her shoemaker lover but '*kept the shoes*' (Hardy 1928, 285; Hardy's italics). The fine essay by Scarry (1983) is a valuable analysis of the way the body and the material world rub off on one another in Hardy.

[9] For Hardy's interest in the gravedigger scene, see Hardy (1928), 312; Orel (1966), 141.

Penny recognizes the dead body of John Woodward's brother
by his foot but fails to recognize, in the foot he introduces to the
assembled choir, a part of the body which will drive them, as a
body, apart. Fancy has her foot in the door; the body which
will follow, dainty and appealing as it looks, will triumph over
theirs.

The novel deals, indeed, with the integrity and the dissolution of bodies. Hardy's theme is the demise of 'orchestral
bodies in the villages of fifty or sixty years ago' (vii); the word is
used of the group the first time they are challenged by the
'intrusive feminine voices' (41) from the schoolgirls' aisle as
well as the last time they act *as* a group, when they go—'the
whole body of men in the choir' (79), 'the ancient body of
minstrels' (88)—to protest their extinction to Parson Maybold.
This male body is dismembered by women—and there lies the
pity of it, and the motive for Hardy's tale. When Hardy in his
Preface describes the passing of the old choir, the process he
delineates is presented as not only a fragmentation (bonds of
community are broken) and a diminishment (fewer music-
makers are involved) but an emasculation: the new musicians
are women and children. It is appropriately emblematic, in the
scene where Robert Penny displays the Day family feet, that
the man's is battered and deformed, the woman's relatively
unscathed and whole. For this powerful body of men is doomed
to be vanquished and disbanded by a mere slip of a girl, to be
disunited by 'united 'ooman' (41), to be 'scattered' (178)
through the congregation at the sides of their wives. There is
the suggestion of figurative dismemberment as well as emasculation: in losing its 'Dick'[10] (who *plays*, as Thomas Leaf *sings*,
treble) the choir might as well lose its *head*: as a body it will
wither away like the skeletal Thomas, its weakest member.
One of the subjects of *Under the Greenwood Tree* is the fragmentation and diminution of male *things*.

The way Hardy deals with the body is idiosyncratic and deeply
suggestive. There is considerable emphasis on isolated bodily
parts: the human body, especially the male body, seems potentially fragmented or disconnected, ready to come apart. Hardy

[10] Goode (1988), 12, notes this pun.

describes male characters rather differently from the way he does females. To Robert Penny, a man can be represented by one of his members ('show *me* a man's foot, and I'll tell you that man's heart', 20); and the narrator often seems to be trying to do what Reuben Dewy says is impossible, read a man's character from 'all his members put together' (21). Parson Maybold has a 'courageous eye, timid mouth and neutral nose'; Dick, silhouetted against the night sky, has 'a low-crowned hat, an ordinary-shaped nose, an ordinary chin, an ordinary neck, and ordinary shoulders. What he consisted of further down was invisible' (5). Even leaving aside the irony, as well as the ambiguity about what Dick consisted of further down, there is something slightly dehumanizing about this kind of list. Indeed, because we are introduced to the members of the choir in the dark and perceive them first as mere black silhouettes against the sky, all of them impress us at first as visual objects rather than as whole personalities. Robert Penny for example is presented as

a little man who, though rather round-shouldered, walked as if that fact had not come to his own knowledge, moving on with his back very hollow and his face fixed on the north-east quarter of the heavens before him, so that his lower waistcoat-buttons came first, and then the remainder of his figure. His features were invisible; yet when he occasionally looked round, two faint moons of light gleamed for an instant from the precincts of his eyes, denoting that he wore spectacles of a circular form. (5)

The effect, with the accent on the grotesque and with the strong focus on accessories like buttons and spectacles, is to make Robert Penny a somewhat puppet-like figure, less individual and vital than his clothing.

The puppets can come apart. The head is particularly vulnerable. Hardy's text is full of casually used figurative language, the implications of which are consistent and startling. Thomas Leaf, notoriously, has 'no head at all'. Geoffrey Day has a nose so misshaped by a blow that 'when the sun was low and shining in his face people could see far into his head' (98). Spinks the schoolmaster's complacent observation that 'by the time a man's head is finished 'tis almost time for him to creep underground' (20) is disconcerting, especially since his own head is eminently finished. The parts of men's bodies tend to have a will of their own. Dick continues to whistle when greeted by Michael Mail, 'implying that the business of his mouth could not be checked at a moment's notice by the placid emotion of friendship' (4); Mr Penny, as he discusses whether Geoffrey Day will want 'his bunion altered or made bigger', lets his left hand wander 'towards the cider-cup as if the hand had no connection with the person speaking' (18); Thomas Leaf lets 'his mouth continue to smile for some time after his mind had done smiling, so that his teeth remained in view as the most conspicuous members of his body' (10). The effect is quite the opposite of Ann Dewy's mechanical smile (11), which implies a body language very much under the control of the will and the total personality.

The portrait of Penny is a reminder of how often the parts of a man's body are presented as details no more nor less import- ant than the details of his clothing. Grandfather William is said to 'wear' his bass viol along with his best clothes on Sunday, so that Reuben Dewy wonders whether the vicar will recognize him without it (82); Reuben Dewy's own commodious trousers, as described by his wife (45), suggest his size as vividly as her comments about his excessive sweating. Some characters, indeed, exist mainly as clothing: Grandfather James's coat has a good deal more character than he has—or, to put it another way, all we need to know of his character is suggested by his coat (16). In this novel masculine character is a product of history, family, vocation, and function in the community, and clothing, which reflects all these factors, can epitomize it.

The 'character' of men, so delineated, is felt as worth record- ing as an end in itself. Men *embody* the *spirit* of the community, its values, its history, its pattern of association, its institutions. The description of some of the men is out of proportion to their function in the narrative. There is no particular connection between Robert Penny's posture and the part he plays in the novel; Grandfather James does almost nothing except serve as a scaffolding on which to hang his coat. But because individuals like Penny and James exist as the reflection of a certain com- munity at a certain moment in time, they are worth memorial- izing. But the corollary is that the 'characters' of such men depend in a fundamental way on the continued coherence of the community which has given them being, the uninterrupted continuance of history which has shaped them. They are in a very literal way the sum of their parts, so that what destroys a part threatens the whole.

Women are described in quite different terms. A woman, for Hardy, is not constituted by her role in the community. Female clothing, accordingly, denotes not vocation but occasion. Hardy's particular eroticism depends on the sense of moment. It is appropriate that Fancy refuses to wear the same dress twice: a woman never does in Hardy's imagination, for a distinct, unique phase of her (and his) emotional experience is figured for ever by a certain costume.[11] Fancy's clothing is described impressionistically rather than precisely—'a white robe of some kind' (29), 'a gauzy dress of white with blue facings' (48)—but the body that it covers is unified in a way that the strongest man's is not, permanently vital, coherent, and enticing.

This feeling is reflected in the way women are described. Nouns referring to female characters, when they do not denote family relationships (wife, daughter, grandmother, step-mother), usually convey the impression the woman makes in the eyes of a (male) beholder. The phrases applied to Fancy are unusually varied and vivid, and most of them suggest her power over male emotion and imagination: she is a 'rale wexwork' (30), a 'neat . . . figure of fun . . . just husband-high' (18), one of the 'brazen-faced hussies' (41), 'the owner of the foot' (19), 'the little unknown' (19)—or, more rhapsodically, 'the Vision' (36), 'bright maiden' (40), 'our heroine' (48), 'his Love' (53), 'his Lady Fair' (60), 'the lively goddess' (56), 'the Angel' (64), 'this lovely Fancy' (59). Though some of these terms are sardonic enough, expressing in free indirect discourse the narrator's implicit criticism of Dick's delusory infatuation, they do suggest the kind of impression Hardy's women tend to make, on his own imagination as well as on the reader's.

Although woman is presented through the male eye, she is not constituted by it. The phrase 'united 'ooman' (41), in

---

[11] See *A Pair of Blue Eyes*, 18: 'Every woman who makes a permanent impression on a man is usually recalled to his mind's eye as she appeared in one particular scene, which seems ordained to be her special form of manifestation throughout the pages of his memory.' The narrator goes on to describe in some detail the dress Elfride is wearing.

which Mr Spinks expresses his outrage at the schoolgirls' rebellion, suggests something fundamental about Hardy's feelings for the feminine. For Hardy, women are united, and so is Woman. A woman is more than the sum of her parts, and her wholeness is mysterious and uncategorizable. The result is that when Hardy tries to use his 'male' method of characterization on a woman, describing Fancy's body item by item—as he does, for example, when 'our heroine . . . advances to her place in the ladies' line' at the Christmas supper (48)—the result has none of the vigour of the masculine descriptions, but tends to become arch and vapid. Fancy in despair may perceive herself piecemeal, comparing her hair to that of the blonde Dick danced with—but the very irrelevance of her concern dramatizes how impossible it would be for Dick to make such a comparison; and Hardy, while putting Dick's idolatry into ironic perspective, shares his erotic sense of woman's mysterious wholeness. It is emblematic of his vision of woman that the local 'witch' should be called a 'Deep Body' (167); that Dick should be disturbed, during the cart-ride which seals his engagement to Fancy, by the premonitory spectacle of a woman whose huge body pushes her husband and son off the seat of the cart in which they ride; and indeed that young Charley should be fascinated both with the mutability and alienness of his own body (the expressions, as he weeps, of his own face in the mirror, 8) and with the deep threat and mystery of the more integral female one ('Idd it cold inthide te hole?', 13). Woman is (w)hole in a way that man can never be; and her wholeness is for him a deep threat and a deep attraction.[12]

Thus in spite of the fact that we get a more precise visual impression of the male characters, woman paradoxically becomes associated with body, man with spirit. This is not, of course, what the women themselves feel, nor what a man in love believes about them. To Ann Dewy, who prides herself on her superior refinement, her husband's sweaty body makes him a coarse and physical creature; and Fancy seems like a 'Vision' (30), an 'Angel' (64), a spirit, to Dick. But Dick is wrong about Fancy; and Mrs Dewy's obsession with physical coarseness makes her in a sense coarser than her husband, more

[12] On woman as (w)hole, see Gallop (1982), 9–11, 20–2; Benvenuto and Kennedy (1986), 186–7, 194.

closely focused on the physical. Women are more materialistic in every sense of the word in this novel, more interested in material things, and more aware of the body, both their own and others'.[13] Men, on the other hand, just because they are parts of a *body*, transcend body and come to represent the *spirit* of the community.

Accordingly, when a woman displaces the men of the choir, the change represents a loss of spirituality. The men's music stands for everything Hardy values. It is communal, in both its appeal and its social organization—that is, it is made of *parts* which form a whole greater than their sum. It is masculine: not only made by men, but plain, 'in keeping with the simplicity of the old church' (178), and challenging to perform (requiring 'Half-an-hour's hammering' to 'conquer the toughness of en', 17—portrait of the artist as blacksmith and soldier!). And it is the one glimpse the villagers have of the possibility of transcending the body. To be sure, not everybody wants to transcend the body: Michael Mail offends Ann Dewy by his vivid description of chewing in time to music. But Grandfather William prefers music to food, even to life itself; and his son attempts to awaken the less sensitive members of the choir to the effect they want to make on their hearers by urging them to 'go quietly, so as to strike up all of a sudden, like spirits' (23). Fancy's music, on the other hand, is individualistic rather than communal, 'fancy' rather than plain, and physical rather than spiritual, in that an analogy is suggested between her sartorial artifice on the day of the performance ('disgraceful! Curls and a hat and feather!'—177) and the 'crowded chords and interludes it was her pleasure to produce' (178). When a woman unmakes male music, emasculation is also the spiritual defeat of the community.

Dismembering a group of men emasculates all the individuals in it, since men are defined by their group identity. What about women? On first glance it would seem that group membership is not essential to them in the same way. There is no female

---

[13] Millgate (1971*b*), 52, notes that 'Hardy anticipates Lawrence in stressing the perpetual conflict between the women's striving for gentility and the unregenerate "animality" of the men'. On coarseness as critique, see Wotton (1985), ch. 5, and Goode (1988), 12–13.

relationship in the novel comparable to the male friendships. Fancy's desires tend to set her against rather than align her with other women, since what she wants is male admiration, status in the community, and a piece of male 'property' (200) which will make the other girls jealous. Indeed, Fancy is more deeply stimulated by the idea of rivalry with other women than by almost anything else—with the possible exception of Parson Maybold's offer of social and economic aggrandizement. The high point of the whole business of marriage for a woman, it is suggested, is the moment when the banns are read, for that is when her triumph over the other girls is first and most dramatically revealed, and she can revel in the 'sorrowful envy on the maidens' faces' (195). The wedding itself must be anticlimactic after such a triumph: as Mrs Dewy says, 'The edge of the performance is took off at the calling home' (196).

Consequently, women's friendships are scarcely depicted in the novel. Fancy is not usually shown working with other women, nor are women seen co-operating or even communicating very much with one another. Although when Dick and Fancy unite, the two fathers become friends, the two mothers are never shown speaking to each other; they remain isolated figures, imperious rulers of their own domains. Fancy has no maternal support: her own mother is dead, and she gets no help from her eccentric stepmother, whose household she wants to escape as soon as she can. Yet although the men's bonding is dramatized and celebrated, the men's group breaks up. Women's contacts with one another are underplayed, but the women get their way in the end.

Every woman desires marriage, and if she sets her mind to it, almost any woman can get it—as Geoffrey Day says grimly about his own second wife, 'Doom is nothing beside a elderly woman' (103). And getting one of their own married is something that women as a group somehow mysteriously succeed in doing. Moving towards marriage means tapping the power of the collective female will. At the opportune moment, Fancy finds herself a surrogate mother readily enough, learning from the 'witch' Elizabeth Endorfield how to exploit her father's good nature. And on her wedding-day she begins to identify, apparently for the first time, with her own mother, acceding to some of the old-fashioned customs because 'mother did' (202).

Is the comic irony here at Fancy's expense, suggesting that as she pairs off and joins the procreative throng of couples, she loses her uniqueness and becomes assimilated to the world of her parents? Or is it at Dick's, suggesting that when the ceremony is over the essential solidarity of all women with one another will reveal itself with a new explicitness? Certainly Fancy's determination to do things 'as mother did' is not a promising sign for Dick, since the one thing that all three mothers in this novel share is the conviction that they have married beneath them; but then it has already been made clear that Fancy thinks she has too. In their condescension towards husbands, it seems, women are united. It is significant that the only occasion on which women are shown acting as a group is the gathering of the bridesmaids and the mothers on the day of the wedding—a ritual of female solidarity treated with broad and somewhat hostile irony by the narrator.

The novel begins with Dick and his father and grandfather; it ends with the prospect of Dick's eventual fatherhood. Procreation is an important and ironic motif in the novel, an aspect of that imagery of expansion and diminishment, consolidation and fragmentation, which is its central rhythm. The subject is treated with a complex ambivalence. Certainly the consequences of married sex for women are not presented as self-evidently appealing. It is rather odd that Hardy pictures 'certain young daughters of the village' (38–9) surreptitiously studying the service for the churching of women in their prayer-books, curious that he shows them anticipating childbirth with (is it prurient?) interest, since he makes clear that this phase of a woman's life can be a martyrdom. One might deduce the author's real sympathy with women from the references to Brownjohn's daughter, who, 'not much more than a maid yet' (10), has buried three children and is pregnant for the fifth time, having learned, as her father callously remarks, 'the multiplication table onmistakable well' (10); or of the mother of Thomas Leaf, who lost eleven children in infancy, and who still mourns Jimmy, who died at the age of 'four hours and twenty minutes' (77). Such women can be seen as victims of married life: indeed, when Mrs Penny gives Fancy the talismanic phrase—' 'Tis to be, and here goes' (196)—with the observation that ' ''Twill carry a body through it all from wedding to churching' (196), the humorous suggestion is that male demands on the female body may take a certain amount of 'spirit' (196) to endure.

We do not, however, actually meet Mrs Leaf or Brownjohn's daughter, or any woman victimized by male sexuality. What we see dramatized is, unexpectedly, the debilitating effect of excessive childbearing on *men*. The real victim of the philo-progenitive Mrs Leaf, so 'romantical on the matter o' children' (77), seems paradoxically to be her enfeebled and emasculated son, withered leaf of exhausted stock, who 'can sing my treble as well as any maid, or married woman either' (76), and whose excessive identification with his sorrowing mother creates in his mind a sibling *doppelgänger* of whom he himself is doomed to remain only an ineffectual shadow.[14] Thomas Leaf is a particularly interesting figure. As the first of a line of young–old castrati (like Joseph Poorgrass in *Far from the Madding Crowd* and Christian Cantle in *The Return of the Native*) who express emblematically some of the anxieties which motivate the narrative—as a single *leaf* of a scattered 'quire' (Hardy uses both spellings apparently arbitrarily[15])—it may not be irrelevant that Thomas Leaf shares his authorial father's Christian name (the only character in Hardy's fiction to do so), and that Thomas Hardy, whose only children were *leaves*, was believed to be dead at birth.[16]

The real victim of the mother of live children is the husband who has to provide for them. Although Dick is expected to do well financially by the standards of Mellstock, 'the stores of victuals and drink' that he has laid in being 'enough for Noah's ark' (198), his energy is instinctively linked by the male

[14] On the double as a manifestation of mirror-stage illusions, see Lacan (1977a), 3.

[15] The first usage, at the beginning of ch. 2, is 'choir'—'The choir stamped severally' (7). The title of ch. 3 is 'The Assembled Quire' (15); at the end of this chapter Spinks speaks of having read 'a leaf or two in my time' (20), and five pages later the spelling becomes 'quire' in the text (25). Charles Lock brought this change to my attention.

[16] Hardy (1928), 18. Millgate (1982) notes that while this detail may be apocryphal, it reflects the infant's feebleness as well as family fears that he would not live to grow up (16). On Hardy's possible feelings about fatherhood, see Millgate (1982), 192, 253. Beach (1922), 72, discussing the rustics, was the first to link together the 'fools' Thomas Leaf, Joseph Poorgrass, and Christian Cantle. Draffan (1973), 58, and Howe (1967), 51, find the treatment of Leaf grotesque or distasteful.

community with the demands children will make upon it: his best man Nat Callcome remarks that it is as if he and Fancy were planning to 'begin wi' a grown-up family' (198). Reuben Dewy, father-figure though he seems to be to the community as a whole, and father, as his wife observes, of a very well-spaced family, nevertheless sees the pressures of marriage in terms of fatherhood, observing that the real pinch for a man comes 'when the oldest daughter's boots be only a size less than her mother's' (209). The image his words create of a monstrous regiment of growing *women* treading on each other's heels and draining a man's economic vitality is both comic and rather touching, neatly picking up the image of Fancy's boot at the beginning of the book, hinting at the possibility of the bride herself as the future mother of a grown girl, and reminding the reader that when a girl's boot is nearly as big as her mother's she in turn will be just about 'husband-high' and ready to begin the cycle all over again. The image can point to Fancy's diminishment as well as Dick's, and the tone never tips away from good-natured humour. But we register nevertheless that Dick, industrious and ambitious though he is, is also a bit of a dupe, that he will spend his life working to support Fancy and her daughters in the style to which she has become accustomed. And we may suspect, considering the discrepancy between the life Maybold offered her and the activities outlined with such naïve pride on Dick's business card, that she will always secretly despise him a little for it.

The same balance between humour and irony characterizes the brilliantly controlled 'Conclusion' to the novel. The negative and positive aspects of the wedding are flawlessly balanced, the rhythms of consolidation and fragmentation, disbanding and coalescing, communality and individualism upon which the whole novel turns, perfectly poised. The guests gather, the groom is late; but he is late because his bees have swarmed—a good omen which reminds us nevertheless of their inevitable dispersion and death. Leaf is reluctantly included in the ceremony, as he was always reluctantly included in the activities of the defunct choir; but drunken Enoch—whose fragmented replies, echoing across the field, have a slightly disturbing quality—will not come to the wedding, having split off from 'the family' (205).[17] Fancy wants to do things the new way, but agrees to do as her mother did. And in a moving paragraph, the united community make their way together to the church: 'Now among dark perpendicular firs, like the shafted columns of a cathedral; now through a hazel copse, matted with prim- roses and wild hyacinths; now under broad beeches in bright young leaves' (204). The picture, with its sudden widening of the field of focus to show the human figures dwarfed by the overarching trees, is just as poetic and considerably more subtle than the more self-conscious description of the green- wood tree itself, symbol of inclusiveness and continuity.

The novel apparently concludes with the same balance. The last two pages focus on two untold stories, one a man's, the other a woman's. On the one hand there is Thomas Leaf's non-narrative of how a man made a great fortune, doubling and redoubling his money, from ten to twenty to forty to eighty to a thousand (210); on the other, there is Fancy's secret 'which she would never tell' (211). Leaf's story seems to be about male success in male terms (potentially though not explicitly about Dick), Fancy's about female success in female terms: the scatheless consummation of her marriage project. Yet read in context—in view of Leaf's association with excessive but enfeebled parturition, and the Noah's-ark imagery just a few pages earlier—Leaf's vision of how money increases sounds less like a financial exploit than a population explosion. *His* 'multiplication table' (10) suggests a process in which the individuality of the breeding pair is irrelevant, a process which dooms them even at the moment of their union to be eclipsed and outnumbered by their descendants. Read this way, Thomas Leaf's story works in the same direction as Fancy's withheld secret—towards the emasculation of the bridegroom.

In a fable about Dick's failure to inherit the great tradition of his father and grandfather, the suggestion of his personal irrelevance as paterfamilias is ironically appropriate; and in a fable about the battle of the sexes, a story of male success which covertly images female triumph is nicely self-reflexive. What looks like male expansion turns out to be male marginalization —a fitting final outburst from Thomas Leaf before he subsides

[17] Millgate (1971*b*), 49, 54, notices this and other ominous details at the conclusion of the novel.

again into 'nothingness'. It seems to me that Thomas Hardy is telling the same story.

What I am suggesting is not only (what would surprise no one) that there is a misogynistic streak in Hardy's eroticism, but that his feelings about male and female, and about bodily integrity and vulnerability, are crucial to his vision. Indeed, they shape his imaginative structures in a fundamental way, inform his methods of characterization, and have something important to do with the way he perceives those celebrated abstractions—like Fate, Time, and Nature—to which so much critical attention has been directed.

Far from the Madding Crowd, a longer and in some ways richer and more complex novel than *Under the Greenwood Tree*, is also built around a beautiful and wilful heroine with a trio of male admirers. The man who finally wins Bathsheba, however, is granted a less ambiguous happy ending than is Dick—largely because of his relationship with a female presence not really evoked in the earlier novel, the Great Mother Nature herself. In *Under the Greenwood Tree*, fathers nurture sons, and 'mothers', in a more mysterious way, promote the projects of daughters. The protagonist of *Far from the Madding Crowd* is the son of a powerful mother and is wise enough to defer to her: therein lies his strength. What has to be displaced for him to succeed is the subject of the next chapter.

2

Far from the Madding Crowd: Venus' Looking Glass

Far from the Madding Crowd is constructed upon a pattern of binary opposition. Hardy evidently conceived the novel in terms of contrast between the characters, setting the reliable but unromantic Oak against the dashing and dangerous Troy, the spirited brunette Bathsheba who resists marriage against her passive, blonde foil Fanny Robin who fails to achieve it, and Bathsheba's wilful self-sufficiency against the rigid monk-like celibacy of Boldwood, which is its parody.[1] Individual characters are analysed in terms of their inner duality: Boldwood's 'stillness' results from 'the perfect balance of enormous antagonistic forces—positives and negatives in fine adjustment' (137),[2] Troy combines the English 'inelasticity' of his mother with the French 'mawkishness' of his father (358), while Bathsheba is an 'Elizabeth in brain and a Mary Stuart in spirit' (149). A number of chapter headings ('An Interior—Another Interior', 'One Solitary Meets Another') encourage the reader to set character against character, scene against scene, in a counterpoint which usually has obvious thematic implications.[3]

[1] The story was conceived as a triangle involving Bathsheba, Oak, and Troy (Hardy 1928, 125); Fanny Robin and Boldwood developed later. See Schweik (1968), 415–28.

[2] *Far from the Madding Crowd* (London: Macmillan, 1912), Wessex Edition, vol. ii, 137. All subsequent quotations from the novel are from the same edition. The title of my chapter alludes to Spenser, *The Faerie Queene*, III. i. 8. 9.

[3] On the symmetries of Hardy's plots—variously characterized as 'architectural' or 'dialectical'—see Proust (1954), iii. 376; Johnson (1894), 44; Abercrombie (1912), 34–42; Guerard (1949), 12, 61–2; Miller (1970), 205–12; Gregor (1974), 47, 63; Johnson (1983), 26. Hardy comments on his own sense of the importance of structure in 'The Profitable Reading of Fiction' (Orel 1966, 120–1). Morgan (1986), 1–3, and Pickrel (1988), 231–50, discuss the psychological benefits to the author of using highly defined forms.

Hardy's scheme calls attention to itself not only at the structural level but also at the rhetorical. *Far from the Madding Crowd* is marked by passages of sententious generalization, often apparently generated by antithesis:

Such imperiousness would have damned a little less beauty; and on the other hand, such beauty would have redeemed a little less imperiousness. (160)

The great aids to idealization in love were present here: occasional observation of her from a distance, and the absence of social intercourse with her—visual familiarity, oral strangeness. (141)

The novel is punctuated with balanced aphorisms of varying relevance and shrewdness:

Love is a possible strength in an actual weakness. (27)

the more emphatic the renunciation the less absolute its character. (37)

moral or aesthetic poverty contrasts plausibly with material, since those who suffer do not mind it, whilst those who mind it soon cease to suffer. (191)

Antithesis can become mechanical. Occasionally the narrator's rhetorical reflex infects the language of the characters. Boldwood, for example, is uncharacteristically ingenious when he complains:

Your dear love, Bathsheba, is such a vast thing beside your pity, that the loss of your pity as well as your love is no great addition to my sorrow, nor does the gain of your pity make it sensibly less. (232)

But it can also generate subtle analysis of motive, like the commentary on Troy's feelings as he flatters Bathsheba:

Her beauty, which, whilst it had been quiescent, he had praised in jest, had in its animated phases moved him to earnest; and though his seriousness was less than she imagined, it was probably more than he imagined himself. (202)

For Hardy, aiming as he said only to make himself 'a good hand at a serial', this strategy provides certain kinds of support. The oppositions between and within characters generate lively plot complications and melodramatic confrontations well calculated to hold the attention of the reader from instalment to instalment.[4] At the same time, the patterning of the prose style provides a ready-made sententiousness which a young author who secretly aims a good deal higher than handiness at a serial might feel gives his effort some claim to a more serious kind of art.

Binary opposition also provides a direction for the plot development. It is clear from the very terms in which the novel is set up that the polarities must be erased, the self-divided characters must either get themselves together or be disposed of, and that the movement towards unification and a happy ending is going to be achieved through Gabriel Oak. While helping him create glamorous and striking individuals like Bathsheba, Boldwood, and Troy, Hardy's formula also allows him to focus in a positive way on the character whose virtues the narrative is endorsing, and to depict Gabriel as the locus of a unifying movement which will bring the novel to a satisfactory moral and emotional conclusion.

Gabriel is a foil to all the other main characters in that, although thwarted, he is not self-divided. A mature man when the novel begins, Gabriel is eminently 'together'. The very polarities of the rhetoric tend, when the narrator is describing Gabriel, to work towards dialectical resolution. The second paragraph of the novel, introducing Gabriel in terms of his community reputation, explains that

when his friends and critics were in tantrums, he was considered rather a bad man; when they were pleased, he was rather a good man; when they were neither, he was a man whose moral colour was a kind of pepper-and-salt mixture. (1)

Gabriel's age is described in similar terms:

He was at the brightest period of masculine growth, for his intellect and his emotions were clearly separated: he had passed the time during which the influence of youth indiscriminately mingles them in the character of impulse, and he had not yet arrived at the stage wherein they become united again, in the character of prejudice, by the influence of a wife and family. (3)

Oak's condition after the loss of his sheep is presented as a midpoint between optimism and despair:

[4] See Jones (1978), 320–34, on Hardy's efforts in this direction.

He had sunk from his modest elevation as pastoral king into the very slime-pits of Siddim; but there was left to him a dignified calm he had never before known, and that indifference to fate which, though it often makes a villain of a man, is the basis of his sublimity when it does not. And thus the abasement had been exaltation, and the loss gain. (43–4)

The very rhythms of the narrator's language set Gabriel up as a balanced and integrated figure.

Indeed Gabriel functions as a 'connecter'. The mentor and confidant of individuals at all levels of the social scale, Gabriel forms a link between the working class and the gentry, himself eventually moving from one class to another.[5] He links the community to its own past, as is suggested when his arrival among the Weatherbury folk evokes a flood of reminiscences from the old men who knew his father. His principal virtue, the fidelity upon which Bathsheba comes to rely, is a kind of temporal connectedness: because he is single in intent, he is able to make promises, to bind the present to the future in a structure as tight as that of the chiasmus with which he declares himself: 'whenever you look up, there I shall be—and whenever I look up, there will be you' (33).

And finally, unlike Bathsheba who is nearly destroyed by the conflict between her 'masculine' desire for independence and her 'feminine' desire for love, Gabriel is all the stronger for possessing both masculine and feminine qualities.[6] Valiant battler though he is against fire and storm, Gabriel, as a shepherd, is also a nurturing figure, a kind of mother to his sheep; indeed we initially see him practising midwifery under the aegis of Lucina and getting up at night to feed the baby.[7] He is on good terms with the 'Great Mother', Nature herself, whose reliable signs he alone reads.[8] These female identifications give Gabriel's character stability and maturity; indeed, it

[5] See Goode (1988), 28, on the novel's 'bourgeois fantasy'.

[6] See Showalter (1979), 101, who argues that 'For the heroes of the tragic novels . . . maturity involves a kind of assimilation of female suffering, an identification with a woman which is also an effort to come to terms with their own deepest selves'. Gabriel Oak seems to have this balance without having to suffer for it; I detect in the tragic novels, however, a more negative attitude to such 'unmannings' than does Showalter.

[7] See Beegel (1987), 221–2.

[8] Johnson (1894), 172–5, was one of the first to comment on Oak as a reader of nature; see also Miller (1970), 83; Bullen (1986), 69–74, 114–15, 186–8.

is his solidarity with the Great Mother which is the basis of his own inner unity.[9]

Gabriel seems to owe this connectedness to his sense of where he fits into the scheme of things. Unlike the other characters, all of whom tend to be self-conscious if not downright exhibitionistic, 'Oak meditatively looked upon the horizon of circumstances without any special regard to his own standpoint in the midst' (338). In the moral structure of this novel, psychological and moral unity involves submission to the realities of a fallen world.[10] The self-divided characters are all egotists, convinced they can make the world accede to their demands. Gabriel, on the other hand, is shown learning that the cosmos has no particular tenderness for human aims and desires. When his sheep are killed, Gabriel has a vision of nature as demonic which is evidently intended to be read as an epiphany and to signal a positive stage in his moral development.[11] Gabriel's is a happy fall—his 'loss gain' (44). He eventually prospers because, like Adam, he has learned he has to *work* and to adjust his behaviour to 'weather' in the widest sense (it is suggestive that the site of Gabriel's testing is called Weatherbury, since weather begins with Adam's fall[12]). The most important polarity in the novel is between man and nature, and only Gabriel, bowing to Adam's curse, can bridge the gap.[13] Precisely because he accepts the otherness of the natural world, its indifference to his desires, Gabriel is able to be in harmony with it as is no other character in the novel.

[9] See Steig (1970–1), 55–62, on the 'fantasy' of the all-nurturing Great Mother upon which this novel is based.

[10] The notion of the Fall is noted by Meisel (1972), 46; Gregor (1974), 59; Wotton (1985), 135. Hardy was probably reading *Paradise Lost* as he was writing *Far from the Madding Crowd*: Paulin notes that the phrase 'gutta serena', used by Hardy to describe Bathsheba's state of mind just before Boldwood murders Troy, occurs in a note on the Invocation to Book III in one of Hardy's copies of Milton (1975, 148–9). On Hardy and Milton, see also Björk (1985), i. 360–1 n. 1144. See Johnson (1983), 28, on Oak as good shepherd.

[11] There are many epiphanic moments in Hardy's writing. On the ideological nature of the conviction that one can lift the veil and disclose essential truth, see Wotton (1985), 7–8, 89–111.

[12] Spelt 'Wetherbury', this is the name of an ancient earthwork in Dorset, Wetherbury Castle.

[13] Hardy used the phrase 'curse of Eden' to refer to agricultural work in 'The Dorsetshire Labourer' (Orel 1966, 181). On the importance of work in the novel, see Howe (1967), 52–4; Gregor (1974), 43–76; Beegel (1987), 221–6; Williams (1973), 212–13; Snell (1985), 399–400; Wotton (1985), 138.

The paired episodes in the first two chapters brilliantly and succinctly dramatize these suggestions. The vignette of Bathsheba with her mirror informs us from the opening pages that her pride will have a fall: because she is looking at herself, we know that she is going to have to learn to look elsewhere. Gabriel, on the other hand, is looking at the stars; he is looking out at a cosmos which seems quite apart from and independent of him. Hardy draws a sharp contrast between the sounds the wind makes among the various bushes and grasses and the notes sounded by Gabriel's flute—'a sequence which was to be found nowhere in nature' (10). In putting down the flute and moving out of the hut, Gabriel is exchanging one sort of order for another, shifting his attention from man-made patterns to natural ones. The fact that he is at home with both musical and stellar patterns confirms his status as connecter, but this very status depends upon the clear distinction between the two realms. Gabriel can read nature because he does not expect her to mirror him—because he looks at her, not as a projection of his own desires, but in terms of her own patterns.[14]

Time-telling is a useful motif for Hardy in this novel because the notion of time raises the question of the relationship between subject and object upon which Hardy's delineation of Gabriel's particular strength depends.[15] Gabriel is the hero of the novel because he knows where he stops, as it were, and where the Other begins. That such a distinction is precisely untenable complicates the reading of the time-telling scene, to which I wish to return in a moment. For 'time' is paradoxical— at once an abstraction created by the human mind and the cause of concrete effects working on the human body; arbitrary in its divisions, yet inexorable in its effects. Mechanical clocks and watches tend to be unreliable in *Far from the Madding Crowd*, and characters who think they can impose their own timetables upon nature tend to fail. In the gap between 'man-made' and

[14] The scene in which Gabriel tells time by the stars is discussed by Eastman (1978), 20–33. On Bathsheba with her mirror, see Carpenter (1964), 331–45; Eastman (1978), 22; Bullen (1986), 69–70. Johnson notes that the telling-time scene 'is no doubt meant as some sort of counterpoint to Bathsheba's gazing in the hand mirror' (1983, 12–13).

[15] Osborne discusses the contrast between clock time and natural or cosmic time in Hardy's poetry and prose (1972, 543–4); see also Sullivan (1974) and Eastman (1978).

'natural' time Hardy locates the fate of the major characters, all of whom are developed, in a scheme both elegant and comprehensive, in terms of their willingness to surrender their own schedules to the rhythms of nature. Introducing Gabriel Oak by having him tell time by the stars provides not only a striking introduction to the novel's hero but a criterion against which Troy, Boldwood, and Bathsheba will in turn be measured and found wanting.

Frank Troy assumes he can master time as easily as he masters women, but in a novel where ignoring time and timing things too closely are equally signs of a dangerous hubris, his timetable leads to his own destruction.[16] Troy acquires power over Bathsheba by techniques of seduction—both verbal, like his flirtatious repartee, and physical, like the sword exercise—which depend upon an instinctive sense of timing, honed by practice. His essential falsity is suggested however by Troy's consistent association with mechanical timepieces. His proper emblem is the manikin in the All Saints' clock-tower, for Troy—who himself compares the beating of Bathsheba's heart to the ticking of a clock—treats people like puppets and enjoys getting them wound up. He abandons Fanny when the clock at All Saints' has struck its three quarters; he offers his father's watch—the only token of his family he himself possesses—to Bathsheba on their second encounter;[17] he flaunts his lack of reverence for the past when he proposes to modernize Bathsheba's Elizabethan mansion;[18] he ignores the danger of seasonal rain to his ricks, even though his losses at the racetrack should have reminded him that 'the time of year is come for changeable weather' (298); and, by the melodramatic timing of his final entrance, he brings about his own death.

Fanny is his victim not only because he has seduced her but because he is oblivious to the natural rhythms in which she,

[16] Morrell (1965), 31. On Troy's attitude to time, see also Eastman (1978), 28–9, and Johnson (1983), 38–9.

[17] See Gregor (1974), 48.

[18] Hardy later accused himself of doing, as a young architect, what Troy wishes to do, admitting ruefully that 'Much beautiful Gothic, as well as Jacobean and Georgian work, he was passively instrumental in destroying' (Hardy 1928, 40–1). Bathsheba's house is described in the novel as having 'traces of . . . Gothic extraction' (80); the Preface to the 1895 edition refers to the 'heroine's fine old Jacobean house' (Orel 1966, 10).

as a woman, is inexorably caught. An archetypal victim of sexuality almost wholly absorbed into nature, Fanny nevertheless finds her life ruled by artificial time and by clock-like rhythms, counting the windows at the barracks as she counts the final milestones to Casterbridge and her inevitable union (in the Union) with the earth she has measured with her steps. Fanny indeed is destroyed as much by Troy's temporal demands as by his sexual predatoriness. But Troy is also his own victim; and the callous egotism which destroys her dooms him, too, to eventual defeat.

While Troy believes he can dominate time and women alike, Boldwood believes he can ignore both, idealize them out of existence. A 40-year-old bachelor still attached to the memory of his parents and oblivious to the local women who are attracted to him, Boldwood is presented as out of step with the rhythms of natural development.[19] Oblivious to fashion, grotesquely biblical in his mode of expression, and unaccustomed to observing communal festivals like Christmas, he is deeply alienated from the rhythms of the community. Bathsheba is irresponsible in sending Boldwood the valentine, but surely unlucky in sending it to the only man in Wessex who would fail to realize that 14 February is the one day of the year when one does not take the invitation to 'Marry Me' wholly seriously. It is appropriate that Boldwood places the valentine against the clock on his mantel, and that his falling for Bathsheba is presented as a literal descent into time and nature, in the scene when he goes down the stairs and out into the winter sunrise to find the sender of the missive.

Like Oak's, Boldwood's could be a happy fall, if he were able to negotiate the transition into natural temporality. His failure to do so assures not only his own destruction but the suffering of Bathsheba, whom he torments, as Troy does Fanny, by pressuring her to submit to his own bizarre timetable. But while Troy's attention span is very short, Boldwood's is grotesquely long. The discovery, after his death, of a room filled with gifts bought seven years in advance—and marked, in defiance of popular taboo, with what he had trusted would be Bathsheba's married name—confirms the feeling that what

---

[19] Beegel notes Boldwood's 'regressiveness . . . a desire to stop the earth from turning and the clocks from ticking' (1987, 210).

is wrong with Boldwood can be expressed in terms of his relationship to time.[20]

In contrast to his rivals, Oak is presented as having an exemplary attitude to fallen nature. By observing and accommodating himself to the rhythms of time and weather, he can get along with the Great Mother. The shepherd's-calendar[21] sequence of vignettes (Gabriel with the new-born lamb in his arms, Gabriel at the sheep-washing, Gabriel at the sheep-shearing) suggests biblical and sometimes ecclesiastical analogies. Gabriel seems in tune not only with the changing year but with the church calendar (literally in tune at the end of the novel, when Bathsheba intercepts him on his way to choir practice). His approach is mimetic: he acknowledges and subordinates himself to the Other by mirroring its rhythms in cyclical and ritualized activities. It is this highly structured and committed labour which is the source of his power (Hardy's hardy protagonist was, in the manuscript, originally called 'Strong'[22]). Gabriel Oak is an attractive self-projection for a writer whose 'Wessex' holds a mirror up to a vanishing Dorset and who sees himself perhaps as conquering time by miming it in fiction.

Bathsheba's orientation to time is less extreme than that of her two unlucky suitors. Unlike Troy and Boldwood, she is practical enough to sense the ways in which luck and nature can contravene human projects. Her reply to Troy when he asks her if she knows French—'I began, but when I got to the verbs, father died' (198)—shows how much poetic power Hardy's consistent use of a motif enables him to get from a single line. As a milkmaid and then a farmer, Bathsheba is vocationally more in tune with natural time than they are. It is accordingly ironical that she is on her nightly patrol of the farm when she first meets Frank Troy; for if as a farmer Bathsheba is in tune with nature's rhythms, as a woman she of course is not. In her insistence on postponing marriage once she has reached marriageable age, in her determination to keep her future open and at the same time to discover what that future holds,

[20] Millgate (1971*b*), 85, draws attention to this episode; see also Giordano (1978); Clarke (1970). Eastman discusses Boldwood's attitude to time (1978, 30–1).

[21] The phrase is R. L. Purdy's, cited by Millgate (1971*b*), 93.

[22] See Millgate (1982), 153, who notes the similarity of Oak's name to Hardy's.

Bathsheba is attempting to control time in a way not permissible in Hardy's universe. For a woman, both sexuality and its postponement involve risk and invite failure. Fanny, a figure associated, like Ophelia, with flowers,[23] dies when time and nature catch up with her; Bathsheba, whose mythical associations are rather with Diana, is no less destined to fall, for a Dianine stance is as untenable as sexual surrender is perilous.

None of Hardy's characters is more schematically self-divided than his heroine. Defined by the conflict between her desire for independence and her need for love, Bathsheba is consistently described in terms of her allegiance both to Venus and to Diana.[24] Even her Dianine attributes imply a tension: while Bathsheba's boyish qualities—her horseback-riding, for example, and her distrust of marriage—derive from the Diana side of her nature, so too do details (usually associated with the image of the moon) which already imply her ineluctable link with nature and with sexuality. When Bathsheba assists at the birth of the little calf who mistakes the lantern for the moon, the narrator evokes Lucina (15); the night of Fanny's elopement with the man who will subsequently woo her as well, Bathsheba is 'dimly seen' at her window, 'robed in mystic white' (77); she illuminates Boldwood 'as the moon lights up a great tower' (139), and hypnotizes him from afar in the moon-haunted scene in which he broods over her valentine. Yet other details link her even more explicitly with Venus. Gabriel discovers that the lady farmer he has heard about is Bathsheba herself—that 'this Ashtoreth of strange report was only a modification of Venus the well-known' (55); in the Great Barn, the newly shorn ewe, metaphorically associated with Bathsheba, is described as 'Aphrodite rising from the foam' (168); and indeed the first time we see Bathsheba she is characterized by Venus' colour, her flower, and her emblem: dressed in red, surrounded by myrtle plants, and looking at herself in a mirror. Perhaps

[23] Brooks (1971), 174.
[24] On Bathsheba as Diana, see Carpenter (1964), 89–90; Casagrande (1979), 64; Johnson (1983), 41–7. Wotton (1985), 134, notes the identification with Venus. Hardy comments that a man may see 'the Diana or the Venus in his Beloved' (Hardy 1928, 314). Bathsheba's name invites comparison with her biblical prototype: see Miller (1970), 124, and Bullen (1986), 73–4. She is also an Eve: see Meisel (1972), 46; Casagrande (1979), 55.

the most subtle example of the Venus–Diana polarity occurs in the scene in which Bathsheba chooses the seal for the valentine she is sending to Boldwood. Rejecting both a unicorn's head ('There's nothing in that') and a pair of doves, Bathsheba, in quest of 'something extraordinary' (111), lights upon the verbal motto 'Marry Me'. The sequence points to Bathsheba's wilful refusal either to think of herself as an 'ordinary' woman or to recognize the dangerously contradictory impulses in her own nature.[25]

On the whole, this scheme serves Hardy's purposes well. By comparing his heroine to two goddesses, Hardy whimsically elevates her; by locating Bathsheba within the polarities of ancient myth, he lends authority to his paradigm, and suggests that the contradiction he analyses in his heroine is a universal and permanent aspect of female nature. And the Venus–Diana split buttresses Hardy's plot. The way the novel begins makes it clear that Bathsheba must drop her Diana stance and acknowledge her desire for marriage and her need for Gabriel Oak before the narrative can arrive at its happy ending. It will be the very talent which marks Bathsheba out as unusual—her competence as a farmer—which will lead her eventually to respect Gabriel's strength and prudence and to realize that she needs his help. As her story unfolds Bathsheba is going to have to realize that her deepest needs proceed from the Venus and not the Diana side of her nature.

Yet it is not as simple as that. Though Venus and Diana seem to pull Bathsheba in opposite directions, the text undermines the very opposition which has been so carefully set up. The Venus–Diana paradigm has a unifying force upon which Hardy equally relies. Bathsheba's independence evokes anxiety about whether she is too 'mannish' (227). Hardy wants to erase any hint of the tomboy about Bathsheba, and the Venus–Diana imagery enables him to describe a split which might too readily be conceptualized as masculine–feminine in terms of reassuringly feminine prototypes. Though split in two, Bathsheba is whole-ly female. His simultaneous insistence both on her unity and on her duality expresses in fact a fundamental contradiction in Hardy's attitude towards his heroine.

[25] Goode (1988), 24, points out that Bathsheba has no way of expressing her own desire except through the coded language of patriarchal monogamy ('Marry Me').

The very vignettes which seem intended to establish tensions in Bathsheba's character function at the same time to *image* her unity. Each 'half' seems radiantly whole, and each aligns Bathsheba with nature. Bathsheba/Venus, complacently looking at herself in the mirror, is self-sufficient: she carries blooming nature along with her, as well as all her household goods; the very horses, 'sensible' (4) of her will, do as she wishes. Bathsheba/Diana on horseback is a vital and attractive figure, and the way she handles the horse—her habit of riding astride, and of dropping 'backwards flat upon the pony's back' (18) as she passes under a low-hanging bough, as swiftly as a kingfisher and as silently as a hawk, springing back 'to her accustomed perpendicular like a bowed sapling' (18)—suggests, more compellingly than Hardy's tendentious mythological allusions, *both* the Venus and the Diana in Bathsheba, both her unconventionality and independence of mind, and her unselfconscious physicality and sexuality. Again and again, Bathsheba's Venus and Diana sides reinforce one another, and seem to proceed from the same source: her instinctive sense of her own powers and her own needs. More winningly than Oak, who is androgynous in his moral nature, Bathsheba is an erotic androgyne, a figure fusing 'feminine' beauty, wilfulness, and naïveté with 'masculine' energy, independence, and athleticism. The narrative tells us about dividedness but shows us a whole woman whose vitality derives from both sides of her nature.

Venus and Diana, then, cannot be separated. Hardy has set up the myth to suggest that Bathsheba must grow out of her Diana phase and recognize her need for Oak. But because the Venus in Bathsheba has been equated with specular narcissism, it too must be abandoned. Bathsheba must outgrow not only her desire to run her own life but also her desire to be looked at, if the novel is to have a happy ending. And she does: the woman who had wanted all her babies' names in the newspaper insists on creeping anonymously to church in the last chapter. But a Venus/Diana who ends up neither Venus nor Diana may be felt to be left with no character at all. The problem is that a Bathsheba who does not want to be looked at is simply a different 'character' from the one we met at the beginning of the novel, for Bathsheba exists in a specular relationship both with the other characters and with the reader.

Much of the vitality of this lively novel derives from the visualness of Bathsheba—the almost extravagant way in which she satisfies the text's scopic desire.[26] Her construction is deftly adumbrated in Troy's mirroring language: she is a woman looked at by a man who tells her that 'you have never been a man looking upon a woman, and that woman yourself' (200). There is a dramatic, even theatrical dimension to her presentation: many of the novel's episodes are visualized like scenes in a play, with Bathsheba at stage centre. When she appears on the wagon, for example, 'the apex of the whole' composition (4), or framed in the second-storey window on the night Fanny disappears, or in the ground-floor window during the shearing supper, or in the 'passionate scene' enacted in the parlour on the same night (180), Bathsheba's *power* to draw and focus the male gaze confers upon the tableaux of which she forms the centre their formal composedness, even while the *desire* to attract the male gaze evokes the criticism of the male narrator.

It is the impression of Bathsheba's wholeness which sets her apart and places her as the heroine of the novel. Unlike Fanny, who is a barely visible 'form' (97), 'shape' (97), or 'spot' (98), glimpsed only in culturally coded fragments (a lock of hair, a rapid pulse, a plaintive voice), and who finally, in childbirth, splits into two and expires,[27] Bathsheba is an emphatically unified figure. Whereas Tess's body is described in terms of unfathomable depths to be penetrated, Bathsheba's seems sheathed, impenetrable, contained. There is strong visual emphasis on her silhouette and outline. Her wardrobe gets more attention than that of any other Hardy heroine, and the emphasis is on binding or enclosing surfaces: on contour, sensuous texture, trim. Dressed in a 'black silk dress' which as she 'surged' out of the room '[licked] up a few straws and [dragged] them along with a scratching noise upon the floor' (93), in 'a rather dashing velvet dress, carefully put on before a

[26] See Bullen on looking and watching in *Far from the Madding Crowd* (1986, 61–87); Wotton on the way in which 'the woman [is] obliged to play the role in which she has been cast by being seen' (1985, 128–30); also Sénéchel's (1980) Lacanian analysis of focalization in the novel.

[27] On Fanny as an undefined 'spot', see Brooks (1971), 172. For the serial version Hardy had to blur the issue of how many bodies were in Fanny's coffin. The words 'one' and 'two' recur with a curious insistence in both the serial version and the final (Wessex Edition) version of the novel: see Jones (1978), 322–3; Gatrell (1979), 86–8.

glass' (156), or in 'a beautiful gold-colour silk gown, trimmed
with black lace' (253); catching Troy by the gimp on her skirt;
'standing by' at the sheep-washing, 'in a new riding-habit—the
most elegant she had ever worn—the reins of her horse . . .
looped over her arm' (142)—Bathsheba stands out visually
from her background with the sharpness of a fashion-plate
illustration. At sheep-shearing—in the context of the description of Oak's technique, as he traces the outline of sheep's body
to 'open up' and remove its fleece like a 'garment' (168), and of
the lush June vegetation, where 'Every green was young, every
pore was open, and every stalk was swollen with racing currents
of juice' (163)—she appears in yet another riding-habit 'of
myrtle-green, which fitted her to the waist as a rind fits its fruit'
(169). The patently erotic quality of such description depends
partly on the Venus–Diana tension between Bathsheba's
potentially explosive nubility and the visual boundedness of her
clothed figure, partly on the implied analogy between Bathsheba's green form and the swollen plant-shoots, which gives
her a specifically phallic dimension.

The narrative develops a peculiarly intense 'skin-sense',
deriving from this boundedness and from Bathsheba's preter-
natural sensitivity to the male gaze, which awakens her own
sense of her body's boundaries.[28] The narrator's impulse to
run his eyes over the surface of her body is expressed in her
awareness of being so enwrapped. When Boldwood approaches
her, 'She heard footsteps brushing the grass, and had a consciousness that love was encircling her like a perfume' (143).
Oak's gaze becomes a caress: 'Rays of male vision seem to
have a tickling effect upon virgin faces in rural districts; she
brushed hers with her hand, as if Gabriel had been irritating its
pink surface by actual touch' (20). The paradigm of the Fall
can accommodate such moments: as Adam's and Eve's embar-
rassment about being looked at marks their fallen state, so
Bathsheba's self-consciousness can be read as a sign of her
fallen nature, her ' "Vanity" ' (7). But something else may also

---

[28] Boumelha (1982), 35, links skin-sense and clothing, citing the remarkable
passage from *Desperate Remedies* in which Cytherea Graye's dress is said to have
'sensation . . . Delicate antennae, or feelers, bristle on every outlying frill' (Wessex
Edition, 151). On Hardy's personal response to the rustle of silken ruffles, see Millgate
(1982), 47–8. Anzieu's (1989) insights seem particularly relevant to Hardy.

be at stake here, and the myth of the Fall, and particularly of the fallenness of woman, perhaps functions for Hardy precisely to control and repress that something else.

What it might be is made clearer by a consideration of two parallel episodes, the sheep-shearing and the sword exercise, in which Oak and Troy metaphorically act out their different styles of love-making.[29] Though Gabriel's tender expertise is set against Troy's flashy display, both techniques involve roving over the surface of the female body. At the sheep-shearing, Oak 'opened up the neck and collar', 'running the shears' expertly over the ewe's body—as Bathsheba's eyes follow his hands (167); in the sword exercise, Troy follows the contours of Bathsheba's body so closely that 'had it been possible for the edge of the sword to leave in the air a permanent substance wherever it flew past, the space left untouched would have been almost a mould of Bathsheba's figure' (211). The two scenes taken together constitute a composite tribute to female wholeness: potential male threat is warded off by a magically impregnable female body which emerges intact, even renewed, from phallic assault. (Troy's oddly schoolboyish tribute of 'scarf-skin', 212, seems an uncannily appropriate acknowledgement of his own fragmentation, her wholeness.[30]) The symbolic function of Bathsheba as a figure is finally made startlingly clear in the strangely unselfconscious comparison between the 'liquid stream' released by Moses' rod and Bathsheba's 'stream of tears' (213):[31] her glowing unitary body with its sensitized surface figures a lack in the males who desire her.

But in becoming the object of masculine desire, Bathsheba herself has disappeared. From Gabriel's hands there emerges not a woman but an animal/goddess; and the figure carved out

---

[29] Among the many discussions of the sword exercise are Carpenter (1964), 331–45, who establishes the parallel with Gabriel's shearing of the sheep; Gregor (1974), 48–9; Johnson (1983), 35–7; Beegel (1987), 211–12; Bayley (1978), 117–23; Bullen (1986), 85–6; Wotton (1985), 134–5.

[30] Bayley (1978), 120–1, comments on the 'scarf-skin'.

[31] Whether Hardy was aware of the sexual symbolism has always puzzled readers. The way Bayley puts it seems to me exactly right: 'Hardy knew quite well here what he was up to, one imagines, as he does in other novels, but his text saves him from any appearance of intention or insistency . . . to be effectively symbolic of sexual relation the scene would require purposive unity, such as D. H. Lawrence would have given it . . . a greater degree of organization than Hardy's prose texture knows about, or cares about' (1978, 117).

by Troy's sword is empty space (like the figure inside the black-and-gold dress, which, as Cainy Ball observes, would have stood alone 'without legs inside if required', 253). Again it is one of the rustic characters who voices most explicitly the deep impulse of the narrative. The heroine as a figure exists to be deployed in a male plot—Troy's, or Cainy's, or Hardy's. The empty dress need not, indeed cannot, have a real woman inside it, if it is to function as a counter in a male fantasy or fiction.

Cainy Ball's description of Bathsheba sounds like a traditional ballad, the narrative shape of which is adopted, as many readers have pointed out, by Hardy himself in the novel as a whole.[32] The woman's place in a ballad plot is usually (as it is in the particular ballad to which Hardy alludes) that of a victim of male power. Hardy seems to have used Fanny to occupy this space in his novel, allowing Bathsheba to move beyond it. The irony of the plot is that such different women fall for the same predatory man, but the point of its denouement seems to be that Bathsheba survives the experience, as Fanny does not. But as she becomes an emptier and emptier sign, there is a sense in which Bathsheba herself comes to occupy the space of the victim.[33] By the end of the novel Bathsheba has lost the visual presence which distinguished her from Fanny, and turned (as Troy complains) into a plaintive voice, finally into a moral emblem. Holding the dying Troy in her arms in a '*pietà*' posture, she is praised by the narrator as exhibiting the stuff of which great men's mothers are made (437).

Troy made Fanny a mother; Hardy has made one of Bathsheba. 'Mother' in this context erases 'woman', repressing her threatening eroticism and her disturbing physical integrity. Indeed, Bathsheba is doubly displaced by the figure: it is because Oak's deepest allegiance is not to Bathsheba but to the Great Mother that he can possess her in the end. Idealized female figures like Dame Fortune or Mother Nature or the Virgin Mary marginalize individual women.[34] Hardy uses the *pietà* tableau to render Bathsheba, as a body, invisible. The (m)Other, whose gaze constitutes the male subject, is appropri-

---

[32] See Davidson (1940); Brown (1961), 48–9; Williams (1973), 203–4, who finds the ballad stereotypes condescending.

[33] See Boumelha (1982), 44–5, on the 'crossing curves of their fortunes'.

[34] Culler (1982), 166–7.

ated by him to unmake his heroine, whose being depends upon her author's decision to look at her or not to look.

For Hardy his heroine is a compelling and yet a threatening figure—compelling because she images wholeness, threatening because, being female, she cannot be allowed to embody it permanently. The intimation of female self-sufficiency fascinates but emasculates; it must be resisted. By dismissing the mirror as an emblem merely of female vanity, Hardy has projected mirror-stage narcissism on to Bathsheba and contained the specular threat. But his success is at the expense of his heroine. The narrative knows that there is no self except what is constituted by the gaze of the Other: that it 'is not the rays which bodies absorb, but those which they reject, that give them the colours they are known by' (171); that 'I look double to you' may mean the same as 'you look double to me' (330). While it enacts the interdependence of subject and object, self and Other, it also dramatizes, in its anticlimactic and antierotic ending, the cost of attempting to evade that knowledge.

Although the literal mirror is associated only with Bathsheba, there are other specular moments in the novel, in which the anxiety denied by the surface of the narrative returns in disquieting ways. Two of these—Frank Troy's encounter with the gargoyle, and Bathsheba's vision in the swamp—have always attracted critical commentary.[35] These episodes invite comparison as demonic epiphanies: Bathsheba and Troy, who, in the Gothic encounter before the open coffin, have had to confront their real feelings for Fanny Robin and the hollowness of their relationship with each other, are now called upon to face not only the failure of their projects but some essential shapelessness and chaos in the nature of things. But what chiefly interests me is not only that both visions involve the deformed or dismembered human body but that the narrator oddly enough does not seem to notice this.

While the narrator draws attention, in luridly heightened

---

[35] Critics who have discussed the swamp scene include May (1974), 152; Gregor (1974), 54; Vigar (1974), 108–9; Kramer (1975), 36–7; Bayley (1978), 114–16; Casagrande (1979), 57–9; Johnson (1983), 44–5; Beegel (1987), 213–14. On the gargoyle, see Carpenter (1963–4), 338; Morrell (1965), 66; Gregor (1974), 59–61; Beegel (1987), 214–15.

rhetoric, to the apocalyptic associations he wishes to fore-ground—he has the mushrooms, springing up from the 'moist and poisonous coat' of the 'malignant' swamp, exhaling 'the essences of evil things in the earth and the waters under the earth'—their sinister effect depends more for the reader on their sharing the shape, colour, and texture of human flesh (in a context which had originally established an association between mushrooms and the cheeks of Fanny's dead baby).[36] 'Tall and attenuated, with stems like macaroni', 'leathery', 'marked with great splotches, red as arterial blood', 'exhibiting to her listless gaze their clammy tops . . . their oozing gills' (348), the mushrooms are weirdly phallic. In the gargoyle episode, Troy observes the uprooted seedlings, which have begun 'to move and writhe in their bed' (362), 'washed white and clean as a bundle of tendons' (363). The background to Troy's observation is the narrator's demonic description of the gargoyle itself, a kind of disembodied head, 'too human to be called like a dragon, too impish to be like a man, too animal to be like a fiend, and not enough like a bird to be called a griffin' (361), with its lower teeth worn away, spitting and vomiting forth a deluge of rainwater. Part of the horror here seems to come from the unclassifiability of the creature, its crossing of taxonomical boundaries: at once 'impish', 'animal', and 'human' (361), it stares back at us like a face in a horror-house mirror.

But the text undercuts the implications of such imagery by supplying a qualifying context. In both episodes, the point of view is ambiguous. In the swamp scene, although the focalizer is Bathsheba the rhetoric seems to be not hers but the narrator's: it is as if for a visionary moment the consciousness of the character were invaded by the consciousness of her observer.[37] At the same time, however, he undermines his own response, framing it with much more conventional images of benevolent nature and new beginnings: the rising sun, the cosy chatter of the woodland creatures, the little ploughboy on his way to church memorizing a psalm (images with stock associations so compelling that their message of uplift completely dominated

[36] See Jones (1978), 322–3.
[37] On this point see Casagrande (1979), 57–9, and Bayley (1978), 114–16.

the scene in the film version).[38] Primordial chaos is evoked again as Liddy appears—only to be suddenly and disconcertingly dispersed as she crosses the treacherous surface without difficulty:

Bathsheba never forgot that transient little picture of Liddy crossing the swamp to her there in the morning light. Iridescent bubbles of dank subterranean breath rose from the sweating sod beside the waiting-maid's feet as she trod, hissing as they burst and expanded away to join the vapoury firmament above. Liddy did not sink, as Bathsheba had anticipated. (349)

What are we to make of this anticlimax? Is Liddy's invulnerability intended to negate the demonic vision—imply that it was all in Bathsheba's mind? Or does it suggest that those who perceive no evil suffer no evil?—a reading which not only shifts the narrative into a kind of allegory out of keeping with its predominantly realistic texture, but which seems to validate innocence and ignorance over the insight Bathsheba has apparently earned by experience. The swamp vision apparently represents something Bathsheba has to acknowledge and come to terms with, not 'pass over' as Liddy does. Yet the conclusion of the chapter, which has Bathsheba deciding to repudiate tragic books which *mirror* her situation in favour of optimistic ones which will cheer her up, does seem to imply that repression is the way to a happy ending.

The gargoyle vision is similarly ambiguous. In this chapter the narrator's point of view is even more clearly distinguished from the character's, because the really repellent image, that of the gargoyle itself, is described before Troy himself wakes up. Yet the text seems to be ambivalent about the attitude one should take to the kind of insight Troy achieves. On the one hand, by having Bathsheba simply replant the flowers and arrange for the water-pipe to be moved, he seems to be suggesting that Troy's is an infantile overreaction. Much judgemental commentary confirms this impression. On the other hand, whether or not the flowers are replanted is, for Troy, not really the point. What matters is that he has been made to see himself and his own projects from a different perspective—decentre

[38] Appia-Via film, produced by Joseph Janni, directed by John Schlesinger, 1967. On its upbeat 1960s ambience, see Widdowson (1989), 103–14.

himself in a radical way. Nature's failure to confirm his senti-mental gesture strikes Troy with the force of an existential revelation. Having always taken himself for granted as subject and accepted the vicissitudes of his life as tolerable because they 'appertained to the hero of his story, without whom there would have been no story at all for him' (364), Troy is suddenly forced to perceive himself as object. The narrative as a whole suggests that his own insignificance is something Troy some-how has to learn, though his response is to hate himself, to '[throw] up his cards' and forswear 'his game for that time and always' (365). That the narrator considers this cowardice is made tiresomely clear; but that he shares Troy's dismay is equally obvious. The novels indeed often express a certain ambivalence about the 'villainous' characters, apparently validating their alienation even while condemning their moral-ity. What is not clear in the end is how seriously we are to take the apparent meaning of the gargoyle vision—to what extent we are to see its quasi-human face as mirroring in some funda-mental way the human situation. It is in the undermining of these epiphanies, even more than in the last-minute reprieve of Boldwood, that the novel is prevented from turning into tragedy. The two scenes enact the process by which Hardy wills his narrative into comic shape, while at the same time dramatizing the cost of this decision.

There is a third episode which, though it has attracted less critical attention, poses some of the same problems as the episodes in the swamp and the churchyard. That is Gabriel's brief vision of an alien universe after his sheep have been killed:

Oak raised his head, and wondering what he could do, listlessly surveyed the scene. By the outer margin of the pit was an oval pond, and over it hung the attenuated skeleton of a chrome-yellow moon, which had only a few days to last—the morning star dogging her on the left hand. The pool glittered like a dead man's eye, and as the world awoke a breeze blew, shaking and elongating the reflection of the moon without breaking it, and turning the image of the star to a phos-phoric streak upon the water. All this Oak saw and remembered. (41)

Perhaps because this passage is so short it does not draw attention to itself as insistently as do the swamp and gargoyle

scenes, but it does share with them not only its epiphanic function but also the somatic imagery—the 'skeleton' moon distorted by the breeze on the water, the pool glittering 'like a
dead man's eye'. Like Bathsheba's, Gabriel's epiphany is
incongruous, for his modified awareness is not really dramatized in the rest of the novel, where he seems to look at nature as
a source of clues rather than of emblems. Indeed, the vision of
the personified moon as demonic—a sinister Diana—is out of
line with the suggestion, consistently developed elsewhere, that
Gabriel is in harmony with his Great Mother. The passage
seems to require a different and more 'metaphysical' kind of
reading than the context in which it is embedded.

Though the explicit echoes in this description are from
Coleridge's 'The Rime of the Ancient Mariner', the informing
presence is that of Wordsworth, specifically the Boy of Winander
episode from *The Prelude*, the echoes and mirrors of which
Hardy consistently parodies with varying degrees of irony.[39]
Wordsworth's image of the stars reflected in the water, with
its suggestions of nature's benevolence and of harmony between
heaven and earth, emerges deformed by Hardy's cosmic scepticism. In Hardy such mirroring moments, with their strong
vertical axis, tend to render the human observer irrelevant, a
looker not looked back at, excluded from nature's mirroring
gaze. Through this moment in Hardy's first major novel can be
traced a direct line from Wordsworth through Hardy to
Lawrence, who picks up and extends the apocalyptic suggestions of Hardy's moon-reflections in the famous scene in
Women in Love.

The *comic* analogue of the Boy of Winander episode is Joseph
Poorgrass's encounter with the owl in Chapter 8.[40] In Wordsworth's world, it is when the echo stops that the revelation
begins—when the owls fail to answer him that the Boy, strain-
ing to hear their call, hears other sounds instead and senses, in
a flash of revelation, the vastness and the otherness of the

[39] This episode has been discussed by Johnson (1983), 17–18, and Gregor (1974),
53–4, who comments on the moments of vision as Wordsworthian attempts to 'render
"unknown modes of being"'. On Hardy and Wordsworth, see Björk (1985), i. 355–6
n. 1102 and 362 nn. 1150, 1151; also Johnson (1894), 180–4; Howe (1967), 24;
Casagrande (1977, 1979).

[40] Something like this apparently actually happened to a Dorset man; see Sherren
(1908), 12–13.

universe. For Joseph, on the other hand, there is no such escape from the self: nature mockingly echoes back his specular anxiety. But the identity denied by nature is given back by the community, in whose eyes, and only in whose eyes, this morbidly self-conscious individual—who pretends to have problems about looking and being looked at—can find his self affirmed. Joseph really is a nobody and the universe knows it, but as long as the community does not, he can hold himself together and keep talking.

His inverted exhibitionism links Joseph with the three main characters who need to find themselves mirrored in the gaze of the Other. Troy is just as exhibitionistic as Joseph, Boldwood just as 'modest', Bathsheba just as aware of being observed. The peculiar role of looking and being looked at in Hardy's novels, their downright voyeuristic dimension, has often been noted, for there seems to be a contradiction between the moral stance Hardy takes against his characters' self-centredness and the tendency of his own voyeuristic impulse to create in them that very egotism which he, as narrator, condemns and, as author, punishes. Joseph Poorgrass—like his analogue Thomas Leaf in *Under the Greenwood Tree*—is one of those minor characters who express in comic terms some of the serious impulses which motivate the narrative, and the way this figure brings together the ideas of natural and societal mirroring is worth examining for the light it throws not only on the narrator's voyeuristic gaze but on the constitution of his protagonist.

Joseph Poorgrass, with his suggestive names (Joseph the excluded father/all flesh is poor grass) is what has to be repressed in order to produce Gabriel—as he is, indeed, in the biblical narrative in which both their names are found.[41] Hardy's hero is a man sturdily independent, it would seem, of echoes and mirrors—a man who does not expect nature either to challenge or to confirm his identity. Yet a closer reading of the very episode in which Oak's relationship with nature is first established suggests a specular dependence apparently denied on the surface of the text. I want to look again at the scene of Gabriel's telling time by the stars in order to suggest how the

---

[41] On demonic parody see Frye (1957), 147–50. Schweik notes that Joseph's surname was originally 'Poorheed' (1968, 422–3).

concept of time deconstructs, on the figurative level, the very moral patterns it seems invoked to establish.

The way this scene is handled undermines the sharpness of the very distinction between man and nature, self and Other, upon which Oak's virtue is founded.[42] If Gabriel is very different from Bathsheba on her wagon, there is nevertheless a sense in which he, too, is looking into a mirror. To 'tell' time is precisely to impose a *fiction* on the bland face of the outer world. The constellations are 'characters' created by the human mind, which has perceived as groups, and mythologized as bodies, the star-patterns which enable Gabriel to relate the sky to clock-time.[43] Indeed the narrator's meditations—as he muses that, however real the movement of the earth, the 'consciousness' of that movement 'derived from a tiny human frame' (10) —tend to jog rather than repress this realization. Though he carefully avoids the more radical Berkeleian implications, and stops short of claiming that the human mind *creates* the speed itself—claiming only (which no one would dispute) that it creates the *consciousness* of speed—Hardy nevertheless charges the passage with a certain ambiguity.[44] Reading the starry sky ('*One* o'clock', 13)—already described by the narrator as '*one* body' (9)—Gabriel seems at *one* with the universe; but since what he 'reads' is already culture not 'nature'—that is, since there was less duality to overcome than Hardy's evocation of the mighty moving globe has tended to suggest—the unity is emptier than it seems. Yet the rhetoric, though it almost reminds us of this, also prevents us from focusing on it. The imagery here is so rich and finally so reassuring because it just succeeds in resolving tensions not always so successfully contained, anxieties not always so successfully rationalized.

For though Gabriel is consistently identified, in an apparently very positive way, with cyclical time, there creeps into even the most positive of cyclical scenes which he dominates the

[42] The question of subject and object raised in this scene has been discussed by Morrell (1965), 16; Meisel (1972), 45; Johnson (1983), 13.

[43] Hardy, asked to identify 'Fine Passages in Verse and Prose', chose from Carlyle's *Sartor Resartus* the 'constellation's-eye view' of the planet earth (Orel 1966, 106–9).

[44] On Hardy's interest in Berkeley, see Bullen (1986), 65–6, 79–81.

suggestion that living naturally in time is not a human possibility. Whenever Hardy's exuberantly figurative impulse seizes
upon the image of the mirror, ironic anti-Wordsworthian
suggestions tend to emerge and undercut the text's broader,
clearer patterns of meaning. Take for example Chapter 19,
in which the spring sheep-washing forms the backdrop for
Boldwood's first proposal to Bathsheba.

One purpose of this chapter is to set up, as a norm, natural,
healthy involvement in time. The structuring contrast is
between flowing, burgeoning, fertile nature—with which
Gabriel is allied—and the obsessive fixation of Boldwood,
which, having no natural 'outlet' (142), seeks both to express
itself and to fix itself in words. The life of the earth connotes
natural sexuality. With its stiffening greenery and coursing
moisture (the flowing river, the plants whose very sap, because
of the microscopic view Hardy takes of them, is like a river
coursing through their stems), the English spring landscape is a
golden world of innocent eroticism. The suggestion is that all
this might possibly rub off on Boldwood, as the 'yellow pollen
from the buttercups' (142) rubs off on his boots; that love,
which has '[opened] the sluices of feeling' (144) in him, might
set it flowing in the right direction. Against the opportunity for
development, however, is the threat of encirclement and stasis:
this is the scene in which Bathsheba senses Boldwood's emotion
'encircling her like a perfume' (143), as he draws her aside and
attempts to bind her to him. By the end of the chapter Bathsheba
is in fact caught, but Boldwood himself is equally immobilized:
he 'stood long like a man who did not know where he was' until
'Realities . . . returned upon him' (147).

The imagery suggests that it is most fully human to move in
time and with time; it endorses Gabriel, whose participation in
the wet, timely, and sequential process of sheep-washing
endows him at once with phallic vitality and an ecclesiastical
virtue (the operation is very like a baptism, with Gabriel as
pastor), and makes Boldwood on the other hand seem rigid,
fanatical, and dangerous. The suggestion is that 'nature' and
'human nature' could form a kind of continuum, and that
sanity and happiness lie in catching nature's rhythms. It is
precisely the intrusion of the human into nature, however,
which generates an image that will deconstruct this illusion.

The image of the sheep-washing pool itself, a perfect circle and an uncanny *eye*, suddenly creates a vertical axis:

The sheep-washing pool was a perfectly circular basin of brickwork in the meadows, full of the clearest water. To birds on the wing its glassy surface, reflecting the light sky, must have been visible for miles around as a glistening Cyclops' eye in a green face. (142)

The Hardyan figure raises the problem of self and Other, presenting a bird's-eye view of an eye which would not be read as an eye by a bird-brain. There follows a very rapid shift of point of view, from the bird's-eye panorama to the almost microscopic close-up: the activity of the grass 'in sucking the moisture from the rich damp sod was almost a process observ-able by the *eye*' (142). It is a case, as Joseph Poorgrass says in another context, of the 'multiplying eye' (330): the eye of the earth and the eye of the sky are locked in mutual gaze, and what their mindless mirroring images is precisely the irrelev-ance of the human eye—which is nevertheless called upon, two sentences later, to watch the sap flow. It is a slightly jarring effect—an emblem of the fact that the human and the natural cannot be assimilated to one another. It is the *unnaturalness*, the perfect circularity of the pool, which turns the earth metaphor-ically into a gigantic, uncanny *body* and puts in question the illusion of the continuity between 'nature' and unproblematized 'human nature' which it is the business of the chapter as a whole to establish.

These suggestions can be assimilated, however, without much strain: the reader registers the idiosyncratic figure, but is not, probably, long detained or much distracted from the read-able message of the chapter as a whole. Other figures are harder to absorb, and it is often the concept of time which seems to generate them. Most fascinating to Hardy is the imagery of man-made time, of clocks and watches.[45] Their materiality tends to generate a comparison with the human body in a way which is sometimes really startling. The 'dead' catachreses we use to describe clocks—'hands', 'face'—spring to life, for example, in *Desperate Remedies*, where the two hackneyed terms

[45] From the time he was a child, Hardy was interested in clocks: see Millgate (1982), 53–4. Cf. also the 'creepy' story Hardy recounts, of a watch that started when its owner died (Hardy 1930, 72–3).

generate a surprising third and fourth, and a Dutch clock is seen with 'its *entrails* hanging down beneath its white *face* and wiry *hands*, like the *faeces* of a Harpy' (350; italics mine). To this bizarre description Hardy blandly appends a quotation—'(fœdissima ventris proluvies, uncæque manus, et pallida semper ora)':[46] there is no more striking example of his technique of blurring and defusing, by means of canonical allusion, passages which testify to his personal obsessions.

Most of the clock imagery in *Far from the Madding Crowd* is considerably blander than this: for example, the implied comparison between Gabriel's huge watch ('a small clock as to size') and its owner's monumental body (and character), or the description of its hour-hand which 'occasionally slipped round on the pivot', so that, 'though the minutes were told with precision, nobody could be quite certain of the hour they belonged to' (2)—a whimsical way of calling attention to the relativity of clock time (since a minute as a unit can have no meaning at all unless it has an hour to belong to). Even at its freshest and most surprising, such imagery generally takes off from the binary patterns of the rhetoric. Consider the portentous opening of the chapter in which Bathsheba is found to have eloped to Bath:

The village of Weatherbury was quiet as the graveyard in its midst, and the living were lying well-nigh as still as the dead. The church clock struck eleven. The air was so empty of other sounds that the whirr of the clock-work immediately before the strokes was distinct, and so was also the click of the same at their close. The notes flew forth with the usual blind obtuseness of inanimate things—flapping and rebounding among walls, undulating against the scattered clouds, spreading through their interstices into unexplored miles of space. (238)

The passage is generated by a series of structuring contrasts: tiny human beings–the huge alien universe; sound–silence; enclosure–expansion; the living–the dead. The central polarity is that between the pure mechanism of the sounds' origin—in the whirr and click of the clockwork—and their emergence

---

[46] Virgil, *Aeneid*, iii. 216–18. In the serial version of *The Mayor of Casterbridge* Lucetta Templeman is described as wearing 'Ear-drops for all the world like the pendulum of the clock that shows his inside in Facey's window': see *Graphic*, 33 (1886), 478.

'with the blind obtuseness of inanimate things' as bat-like *creatures* flying and 'flapping' through space.[47]

It is Hardy's obsession with the body, however—his unorthodox conception of the 'thing-ness' of the sounds—which explodes the paragraph and disrupts its binary neatness. The metaphor of body generates a metaphor of mind: since 'blind' and 'obtuse' only have meaning as applied to animate creatures —creatures which *could* potentially see and think—the very words which declare the sounds to be inanimate personify them and thus endow their journey through space with the attributes of the questing human consciousness. No sooner have they formed, however, than these momentarily animate beings progressively disintegrate—first flying, flapping, and rebounding, like discrete bodies, finally undulating and spreading, like a liquid or gas—indeed, decomposing into the sound waves which, from a scientific point of view, they always were—as they leave behind the 'walls' of the town to pass through the 'scattered clouds' into the 'unexplored miles of space'. Constituting and dissolving animate bodies, Hardy has quickly passed far beyond Weatherbury and the silent dead in its graveyard, but reached nevertheless an equally insistent image of dissolution.

The metaphor is so much more interesting than the story at this point that to return in the second paragraph to Bathsheba's 'crannied and mouldy halls' (238) seems a descent, from air to earth, from mind to body, from poetical speculation to stereotyped plot, the complications of which are beginning to be felt as dead and mechanical, whirring and clicking like the church clockwork itself. As a result, perhaps, the imagery of the grave ('crannied and mouldy halls') connects itself to the main character. As the self-reflexive nature of the figurative language suggests, Hardy's 'free' speculations are caught in the body of a text which cuts them off and cuts them up, disseminating meaning in a way which cannot be wilfully controlled by the careful deployment of binary structures.

Other clock imagery in *Far from the Madding Crowd* seems more controlled, more narrowly relevant to the novel's themes.

[47] 'Flapping' is one of the words Hardy uses rather often, in an idiosyncratic way, to refer to sound or light: e.g. to describe the music of gondoliers echoing against Venetian walls (Hardy 1928, 254).

Such is the clock in All Saints' church, which strikes the quarter-hours as Troy waits, his rage and humiliation exacerbated by its intermittent racket. Though the human shape of the quarter-jack gives an uncanny dimension to the scene, the imagery nevertheless relates cannily enough to the rest of the text. The fact that the mechanism which strikes the blows is a 'mannikin' (130), an anthropomorphic 'puppet' (131), imputes a parodic intent to its 'twitchings' (131), its sequences of 'fussy' (130) movements, and underlines by contrast the 'abnormal rigidity' (130) of Frank—rigidity both physical and moral, for Frank is as strictly programmed by his egotism and callousness as the little figure by its 'creaking . . . machinery' (130). The 'grotesque' (130) quality of the quarter-jack, the 'malicious leer upon the hideous creature's face' and its 'mischievous delight' (131) in its machinations, connect it with the gargoyle. The scene is emblematic of Troy's relationship with time, as Chapter 2 is of Oak's, and its emphasis on the man-made, the artificial, the mechanical aptly characterizes Troy's wilful and manipulative orientation.

Yet the hovering figurativity of the heightened rhetoric releases other meanings which undercut such neat polarities. The scene in All Saints' condemns Troy but its language complicates his relationship both to the narrator and to the author. The description of the clock recalls Hardy's response to the gargoyle, implicating him once again in Troy's dismay. And Troy tends to become a parody of Hardy himself, in his tendency to take frustration personally, literally to *see* as human the powers which thwart human intentions: Hardy's fascination with the humanoid quarter-jack reflects his own sense of cosmic mockery, even while the chapter as a whole condemns Troy for reacting to such mockery with callous bad temper. At the same time, the words which emphasize the materiality of the clock are the very language of criticism—one talks about creaking plots, and their machinery—so that the clock imagery can be read as a self-parodic reference to authorial manipulation.[48] The text which makes Troy a puppet points to Hardy as

[48] See Johnson (1894), 61; Howe (1967), 103; Gregor (1974), 71. Hardy observes in 'The Profitable Reading of Fiction' (1888) that in bad novels we see 'a machinery which often works awkwardly', and sense 'the audible working of the wheels and wires and carpentry, heard behind the performance, as the wires and trackers of a badly

the puppeteer, and to the willed quality of his fictions. Though it is Oak who seems to be Hardy's self-projection, it is Troy who expresses his will to mastery—of time, of narrative, and of women—and his dismay when this will is thwarted, just as it is Joseph Poorgrass who reflects his specular anxiety. The mirror has broken, the 'multiplying eye' (330) has become the multiplying I, and the author finds himself reflected not only in his master/piece Oak but in some of the less heroic fragments as well.

The clock imagery is the other side of the determination to idealize time and to construct Oak as a reassuring mirror-image. Hardy's somatic clockwork is uncanny in the strictly Freudian sense, precisely as the return of the repressed. Shattering his willed parallels and antitheses and setting up others, it undoes the authority of the author, points to Hardy as both manipulating his fictions and manipulated by them. *Far from the Madding Crowd* is an exuberant attempt to invest the male with a wholeness borrowed from the female, and it almost succeeds. Later fictions will testify more directly to the kinds of unease it represses.

---

constructed organ are heard under its tones' (Orel 1966, 113): the church setting of this metaphor links it with the manikin passage. See also Hardy (1928), 184.

3

The Return of the Native,
The Woodlanders: Reading the Body

THE RETURN OF THE NATIVE

In his study of Romantic imagery, Frye records a shift from
heaven to earth, from sublime contemplation of the sky-father
to rapt immersion in the earth-mother.[1] *Far from the Madding
Crowd*, which tries to resist Romanticism, denies the shift.
Balanced and integrated as he is, Gabriel Oak is in tune with
both his sky-father—whose stars he reads and whose thunder-
bolts he can withstand—and his earth-mother, who warns and
protects her loyal son. Accordingly he comes to function as the
universal parent, himself acquiring both maternal and paternal
characteristics and providing the novel with a firm comic
closure.

The Return of the Native, which initially invites a more
thoroughly Romantic response, seems to fit Frye's paradigm
better, the celebrated opening of the novel promising Brontëan
satisfactions. Readers who approach the novel with expectations generated by this impressive opening tend to find,
however, that it too resists a Romantic reading. Although it is
full of moments which satisfy a taste for the sublime and the
uncanny, there are also shocks and dislocations when the text
fails to supply what it seemed to promise. Eustacia turns out
not to be quite the erotic sorceress hinted at in the 'Queen of
Night' chapter, and indeed the chapter itself has enough false
notes to make the reader who wants to take it 'straight' somewhat uneasy. Clym is a disappointment as a romantic hero; the
reddleman is a disappointment because he turns into one.

The question this novel poses is indeed how to read. The
protagonist is a reader—a scholar of sorts whose literacy

[1] Frye (1968), 6–20.

impresses the local people, a nature-lover and amateur anti-
quarian whose sensitivity to the language of the heath is an
important part of his character notation—and both he and the
heath itself are explicitly described as texts. How the heath is to
be read is a question insistently posed by the novel's soon-to-
be-fashionable opening chapter; how Clym is to be read is a
subject to which the narrator will repeatedly return. Reading
the heath not only as a 'character'—a presence and a body to
which some human qualities are attributed—but specifically as
a figure for the parent raises questions both about Clym and
about the parental function in *The Return of the Native*, questions
which invite at least two sets of answers.

On the figurative level, there is something unsatisfactory
about Clym's relationship both with mother earth and with
father sky. When he looks up, the ideal realm he sees in the
shining moon merely confirms his own alienation and loss;
when he looks down—as he does in the famous furze-cutting
episode—he gets *pulled* down into the life of the body at its most
primitive: no Antaeus, Clym is emasculated rather than revived
by contact with the earth. On the literal level, paternal authority is conspicuous by its absence at the beginning of this novel,
and it becomes increasingly clear that neither Clym nor his
mother can fill the paternal gap.

Mothers tend to be redundant, fathers deficient, in Hardy's
fiction: while mother-figures proliferate, fathers tend either to
be lacking, or to signal a lack in their sons, or both. Paternal
figures, threatened in *Under the Greenwood Tree*, have come, by
Far from the Madding Crowd, to stand for a security and vitality
the inheritance of which is at least problematical. Gabriel's
father and grandfather are dead, but the very fact that they are
so warmly remembered implies that Gabriel himself will be
able to fill their shoes. Bathsheba's father died in the middle of
her ladylike education, with the result that she stopped reading
and started farming. It is significant not only that she is eventually relieved to surrender the farm to her husband, but that the
scene in which she begins to turn away from Troy and back to
Oak ends with her resumption of elegant reading. With a
father-figure in his right place, a woman is free to dwindle into
a properly bourgeois wife.

In *The Return of the Native*, there are no effective fathers, and things accordingly unravel: all the plot developments in this novel begin with a missing, or deficient, father or father-figure.

Clym's father is dead—and his mother implies that he was not much of a man when he was alive. His place was taken by the friend who sponsored Clym for the position in Paris which, he comes to feel, is unworthy and effeminate, and from which he must eventually retreat. Thomasin's father, a renowned musician whom the rustics remember with awe, is likewise dead. Although this man—who could play so many instruments that it was hard to believe 'that one body could hold it all and never mix the fingering'[2]—is discussed in just the fond, reminiscent tone used by Gabriel Oak, and in somewhat the same terms as the fathers in *Under the Greenwood Tree*, in this novel such praise is largely irrelevant, his music finally impotent. The important fact for Thomasin is that her father is no longer around, so that when she gets involved with Wildeve, there is no one to force him to make an honest woman of her but her terrible aunt and her absent cousin Clym. Diggory Venn tries to fill the gap, with mixed results, to which I shall return. And Thomasin is not the only young woman virtually fatherless. Eustacia, so different from her rival, is nevertheless in a similar position in one respect at least: she is an orphan, and her grandfather has no authority over her. Although the two women are temperamentally so different, both, without a father's supervision, get themselves into painful romantic dilemmas.

It has often been observed that Clym is an ineffectual creature, and so he is, but it seems worth noting that few of the men in this novel are very successful in achieving either their interim or their long-term goals. Virtually every chain of events in *The Return of the Native* is initiated by someone doing badly or not doing at all something that a masterful man ought to have done decisively. Eustacia 'calls up' Wildeve in the first place when her grandfather fails to prevent her from using up his 'precious thorn roots' (66) to keep her signal going; she is free to join the mumming only because her grandfather's 'prevailing indifference to his granddaughter's movements left her

---

[2] *The Return of the Native* (London: Macmillan, 1912), Wessex Edition, vol. iv, 53. All subsequent quotations from the novel are from the same edition.

free as a bird to follow her own courses' (173)—courses which eventually lead to adultery and three deaths. On Eustacia's final night, it is her grandfather's failure to deliver Clym's letter which contributes to her demise. However, in this instance it is lucklessness rather than carelessness on his part; and indeed it could be argued that Captain Vye's irresponsibility, signalled as it is early in the text, disguises the irresponsibility of other characters who have paternal obligations but whose contribution to the tragedy the narrator is not so ready to analyse.

Diggory Venn is an interesting figure in this regard. Venn is a character who seems to invite a fairly thorough romantic reading.[3] An Ishmaelitish creature emerging from and disappearing into the heath, a man who has chosen to alienate himself from society because of disappointed love, he is never more present to the imagination of the romantic reader than in his numinous absences. We first see the still unnamed reddleman through the curious eyes of Captain Vye (himself anonymous in Chapter 2); we see him next through the terrified eyes of Johnny Nunsuch. If it is the second sighting which more deeply conditions our subsequent reading of Venn, it is not only because the second episode, vivid with chiaroscuro effects, is more fully and romantically described, but because what Johnny fears is what the romantic reader desires. Venn himself discourages such a reading, pointing out to Johnny that 'You little children think there's only one cuckoo, one fox, one giant, one devil, and one reddleman, when there's lots of us all' (87). But his very disavowal tends to link him in the reader's mind with the mythical entities he lists. Venn indeed seems peculiarly 'ab-original', the fact that he is marked with red earth suggesting an Adamic identification. Yet the same detail is also a class notation: the pigment which marks him—rather in the way Jude will later be marked by dust from the stone with which he works—makes him socially invisible when he aspires to Thomasin's hand. Both aboriginal and class suggestions, however, work in the same direction—to make us expect an unveiling of the 'real' reddleman at the end of the novel. The

³ For example, that of Bailey (1946), 1150–5; Paterson (1959b), 111–27; Brooks (1971), 184. Others have seen him as what Lodge calls 'a rather dull "goodie"' (1974b, 251): Brown (1961), 58; Guerard (1949), 117; Wotton (1985), 113–14.

romantic convention of disguise depends on the illusion of the subject, on the assurance of a hidden and genuine *self* underneath.

The reddleman is not only an evocative image, however, but also someone who makes things happen, and the way his actions advance the plot is worth looking at more closely. Venn is placed in a paternal relation to Thomasin, in so far as he continues to try to do what a father would certainly have tried to do had he been alive: compel Wildeve to marry her and then protect her from the consequences of her husband's adulterous affair. His efforts seem to receive the text's approval: his devotion to Thomasin impresses even Eustacia ('a strange sort of love . . . entirely free from . . . selfishness', 160), and his harassment of Wildeve—even when it involves not only tripping him and throwing stones at him but shooting at him—is defended by the narrator, and in peculiarly distasteful terms ('From the impeachment of Strafford to Farmer Lynch's short way with the scamps of Virginia there have been many triumphs of justice which are mockeries of law', 321). Yet the actual results of Venn's meddling, here and elsewhere in the narrative, are so negative as to invite the no doubt perverse conclusion that he is the real villain of the story.[4]

Although the plot line is so intricate that the causal connections are hard to remember, it becomes clear, when Venn's actions are carefully traced, that he consistently achieves the very opposite of what he apparently sets out to do. When he attempts to persuade Eustacia to leave Wildeve to Thomasin, her desire for Wildeve is doubled. When he proposes for Thomasin to Mrs Yeobright, on the other hand, he succeeds only in inflaming Eustacia's interest in Clym and spurring Wildeve to marry Thomasin himself. Having reported the marriage, he disappears. Back on the scene, however, as soon as things begin to go wrong for Thomasin, he contributes in several ways to the final disaster.

The celebrated episode in which Venn wins back Mrs Yeobright's guineas from Wildeve by the light of the glow-worms is an example of the problems posed by this text. Nowhere in Hardy is the voyeuristic dimension of his imagination exercised

---

[4] Bayley notes that 'however chivalrous his motives Venn has behaved in a manner for which neurosis would seem too mild a term' (1978, 114).

to better effect than at the moment when the 'dusky forms' (274) of the heath-croppers emerge from the darkness among the less sentient moths and glow-worms, suddenly establishing with their grave gaze a *scale* of consciousness in the context of which the concentrated purposefulness of the two human figures at the upper end appears alienated and obsessive.[5] To someone reading the reddleman as Johnny Nunsuch does, this uncanny scene will seem his inevitable setting and his luck with dice too appropriate to be worth questioning. Reading him, however, as he asks to be read—as an ordinary human being—one might question his common sense. Since Venn has overheard Wildeve latching on to Christian Cantle, since he knows that the money Christian carries is probably Thomasin's, and since he is watching when Christian begins to gamble with it, he should simply have stepped in and stopped Wildeve before he had won the money from Christian in the first place. By winning back the guineas from Christian Cantle and passing on Clym's share to Thomasin, he creates the misunderstanding which eventually causes Mrs Yeobright's death—to which he also contributes by urging her, in the middle of a heat wave, to visit her son immediately, and by taking potshots at Wildeve by night, a strategy which assures Wildeve's presence in Eustacia's parlour in the middle of the afternoon.

A reader alerted to pessimism, fatalism, and irony in Hardy will observe how poignant it is that so often in his fictional world the best of motives lead to the direst of outcomes.[6] A Machiavellian or paranoid reader, on the other hand, might conclude that Venn, by canny bungling, has brought about precisely the conclusion he desires. Whatever Hardy may originally have intended to do with the reddleman at the end of the novel,[7] in the text as it stands Venn has got what he wants in the only way he could get it: by involving Clym, who had himself been attracted to Thomasin, with Eustacia, and by disposing not only of Wildeve but also of Mrs Yeobright—who, as Thomasin's discussion with Clym at the end of the novel

[5] Bailey was one of the first to discuss this scene; he notes the link between Venn's winning of the guineas and the fatal quarrel (1946, 152–4).

[6] This is the line taken by Hagan (1961–2), who draws attention to these chains of cause and effect. See also Morgan (1988), 66–72.

[7] Paterson (1960*b*), 49–59, argues that the description of Venn as an 'agreeable specimen of young manhood' was already present in the serial version.

suggests, might well have steadfastly opposed her niece's marriage to an ex-reddleman. When Venn emerges in the novel's final pages as a kind of cool and dapper Farfrae, the reader may be disconcerted but should scarcely be offended: the master of metamorphosis has simply done it again, this time in a way which is a genuine surprise. Venn's serene evaluation into the middle class is enough to make one suspect that Hardy is slyly diagnosing as socioeconomic all the premisses and promises of the disguise plot of romantic comedy.

Or is he? The figure of Venn poses fundamental questions about Hardy's method and about how to read him. Is Hardy, as readers have generally tended to assume, simply so enamoured of intricate melodramatic plots that he gets 'good' characters involved in chains of cause and effect which seem to implicate them in ways he never intended? Or is he playing generic games with the reader, altering 'character' by shifting genre, so as to reveal the way our conceptions of character are themselves generic—already, in other words, doing better for himself what Fowles will later attempt to do for him?[8] Or does plotting in a Hardy novel function—as Irving Howe interestingly suggests coincidence does[9]—to delineate unconscious motivation? I tend to lean towards the third point of view, although I am not willing to dismiss the second, and I have not entirely made up my mind whose unconsciousness is involved.

The same kinds of questions can be raised about Mrs Yeobright, the central parent in the novel. Though a woman, she too functions as a father in her attempt to make Wildeve do the right thing by Thomasin. Lacking however both the authority of a man and the tact of a woman, she succeeds in infuriating rather than intimidating him and in making him more rather than less reluctant to redeem her niece's good name. When her interference can do no good, she meddles in Thomasin's affairs, refusing Venn on Thomasin's behalf, but using his proposal to spur Wildeve to action. Even while insisting that the marriage with Wildeve must take place, Mrs Yeobright sneers at Thomasin for defending him. But the moment Wildeve has proposed

---

[8] On Hardy and Fowles, see Bayley (1978), 6–14.
[9] See Howe (1967), 66.

and Thomasin accepted him, she becomes grudgingly and as it were retroactively passive ('I can do nothing. It is all in your own hands now. My power over your welfare came to an end when you left this house to go with him to Anglebury', 184). Harassing and humiliating Thomasin, while consistently failing, except by accident, to bring about the end she apparently desires, Mrs Yeobright is a depressing surrogate parent indeed.[10] It is perhaps not irrelevant that the meek little woman she mothers bears, like Thomas Leaf, her author's name.

In the matter of Thomasin's marriage, it is hard to resist the conclusion that Clym and his mother are in collusion with one another, even at moments when they seem to disagree. Clym, as Thomasin's only surviving male relative, might be expected to protect her interests in such a case, but is absent at the beginning of her troubles.[11] When he does come home from Paris, Mrs Yeobright agrees to Thomasin's request not to tell him about Wildeve's failure to marry her; later, when he is absent 'on a few days' visit to a friend about ten miles off' (183), she also agrees to let the marriage go forward before he returns. Her own ambivalence about this clearly cruel and inappropriate decision seems mirrored by Clym's, for though Clym concludes, quite rightly, that Thomasin should not be deserted by the family on the day of her marriage and goes so far as to chide Mrs Yeobright for not summoning him ('Mother, you did wrong', 189), he almost in the same breath hints that, though he had once thought of marrying Thomasin himself, he is now attracted to someone else. It is as if neither one of them really wants to risk the very consummation Mrs Yeobright is supposed to desire: marriage between Clym and Thomasin.

The bizarre detail of Eustacia giving Thomasin away on her wedding-day—as, in effect, she had already 'given' her back to Wildeve—is a kind of double displacement. Eustacia is presented as replacing Mrs Yeobright, who has declined to

---

[10] Paterson (1960b), 66–75, shows that Mrs Yeobright was even nastier in the serial version. Hardy's subsequent revisions softened her character and strengthened the impression of the bond between her and Clym.

[11] In the early stages of the composition of the novel, Clym, originally conceived as Thomasin's *brother*, had objected to Wildeve's courtship: see Paterson (1960b), 45.

attend.[12] The person she is really replacing, however, is surely Clym himself, whose rather nasty letter ('that such a girl as Thomasin could so mortify us', 184) suggests that his absence at the key moment in Thomasin's life is less accidental than emblematic of his fundamental callousness towards his cousin and alignment with his mother ('so mortify *us*'). Clym's absence allows Eustacia to be cast in a male role, as his passivity will do throughout their relationship; it also positions her as a double for Mrs Yeobright, as she continues to be in various ways in the rest of the novel.

Mrs Yeobright's motivation in the events which lead to her quarrel with Eustacia is equally puzzling. Her attempt to offer some financial support to her son and her niece—something a father might be expected to do without any difficulty—is grotesquely bungled in ways which become deeply illogical. It is careless of Mrs Yeobright to entrust the money to a simpleton like Christian Cantle,[13] irrational of her to go along, even temporarily, with his hopeful suggestion that 'perhaps' Wildeve will give Clym's share to Eustacia (286), and outrageous of her to ask her daughter-in-law whether she had received money from Wildeve. Such a question is innocent if Mrs Yeobright is ignorant of the fact that Eustacia and Wildeve have been romantically involved with each other—inexcusable if she is aware of it. The narrator implies—though he does not actually state—that she is *not* aware: he says that Eustacia's 'own consciousness of the old attachment between herself and Wildeve led her to jump to the conclusion that Mrs. Yeobright also knew of it' (suggesting that Eustacia is wrong, 287). This excuse is supplied, however, only one page after it has been made clear that Mrs Yeobright *is* aware: she has just been described as angry at the thought of Wildeve's 'placing Clym's share in Clym's wife's hands, because she had been his own sweetheart, and might be so still', 286). Yet how could Mrs

[12] Jordan, who in her Freudian reading of the novel compares Mrs Yeobright to Jemima Hardy as the 'figure that stands in our van with arm uplifted to knock us back', notes that Jemima would not attend her son's wedding to Emma Gifford (1982, 108). Hardy told Cockerell that Mrs Yeobright was based on his own mother: see Millgate (1971*b*), 125. On possible autobiographical identifications in the novel, see Millgate (1982), 21, 200, 279.

[13] On this and other improbabilities in the plot, see Heilman (1979), 65–8.

Yeobright know this? Only two people on the heath have apparently observed the affair—Johnny Nunsuch, who does not understand what he sees, and of course Diggory Venn. These discrepancies signal either real carelessness on Hardy's part or a deeply ambivalent attitude to Clym's mother. The reader is left with a somewhat blurred impression that Mrs Yeobright is bound to Eustacia in an enmity which renders her preternaturally perceptive of her daughter-in-law's guilty secrets.[14]

Once again, Clym becomes implicated in the events which follow from his mother's interference. When Eustacia reports Mrs Yeobright's insulting remark, he decides there must be some misunderstanding but does not try to find out what it might be. When he does find out from Thomasin the next day ('Then this is what my mother meant', 293) he does not try to tell Eustacia but acquiesces fatalistically in the women's bitter quarrel ('Well, what must be will be', 294). Later, as Mrs Yeobright stands outside his door, Clym's dreaming cry of 'Mother' (337) at the key moment precipitates his break with his wife—as if, in unconsciously choosing between the two women whose presence he senses, he is initiating the decisive confrontation between them which he covertly desires.[15]

Describing the profound love of mother and son, the narrator will assert that Clym is 'a part of her': 'their discourses were as if carried on between the right and the left hands of the same body' (223). Clym is indeed his mother's left hand, and sinister is one way of describing their handling of the women who stand between them. There is something monstrous about this andro-gynous 'body'—Clym-and-his-mother—and I want to turn now to the first body to appear in the text, the heath itself, in an attempt to understand how the somatic imagery connected with it illuminates the novel's meanings.

[14] There is one subsequent reference to Mrs Yeobright's knowledge of Eustacia's relationship with Wildeve. When Venn suggests Mrs Yeobright should pay a visit to her son because, as he broadly hints, Eustacia is involved with Wildeve, Mrs Yeobright exclaims, 'Then there *was* an understanding between him and Clym's wife when he made a fool of Thomasin!' (322). It is this interview with Venn which sends her the next day to her death.

[15] On Clym's cry, see McCann (1961) and Jordan (1982), 113–15: both read it as a desire to punish the mother.

Hardy personifies the heath in two ways: he presents it as a brooding mind and also as a gigantic body, or rather an incoherent collection of bodily parts. It is the first of these—the impression of mind or will—which dominates the famous opening chapter. [16] The impression of presence is built up by a series of active verbs used to denote processes which might more usually be conceived as passive. As evening falls, the heath does not become brown but '*embrown[s]* itself' (3). A being which can '[take] up its place' (3), '[add] half an hour to evening' (3), 'retard the dawn' (3), 'rise and meet the evening gloom' (4), '[exhale] darkness' (4), '[advance] half-way' (4), seems to have a will of its own. Such a monster dwarfs and dismisses from the scene the tiny furze-cutter, who, 'looking upwards . . . looking down' (3), caught between earth and sky as between two halves of a closing clam-shell, must 'finish his faggot and go home' (3). As at other important moments in Hardy, earth and sky mirror one another and form a closed circuit which excludes the tiny human beings caught on the surface between them. When earth-mother and sky-father get together, their son may be left with no place to stand.

The second impression begins to be established in the second chapter. It is when the plot begins to move and when 'Humanity Appears upon the Scene, Hand in Hand with Trouble' that the heath starts to dissolve into a collection of unrelated bodily parts. In the first paragraph, the white road is said to bisect its surface 'like the parting-line on a head of black hair' (8), and the figure is soon picked up in a series of startling conceits: the barrow on which Eustacia first appears is like 'a wart on an Atlantean brow' (13); human figures emerge on to a crest like 'two horns which the sluggish heath had put forth from its crown, like a mollusc' (99), appear on the side of a ridge 'like a fly on a negro' (149), and rise from the horizon 'like a spike from a helmet' (13); a patch of light-coloured holly shines out in the night landscape like 'the pupil in a black eye' (320); the bonfires lit by the countrymen glow 'like wounds in a black hide' (16), and, 'perishing', become 'living eyes in the corpse

---

[16] Discussions of the opening chapter include Johnson (1894), 50, 118; Miller (1970), 87–92; Benvenuto (1971), 88; Brooks (1971), 177–8; Lodge (1974*b*), 249–50; Beer (1983), 68–73; Bullen (1986), 97–8. Goode (1988), 40–57, points out that the heath, as landscape, is the product of ideology at a particular historical moment.

of day' (59). The somatic imagery reaches its climax on the night Eustacia stumbles across the heath to her death, tripping over 'fleshy fungi, which at this season lay scattered . . . like the rotten liver and lungs of some colossal animal' (420).[17]

Hardy creates, then, two distinct if not exactly contradictory impressions: of the heath as a single integrated conscious being (unified and spiritual) and of the heath as a collection of bodily parts (fragmented and physical). The first way of reading the heath puts it together, the second takes it apart; the first is orthodox—tending towards old-fashioned personification—the second decidedly grotesque. It is the first image of the heath which gets more or less explicitly associated with Clym; the second on the other hand points perhaps to an alternative reading of his life-story.

The gender of the heath-creature is undecidable. The pronoun Hardy uses consistently is 'it'.[18] Mythically, earth is female, and this particular spot is womb as well as tomb in a very literal way—full of the burial urns in which are curled skeletons of men long gone.[19] Yet certain details seem to insist upon a masculine identity. The connection between earth and sky is called 'fraternization' (4), the heath itself is 'Ishmaelitish' (6), and the Ruskinian contrast between sombre brooding North and blooming careless South, which Hardy begins to develop in the sixth paragraph, puts the heath in the space of the male.[20] But the most important determinant is the implied analogy between the heath's 'lonely face' (6), 'full of a watchful

---

[17] See Fleishman's (1987) discussion of the 'buried giant' in Hardy's landscape, a figure for which he supplies a Romantic background. Many readers have noted that Thomasin's matter-of-fact attitude to the stormy heath as 'no monster . . . but impersonal open ground' (433) tends to work against the heightened rhetoric in the last case. Those who see her common sense as a criticism of Eustacia's emotionalism include Eggenschwiler (1970–1); Martin (1972), 621; Jones (1975), 513; Johnson (1983), 71–3; Wotton (1985), 117. Fleishman (1987), 102, on the other hand, describes her perspective as 'rationalistic stupidity'. I take it as another example of the way Hardy tends to draw back from the implications of his most grotesque somatic figures by embedding them in a context which undercuts them.

[18] Cf. the interesting passage in a letter to Edward Wright 'on the philosophy of *The Dynasts*', where Hardy claims that he was the first 'in any poetical literature' to apply the pronoun 'It' to 'the Prime Cause' (Hardy 1930, 124–5). See Lacan on the Other—'ça parle' (1977a, 284–5); MacCannell (1986), 68–9, 85–6.

[19] Psychoanalytic readings of the novel emphasize this identification: see McCann (1961), 150, and Jordan (1982).

[20] 'The Nature of Gothic', paras. 7, 8, in Ruskin (1904), x. 184–8.

intentness' (4), and Clym's own thought-marked visage.[21] The analogy involves the repression of gender difference. When Hardy emphasizes that its sublime sombreness is at this point in human history 'in keeping with the moods of the more thinking among *mankind*' (5), so that it is 'a place perfectly accordant with *man's* nature' (6), three-quarters of the way through the nineteenth century, his language erases the feminine, just as the vision of heath-as-mind erases the mother and the explosive effect of woman on the male body, and just as the figure of Clym-as-mind, Clym-as-face, Clym-as-reader, which derives from his metaphorical link with the heath, erases his body below the neck, erases his sexuality and his dependence upon woman.

Clym seems to read the heath as a whole, integrated *being* to whose spirit it is worth getting attuned, and so does the narrator whenever he is being self-conscious—whenever he uses the 'a-sensitive-observer-might-have-imagined' formula.[22] But the female returns, in a way which is precisely uncanny, in the text's figurative language. A good example is the description of the wind sweeping through the 'mummied heath-bells . . . dried to dead skins' (61). The scene is said to be likely to 'impress a listener with thoughts of its origin' and the narrator insists on the one behind the many:

'The spirit moved them.' A meaning of the phrase forced itself upon the attention; and an emotional listener's fetichistic mood might have ended in one of more advanced quality. It was not, after all, that the left-hand expanse of old blooms spoke, or the right-hand, or those of the slope in front; but it was the single person of something else speaking through each at once. (61)[23]

The 'spirit' must be masculine; yet in this evocative vision of blooms'-end, there is a body which resembles the Clym-and-his-mother figure in having a left and a right hand, and which

---

[21] See Brooks (1971), 177–8; Gregor (1974), 100–1; Johnson (1983), 57–9. On how the 'reading' of Clym's face places the reader, see Wotton (1985), 119–20.

[22] Barrell (1982), discussing Hardy's nostalgic mythologizing of his rustics' perception of their environment, deals with this formula (358).

[23] Hardy's use of 'fetichistic' alludes to Comte: see Björk (1985), i. items 641, 642, 669, 722, 754, 755. Hardy drew a comparison between primitive man and poet, attributing to both what his friend Clodd called the ' "barbaric idea which confuses persons and things" ' (Hardy 1930, 301–2). See also Johnson (1983), 63–4.

is subliminally associated, through the word 'mummied', both with the mother and with death.[24] But the structure of the last sentence is also trinitarian (left-hand/right-hand/slope in front), and the sinister androgyne is quickly left behind in quest of the 'single person', the transcendent one-in-three, who breathes music into the 'tiny trumpets' of the 'mummied' flowers. The narrator's reading swerves away from the figurative language which points to the death-dealing mother and into transcendental rhetoric which testifies, by its sense of the immanent Father, to his own rapid progress from 'fetishism' to the 'more advanced' spirituality of 'the more thinking among mankind'—the very progress exemplified, evidently, in Clym himself.

This way of reading the heath seems to be endorsed by the plot of the novel. Those characters whose failure to respond to the spirit of the heath is expressed by their willingness to exploit its bits and pieces are in the end undone. There is something sinister in the mendacious way Eustacia appropriates and distorts nature's language: to tell Johnny Nunsuch that when he hears a frog jump into the pond he will know it is going to rain is to turn the signs Gabriel Oak read with patient good faith into a manipulative lover's code. So Wildeve, himself Eustacia's moth, sends the moth to its death in the candle and uses the glow-worms as light to gamble by; so Clym himself, ominously captivated by Eustacia, uses the moon's eclipse as a lover's clock. These scenes derive their eerie power from the sense of profanation—from the impression of nature as a living whole from which it is dangerous to appropriate parts at will— and they effectively suggest that those who cannot respond more appropriately to the heath as a numinous presence will come to no good.

On the other hand, the novel does not seem to offer any image of how to get in touch with nature as a living whole. When Eustacia exploits for her own private ends the traditional fertility rituals of the heath, the bonfire-lighting and the mummers' play, she seems to be trivializing them by divesting them

[24] I owe this observation to Judith Williams. Jordan (1982), 105, comments on the name of Clym's mother's house, Bloom's-End. On the map Hardy drew for the novel, the site of this house was roughly that of Hardy's birthplace: see Millgate (1982), 199, 201.

of communal significance. Yet community and ritual offer in this novel no saving contact with the life of the earth. Although fire-lighting on the fifth of November is said to express 'promethean rebelliousness' against 'foul times, cold darkness, misery and death' (18), the actual bonfire presided over by the geriatric crew of rustic characters seems to foretell their extinction rather than forestall it. Lit to keep mortality at bay, the dancing flames reveal the skull beneath the skin and turn the rustics' dance into a dance of death.[25]

All was unstable; quivering as leaves, evanescent as lightning. Shadowy eye-sockets, deep as those of a death's head, suddenly turned into pits of lustre: a lantern-jaw was cavernous, then it was shining; wrinkles were emphasized to ravines, or obliterated entirely by a changed ray. Nostrils were dark wells; sinews in old necks were gilt mouldings. (18)

The dancers talk about old age; about the failure of human projects (Clym has arrived too late to prevent Thomasin's marriage, Wildeve's training as an engineer is 'no use to him at all', 24); about the melancholy outcome of most marriages; and, with surprising directness, about sexual impotence, impersonated by Christian Cantle, the 'man no woman will marry' (26), born in the dark of the moon ('No moon, no man', the local people say). Though the rustics as a group are so schematically contrasted to the solitary figure of Eustacia in the opening scene of the novel that they seem set up as a critique of her manipulative individualism, they offer, on closer inspection, no very creative alternative to it.[26]

The rustics also talk about reading and writing, and it is here perhaps—in their dialogic intervention into the idealizing discourse of the text—that we can locate their most important function. Their remarks on Clym's book-learning, which they instinctively distrust even while they partly revere it, link the image of reading and writing with the image of the stylized, tormented, or distorted human body. Olly the besom-maker implicitly contrasts the finished perfection of the written word with the awkward process of inscribing it:

[25] See Gregor (1974), 82–4; Brooks (1971), 180; Bullen (1986), 98–101.
[26] Goode (1988), 43–50, suggests that rebellion in this novel is invalid—whether romantic-individualistic or communal-orgiastic—and that the novel fails as a tragedy because 'The individual life is marginalized against whatever the setting means'.

And yet how people do strive after it [literacy] and get it! The class of folk that couldn't use to make a round O to save their bones from the pit can write their names now without a sputter of the pen, oftentimes without a single blot: what do I say?—why, almost without a desk to lean their stomachs and elbows upon. (24)

Pens that sputter, bodies that bulge, bones destined for the pit—all the contingencies of the bodily existence of the writer, rendered invisible by the written word, are brought back before our eyes by Olly's concrete language. Timothy Fairway recalls seeing the mark made in the marriage register by the bride-groom whose wedding preceded his own: 'there stood thy father's cross with arms stretched out like a great banging scarecrow. What a terrible black cross that was—thy father's very likeness in en!' (25). The O and the cross have no phonetic function for the speakers: Olly uses O just to denote the simplest possible letter, Fairway sees the cross as a hieroglyph of the human figure. The 'round O' and 'terrible black cross' have cultural resonances for Hardy's readers, however, as emblems of (female) completeness and self-sufficiency (Olly's own initial, Shakespeare's wooden O, the great round world itself, the full moon, in whose absence no man can be made) and male agony and self-sacrifice (the hanged man, the cruci-fied Christ 'with arms stretched out'). Precisely because they are illiterate, the rustics foreground the materiality of language and call into question any possibility of transcendence of the body. (Clym will become at once a nought and a cross—a Christ-figure and a cipher—in the final pages of the novel.) Their reading of Clym's reading foregrounds what Clym's reading of the heath represses—gender difference, dismemberment, and death.[27] I propose, following their lead, to anatomize Hardy's characters by pursuing the motif of anatomization.

The Return of the Native is filled with bodily parts separated either literally (like the 'two or three undulating locks of raven hair' Clym gives to Charley, 481) or psychologically from the body to which they belong. Much of this imagery expresses Hardy's sense of the fetishistic aspect of sexual attraction. The fact that on the night of the mumming, when Eustacia meets Clym, she

[27] See Wotton (1985), ch. 5, on the way in which the language of the workfolk undercuts the discourse of idealizing consciousness.

is attracted first by a disembodied 'masculine voice' (135), then finds herself seated where she can see only his face—and that she, reduced to a voice and unable to show her face, feels as if she has turned into Echo; the fact that when in her dream he takes off his casque to kiss her, 'his figure fell into fragments like a pack of cards' and she awakens crying 'O that I had seen his face' (138); the fact that Eustacia grants Charley, in return for his help with the mumming, a full thirty minutes by the clock of holding her hand, lending him her 'part' (146–7) as he had lent her his—all these details, faintly disturbing in their suggestions of self-alienation and self-fragmentation, corroborate Hardy's ironic theme: the obsessive and delusory nature of sexual attraction. When Eustacia's face framed in a window becomes an emblem of her collision with Mrs Yeobright; when Wildeve sees 'the pale, tragic face' watching him drive away on his wedding day (373); when Mrs Yeobright cryptically responds to Johnny Nunsuch's query about seeing an ooser, 'I have seen what's worse—a woman's face looking at me through a window-pane' (339);[28] when Clym, enraged, confronts his wife's image in the mirror ('Your face, my dear; your face', 386)—the strong, somewhat theatrical focus on the framed face only carries out the tragic implications of the romantic idolatry which has set the plot in motion.

What is disconcerting, however, is the way the narrator himself gets implicated both in the idolatry and in the fragmentation. Eustacia in particular tends to fall apart, the narrator exposing her to the reader's eye in tantalizing bits ('two matchless lips and a cheek only', 63), and—in the 'Queen of Night' chapter, which is organized rather like the traditional blazon—dwelling on her beauties item by item: on her hair, apparently suffused down to the tips with nervous feeling; on her lips, like 'fragments of forgotten marbles' (76), dug up from underground—a somewhat startling conception; on her mouth —'where was a mouth matching hers to be found?' (79).[29] This question is justified, apparently, by Eustacia's own challenge

---

[28] On the importance of the human face in this novel, see Lodge (1974*b*), 251–2; Eagleton (1971), 158–60; Bullen (1986), 98–117.

[29] Among the discussions of the 'Queen of Night' chapter, see Eggenschwiler (1970–1); Gregor (1974), 85–90; Bayley (1978), 87–9. Wotton (1985), 115, discusses Eustacia as produced by contradictory discourses.

to Wildeve ('Have you seen anything better than that in your travels? . . . not even on the shoulders of Thomasin?', 71) and by Clym's adulation of her face ('Only a few hair-breadths make the difference . . . between everything and nothing at all', 231–2). Diggory Venn's sardonic description of Eustacia, in words which could apply with equal plausibility to a woman and a horse—'a beauty, with a white face and a mane as black as night' (315)—reveals the degree to which woman has become in the male imagination merely a catalogue of culturally coded parts. It is as if the narrator were competing with his characters in the overdetermination of that Real Woman which, on the night of the mumming, he has his protagonist detect under Eustacia's phallic disguise. But the rhetorical overkill undoes itself, exposing instead precisely the factitiousness of 'woman' as a male construct. Eustacia herself participates enthusiastically in her own encoding, endorsing and promoting the imagery which she has apparently absorbed from romantic literature. As a result, she can be seen as a victim not only of her husband's misreading but of all male readings of woman as Other (including the author's), and there is genuine pathos in the final words ('How I have tried and tried to be a splendid woman . . .', 422) which reflect her puzzlement when the codes fail her.[30]

When it is sexual fascination which dismembers and the female body which is anatomized, the image of the *corps morcelé* is connected in a straightforward way with specific characters. But when a man comes apart, the figurative dimension of the imagery is less obvious, its application more oblique. Interesting in this connection is the motif of decapitation which recurs at odd places in the novel, both casually—as in the description of the tufts of furze on stems 'like impaled heads above a city wall' (64), or of the pins used by Susan Nunsuch to stick into the waxen image of Eustacia, 'of the old long and yellow sort, whose heads were disposed to come off at their first usage' (424)—and more emblematically, with peculiar force, at

[30] Lacan's concept of the masquerade seems relevant to Eustacia: see Lacan (1982), 84; Rose (1982), 43–4; Irigaray (1985), 133–4, 220. On woman as exclusion, see Lacan (1982), 144, 156–7; Rose (1982), 48–50. Wotton (1985), 172–3, shows how Hardy's writing puts in contradiction its own construction of women.

certain points in the narrative.[31] Wildeve's inn is called the Quiet Woman, its sign representing the 'gruesome design' of 'a matron carrying her head under her arm', with a couplet which suggests the reciprocal relationship of female volubility and male rebellion: 'Since the woman's quiet / Let no man breed a riot' (46).[32] Paris—where Clym fears to be made effeminate—is identified as the place 'where the king's head was cut off years ago', Humphrey recalling how his mother was told, 'They've cut the king's head off, Jane; and what 'twill be next God knows', and the captain relating what did follow: 'men brought down to the cockpit with their legs and arms blown to Jericho' (124). The mummers' play, the occasion of Eustacia's first contact with Clym, features decapitation as its climax: 'the Saracen's head was cut off, and Saint George stood as victor' (162).

Decapitation symbolizes emasculation, and both are linked with blindness. The character to whom such images would seem to point is Clym, whose head—and suffering face—are separated from the rest of his body not only by Eustacia but by the narrator himself (161-2, 197-8), and who ends up as it were nothing but head, a set of stubborn moral intentions, his body almost absorbed into the heath, the huge flies buzzing around him 'without knowing that he was a man' (298).[33] Certainly Clym's emblematic eye-trouble unmans him. Since it is his semi-blindness which reduces him to grubbing for a living on the heath, and since this labour makes him repulsive

Clym's masculinity

[31] The image of decapitation seems to have intrigued Hardy: he informed a friend that five Roman 'soldiers, or colonists' had been decapitated by workmen who were constructing the driveway at Max Gate (Orel 1966, 195); see also his anecdotes about the 'headless' man with the nagging wife (Hardy 1928, 30-1) and 'the man with two heads at St. Pancras' (Hardy 1928, 58-9).

[32] The couplet and the accompanying footnote were added in revisions for the Wessex Edition of 1912: see Paterson (1960*b*), 121.

[33] This scene evokes strong contradictory responses. Some readers see Clym's absorption into the heath as a good thing—'wise indifference': see Miller (1970), 91; also Benvenuto (1971), 91; Martin (1972), 623; Brooks (1971), 187. Those, on the other hand, who find it perverse, self-absorbed, or morbid include Beach (1922), 103-5; Meisel (1972), 83-7; Millgate (1971*b*), 139; Gregor (1974), 90-5. That Clym at this moment becomes linked with the father is noted by McCann (1961), 148, who points out the similarity between this episode and Hardy's description of his own father lying in a bank of herbs, and Jordan (1982), 103-4, who notes that Mrs Yeobright recognizes Clym's gait from a distance as like that of her dead husband.

to Eustacia, the blinding is, practically as well as symbolically, a kind of castration.[34]

Who is responsible for what happens to Clym? Is he, as his mother would have him believe, the victim of a frivolous, selfish wife? Is his decision to be a furze-cutter a wilful de-sexualization, as Eustacia evidently feels?[35] The perverse repudiation of worldly opportunities, as his mother argues? Or the admirable consistency of a man whose melancholy intuitions make him a peculiarly contemporary type, as the narrator suggests? Or is his mother herself somehow involved in his 'decapitation'?

The evidence concerning the eye-trouble seems contradictory. Apparently the result of overwork, perhaps it is meant to be seen as self-imposed—a literal example of the preying of the spirit upon the flesh which the narrator emphasizes when he first reads the 'waste tablet' of Clym's face (161). Or—since its onset follows immediately upon the consolidation of Clym's relationship with Eustacia—perhaps we are to read it as emblematic of moral blindness and in terms of the narrator's comment about 'the blinding halo kindled' for Clym by 'love and beauty' (237) or his mother's ominous words: 'You are blinded, Clym . . . it was a bad day for you when you first set eyes on her' (227). Might we indeed go so far as to suspect Mrs Yeobright of somehow willing the incapacity she predicts? When she says things like 'Probably my son's happiness does not lie on this side of the grave, for he is a foolish man who neglects the advice of his parent' (290) or—with more ominous specificity—'sons must be blind' (251), are her words a magic that 'takes'? The narrator seems to say no, but other details of the text may not corroborate him.[36]

Particularly interesting in this connection is a cluster of images which surround Clym's attempt to explain his vocation to the rustics and to his mother. Meeting his neighbours at one of Fairway's Sunday-morning hair-cutting sessions—humor-ously described as a kind of execution, 'the victims sitting on a chopping block', the neighbours 'idly observing the locks of

[34] As Howe (1967), 63, points out.
[35] McCann (1961), 153, and Jordan (1982), 112, agree with her, suggesting that Clym is punishing himself for deserting his mother.
[36] See Gregor (1974), 93.

hair as they rose upon the wind' (200)—Clym attempts, with little success, to explain why he has abandoned the 'effeminate' business (202) of jeweller in order to return to the heath. The next chapter opens with the description of Clym as a John the Baptist figure, not explicitly in terms of decapitation but in terms of his love of the wilderness—his 'barbarous satisfaction' that attempts to cultivate the heath 'had receded . . . in despair' (205). When he returns home, he has to explain himself a second time to his mother, who like 'the hair-cutting group' (206) is curious about his intentions, and who, as she questions him, is snipping dead leaves from her household plants. Mrs Yeobright's care of her plants is apparently a positive bit of character notation—after her death the plants die and Thomasin has to restore them—but the fact that this care is consistently presented in terms of snipping and pruning, and the juxtaposition of this motif with the reference to Clym's love of uncultivated spaces and with images, however whimsical, of decapitation, execution, and emasculation, qualify the obvious meaning of the parallel encounters—that Clym's idealism is not appreciated by the dull or worldly people around him— with a more sinister suggestion: that his mother, with her 'cultivated' ambitions for her son, is snipping and pruning Clym himself.

Certainly Mrs Yeobright, who calls her son a failure 'like your father' (208) and nags him 'to push straight on, as other men do—all who deserve the name' (207), shows herself willing to assault his masculinity quite directly to get him to do what she wants. And her son's subsequent career suggests that he cannot successfully defy her. Mother and son are one flesh— 'he was a part of her' (223). That his link with this woman is so intense that separation from her means dismemberment, emasculation, sexual death, is one inevitable meaning of the narrative. Unable to contract and maintain a fully passionate relationship with another woman, he retreats from both his wife and his mother into a willed state of emasculation which both women equally deplore, even as they oppose each other. His complacent acquiescence in a disability and a vocation which are blasting his wife's realistic hopes as well as her egotistical daydreams and killing her desire for him seems almost perverse: he is disconcertingly content to have become 'an insect . . . a mere parasite of the heath' (328), 'a brown spot in the midst of an expanse of olive-green gorse, and nothing more' (298). This is unity with nature with a vengeance and it is a question whether—as in Wordsworth's Lucy poems —such unity is not a kind of death. Clym survives on the last page of the novel as a cadaverous figure whose only energy is in his voice, delivering to a half-indifferent audience what appears to be a lecture on filial piety.

Clym has to take the space of the novel's hero, and the narrative voice often seems to approve of him, even if his women do not.[37] But the way we read Hardy's text is complicated by the splitting, displacing, and doubling of characters. Diggory Venn seems to be a kind of unintellectual version of Clym: a rival for Thomasin's hand, an alienated figure isolated in interesting ways from his social environment, a man whose knowledge of the heath allows him to merge unproblematically with it. He is the kind of figure who might, in Wessex, be expected himself to be a reader of nature's signs. But the reddleman is actually shown reading merely the clues which keep him on the track of his beloved's adulterous husband, whom he follows, as it were, back into the community. Venn has ended up 'doing well' (208) in precisely Mrs Yeobright's sense, and he has done it by weaving patiently and imperturbably around the two imperious women who blocked and dominated Clym. Indeed, if we take seriously the notations of primitivism which characterized him in the beginning, we might even see his career as an epitome of social evolution— the reddleman himself as the belated survival of the 'dyed barbarians' whose 'records had perished long ago' (456) at last bleached and 'cultivated' into contemporary anonymity—and his entry into the middle class as Hardy's wry satire both of the

[37] It has been suggested that Hardy identifies uncritically with Clym: see Paterson (1960b), 59, 131; Howe (1967), 102; Collins (1980), 63. Critics who sense that the text betrays a lack of enthusiasm for him include Lawrence (1961), 414–16; Benvenuto (1971), 91–3; Schwarz (1979), 23–4; Millgate (1982), 203; and Jordan (1982), 105, 115. Correcting proof for the Wessex Edition, Hardy 'got to like the character of Clym before I had done with him. I think he is the nicest of all my heroes, and *not a bit* like me' (Hardy 1930, 151). This comment oddly suggests that Hardy in 1912 had virtually forgotten the novel and was being exposed to Clym for the first time.

reader's romantic expectations and of the 'meliorism' in which, in his public persona, he professed to have faith.

The progress Venn embodies, however, parodies the kind which Clym advocates, and which he is so ineffectual in promoting. As Clym moves in the novel from community to isolation, Venn moves from isolation to community.[38] While the canny opportunism of Venn's operations is shown up, especially in the final chapters, by Clym's otherworldliness, the way Clym reacts to Venn's courtship and marriage makes him seem sterile, senile, and self-absorbed. The two figures expose one another, the resolution of each plot-line reflecting unfavourably on the other: neither is very satisfactory to a reader looking either for romantic archetypes or for moral patterns.

Christian Cantle plays a similar parodic role. This old young man, almost exactly the same age as the protagonist, strikingly inferior to his virile father, is mourned over by a mother who did not want him to be born a boy.[39] A 'slack-twisted, slim-looking maphrotight fool' (27), born in the dark of the moon and doomed to 'lie alone all [his] life' (28), Cantle is a shadowy type, perhaps, of Clym Yeobright himself, whose unmanning is consolidated during the moon's eclipse, and whose studied withdrawal from Thomasin and commitment to a lifetime of Christian cant at the end of the novel make him a less attractive protagonist than the Christ-imagery seems designed to make us feel.

As the men are doubled, so perhaps are the women. Who is the real witch in this novel? Hardy seems to use the idea of witchcraft to give a kind of spooky ambience to the narrative without really committing himself to its implications. The narrator casts Eustacia as chief witch (thereby aligning himself, incidentally, with one of the novel's less enlightened characters, Susan Nunsuch, who also firmly believes that Eustacia has

---

[38] Schwarz (1979), 23, notes that Clym and Venn change places.

[39] The word 'maphrotight' was added only in 1912 for the Wessex Edition: see Paterson (1960*b*), 122. The manuscript of the novel shows that Clym and Thomasin were originally to have been brother and sister (see Paterson (1960*b*), 45–7). If the legendary musician the rustics remember was originally conceived as Clym's father as well as hers, a potentially ironical contrast would have been established between a vital father and an enervated son. This contrast remains in the text as it stands only in parodic form, in Granfer Cantle and Christian.

demonic powers[40]). His characterization of her as Queen of Night exploits the metaphor of witchcraft in a rather melodramatic way, to suggest the power of her sexual attractiveness and the damage it is likely to do Clym. A reading of the narrative which emphasizes the demonic power of Clym's mother might, however, raise the question of whether the text has displaced on to Eustacia a charge which might equally well be brought against Mrs Yeobright. The two women are equated with one another in unexpected ways: for example, by the grotesque gift Clym intends for his mother but presents to his bride: one of the burial urns—'like flower-pots upside down'—full of 'real charnel bones' (224), an image which suggests the containing female body, that round O which, even in saving our bones from the pit, preventing them from flying apart like locks of hair in the wind, turns into the body of death.

They are also linked through the Nunsuch family. Johnny connects himself to both women in the same capacity, serving as Eustacia's fool and Mrs Yeobright's Fool (Mrs Yeobright's ordeal on the heath having obvious parallels to Lear's[41]). An odd detail helps establish Eustacia as Mrs Yeobright's double. When Mrs Yeobright describes the horror she felt at seeing Eustacia's face in the window, Johnny recalls the fright he felt when he 'seed myself looking up at myself' from a pond (340)— as though he thought she had been talking about her own *reflection*. Susan Nunsuch's vendetta against Eustacia brings Susan herself into symbolic alignment with the older woman, for Susan, too, believes that Eustacia is harming her son, and undertakes to do on Johnny's behalf what Mrs Yeobright would no doubt like to do on Clym's.[42]

What are we to make of the fact that involvement with the two women is indeed followed by Johnny's decline? Susan blames Eustacia, but in fact Johnny falls ill not after his Guy Fawkes evening with Eustacia but after his encounter with Mrs

[40] Eustacia was originally more thoroughly demonic. See Paterson (1959*b*), 114–15; in his study of Hardy's revisions (1963, 17–30), he notes that some of the more lurid details of her characterization were toned down. The instability of this figure has been much discussed: see Eggenschwiler (1970–1); Evans (1968); Benvenuto (1970), 77–9; Bayley (1978), 87–90.

[41] On Johnny as 'Fool to Mrs. Yeobright's Lear', see Paterson (1960*b*), 69; Brooks (1971), 190–1; and Bayley (1978), 181.

[42] McCann (1961), 154, notes this parallel.

Supernatural.

Yeobright on the heath. Hardy deals very cannily with the supernatural, deferring to the rationalism of his readers by having Clym repudiate folk beliefs, but it is interesting that while he dramatizes the failure of the adder remedy, he leaves the question of black magic up in the air. Susan's malicious activities immediately precede, if they do not cause, Eustacia's mysterious death; and we never do hear whether, after her death, Johnny gets better.[43] Nor is it absolutely clear whether either mother, in her frenzy of resentment, is not doing to her son the damage she attributes to the 'witch'.

Indeed, Eustacia and Mrs Yeobright, though apparently hostile to each other, are aligned in unexpected ways—united in their capacity for damaging sons and lovers. It is indeed possible to argue that Clym, not Mrs Yeobright or Eustacia, is the real victim of the narrative. The two women become not only more sympathetic but more interesting as their stories unfold, and acquire in their deaths if not quite tragic stature at least a monolithic impressiveness and pathos. Clym, though he survives, is diminished, and becomes an attenuated and in some ways inconsistent figure.

The final scene in the novel is particularly interesting in this connection. Having made the cultivation of his mother's house-plants a kind of dead religion, Clym at last fulfils his ambition to cultivate the locals. The fact that the site of Clym's Sermon on the Mount is the same barrow on which some members of his audience merrily danced in Chapter 1 suggests that Clym—who as a boy used himself to be 'a dog . . . for bonfires' (36)—is self-divided in his approach to his fellow heath-dwellers, who embody the very past Clym finds so attractive when he reads it in urns and barrows. If the heath were to be cultivated, its unique records of human history would be lost; if the heathmen (heathen-men) were to be cultivated their folk memory would also die.[44] And once dead it could not be brought back to life: in his distinction between a genuine unbroken tradition and a revival, Hardy's narrator has made clear how much is lost in deliberate 'cultivation' of traditional folkways.

Clym's audience however seems not very vulnerable to

---

[43] Hardy was interested in local stories about witchcraft (e.g. Hardy 1930, 11), and described his own 'poetic' belief in the supernatural (Hardy 1930, 168).

[44] Wotton (1985), 118, makes this point.

cultivation: nobody pays much attention to the content of what he says, though they receive him kindly because 'the story of his life had become generally known' (485). In their response to him, they are not only better Christians but better readers than Clym, who has misread them and also apparently misread the very text from which he is preaching. Clym was a precocious biblical scholar—the first evidence of his childish intelligence was a Scripture riddle (199)—but the quotation upon which his Sermon on the Mount is based proves to be a grotesquely dismembered fragment, which makes the sense Clym evidently intends it to make only out of context.[45] Absurdly irrelevant to the needs of his listeners, his sermon apparently attempts to expiate his own guilt.

That such expiation of guilt towards the mother would mean sexual and intellectual death is a possibility the text seems covertly to be exploring.[46] Clym had imagined weaning his neighbours away from belief in witches, but his talk rather confirms the reality of demonic influence. It is as though his mother, in her death, has put a spell on him, destroying not only his happiness and peace of mind but also his critical intelligence. She has, indeed, taken possession of the male *word*—not only her son's, but also the biblical text's, for his misleading fragment has acquired a feminist emphasis which is the very reverse of its contextual meaning. Through the lips of her son, whom she seems to have transformed into a virtually schizophrenic reader, the Quiet Woman is still talking.

THE WOODLANDERS

Probably the most frequently quoted pair of sentences in *The Woodlanders* is the description of the wood through which Giles Winterborne passes as he follows Grace Melbury and her father to the outdoor auction:

Here, as everywhere, the Unfulfilled Intention, which makes life what it is, was as obvious as it could be among the depraved crowds of a city slum. The leaf was deformed, the curve was crippled, the taper

---

[45] Bayley (1978), 146, and Jordan (1982), 117–18, note this incongruity.
[46] See Millgate (1982), 201.

was interrupted; the lichen ate the vigour of the stalk, and the ivy slowly strangled to death the promising sapling.[47]

This grotesque vision of vegetable nature has always evoked critical explication, and the concept of the 'Unfulfilled Intention' has been picked up and dwelt on by readers interested in Hardy's antipastoralism, his assimilation of Darwin, even his sympathy with the urban slum-dweller.[48] The passage is also easily read as self-reflexive, for *The Woodlanders*, the least admired of Hardy's 'major' novels, seems itself the expression of an unfulfilled intention. Uneasiness with this work is often expressed in generic terms. Although the novel shares certain pastoral characteristics with *Far from the Madding Crowd*— notably, a sympathetic male protagonist who has attuned himself to the rhythms of nature and is able to 'read' her language—its pastoral unity is undercut by other features: by a vision of nature as essentially cruel; by a melodramatic plot which Hardy allows to take over in inartistic and mechanical ways; by an anticlimactic, even cynical ending which possibly reflects the author's own lack of commitment to his heroine.[49] The 'Unfulfilled Intentions' bit is so easy to abstract from its context because it seems to refer to the novel as a whole.

The longer passage from which the two sentences are so often taken is, however, equally characteristic, both of Hardy's sensibility and of this particular novel:

They went noiselessly over mats of starry moss, rustled through interspersed tracts of leaves, skirted trunks with spreading roots whose mossed rinds made them like hands wearing green gloves; elbowed old elms and ashes with great forks in which stood pools of water that overflowed on rainy days and ran down their stems in green cascades. On older trees still than these huge lobes of fungi grew like lungs.

The somatic imagery here (roots like hands, fungi like lungs), though less bizarre and disturbing than the 'Unfulfilled Inten-

[47] *The Woodlanders*, ed. Dale Kramer (Oxford: Oxford University Press, 1981), 53. All subsequent quotations from the novel are from this edition.

[48] See for example Brooks (1971), 217; Gregor (1974), 165–6; Giordano (1984), 138; Johnson (1983), 87–9; Williams (1972), 157; Goode (1988), 96–7.

[49] For readings of *The Woodlanders* in terms of the pastoral, see Lodge (1974a); May (1974); Drake (1960); Jacobus (1979a), 116–34; Johnson (1983), 84–94. Readers expressing dissatisfaction with the formal or generic coherence of the novel include Beach (1922), 158–76; Howe (1967), 103; Peck (1981b); Boumelha (1982), ch. 5.

tion', strikes a note which is even more central to the novel. For
The Woodlanders is a text in which the *corps morcelé* is not only
glimpsed again and again in the landscape but also repeatedly
and uncharacteristically literalized in the narrative. The rape
of Marty South's locks is the subject of the first three chapters;
the villain Edred Fitzpiers is characterized by his desire to get
hold of people's heads; John South dies when the tree which
has become his totem is dismembered and finally felled by
Giles Winterborne; and the heroine and her husband are re-
united at the end of the novel by a grotesque disembodied set of
teeth. These episodes—striking in themselves, but related to
the plot in curiously devious ways—hint at a subtext which
might supply the coherence often felt to be missing on the
surface of the narrative.

The somatic imagery points to the desire for possession—
possession in both the economic and the demonic senses—the
analysis of which is one of the novel's central concerns.[50] The
main 'possessor' is Mrs Charmond, who has the economic
power to buy Marty's hair, to oust Giles from his house, and to
oppose the 'shrouding' and felling of John South's tree—'She
won't allow it' (87)—as well as the sexual power, as her surname suggests, to 'charm' Fitzpiers. Fitzpiers in turn, who is
described as having an almost supernatural influence over
Grace, has 'had' both Suke Damson and Felice Charmond as
well (228). Indeed, Fitzpiers aims to possess not only women
but also forbidden knowledge of many kinds: he sees himself as
a kind of Faust or Prometheus, plumbing the secrets of nature,
discovering by dissection the point at which the ideal connects
with the real. He meets Grace in the first place because of his
lust to possess the head of Grammer Oliver and courts her
while dissecting a bit of John South's brain. Grammer points
the moral: 'Instead of my skellinton he'll carry home her living
carcase before long' (138). Apparently Fitzpiers triumphs at
the end of the novel, not only over Grace's father, who also sees
Grace as a 'possession' (101)—a 'chattel' (105) in which he has
invested heavily and from which he expects a commensurate
'return' (104)—but over his other rival Timothy Tangs, whose
frustration at not being able to possess his own wife has led him

[50] Miller suggests that the hopeless desire to possess another person is the motive
force behind many of Hardy's plots (1970, 74–5 and *passim*).

to set the mantrap which ironically restores Grace to the man he had hoped to harm. Hardy is clearly critical of the will to possess which he analyses in terms of such demonic images; one of his explicit themes is the injustice of an economic and class system which has created such devices as the mantrap and such property laws as the one by which Giles is expelled from his home.

The author's sympathies seem to be firmly on the side of the dispossessed. His two 'good' characters, Marty South—who loses her lover, her hair, her father, and her home—and Giles Winterborne—who loses his houses, his fiancée, his hut in the woods, and finally his life—are distinguished from the 'possessors' by a certain passivity, as well as by a willingness to identify with rather than exploit other creatures. When their love seems hopeless, Marty abjures Giles and Giles abjures Grace with the kind of resigned stoicism for which Hardy apparently feels deep moral approval. At the same time the two are presented as creatively involved with nature, Giles's unique power to make trees grow deriving from a sympathetic identification with them, a desire to help them achieve their own fullness of being. Marty expresses a similar sympathy more fancifully in her comment on the sighing noise the trees make when they are placed upright, 'as if they . . . are very sorry to begin life in earnest—just as we be' (64). It is such sympathy which allows the pair to 'read' the language of trees —Hardy's favourite compliment to his favoured characters. The only 'possession' Giles and Marty exercise is that won by sympathetic observation:

They had been possessed of its finer mysteries as of commonplace knowledge; had been able to read its hieroglyphs as ordinary writing . . . together they had, with the run of the years, mentally collected those remoter signs and symbols which seen in few were of runic obscurity, but all together made an alphabet. (306)

Our positive reading of Giles depends in part on our acceptance of the tree as a plausible emblem of permanence, stability, and organic unity. Hardy's use of the image recalls the Nordic tree of life Yggdrasil, particularly as interpreted by Carlyle, his dual emphasis on its rootedness and on its lofty branches suggesting continuity and interconnectedness.[51] As a kind of 'fruit-god' and 'wood-god' (258), Giles, 'Autumn's very brother' (193), is tied by his sympathy with trees into the ongoing organic life of nature. It is significant, especially in relation to the fly-by-night projects of predatory interlopers like Fitzpiers and Mrs Charmond,[52] that his ability to 'read' them is explicitly connected with temporal commitment, with close observation over the 'run of the years', and that it is based on the pathetic fallacy, the willingness to impute to trees their own being and purposes. Reading as Giles practises it is a unifying and pathetic activity.[53]

All the other readers in the novel, on the contrary, read possessively and fragmentedly in terms of their will to control, grasping bits and pieces of culture and information for their own egotistical ends. Grace, Fitzpiers, and Mrs Charmond have a certain literary bent and even literary ambitions. Grace, with her fancy education, can no longer 'read' the countryside —she has forgotten the difference between bitter-sweets and John-apples (41)—but she has become familiar enough with impressionistic literature to propose a range of literary personae for Mrs Charmond. The older woman, who would like to record her impressions of travel but does not want to use a pen, proposes hiring Grace as a kind of sentimental secretary —a project she drops when a glance at herself and Grace in the mirror gives her a different reading of their potential relationship. Fitzpiers scandalizes Little Hintock with his appetite for esoteric knowledge, and has dipped into a range of literature, as his allusions to Schleiermacher (135) and Prometheus (237) suggest; but the most concentrated reading we see him doing is that of the characters of the women who go through the newly painted gate. Melbury, who interprets everything in terms of the dual obsession with his daughter Grace and with his place in the class system, accurately reads the Homeric riddle posed

[51] Brooks describes John South's tree as 'a kind of Hintock Igdrasil' (1971, 222); Jacobus (1979a), 116, observes that Hardy, like Carlyle, mourned the death of organicism.

[52] On the figure of the sinister intruder in Hardy's fiction, see Bailey (1946); Guerard (1949), 20–2, 96–9; Brown (1961), 30–42, 74; and the character typologies of Johnson (1894), 67–8, 205–6, Abercrombie (1912), 108–12, and Davidson (1940).

[53] See Wotton on this episode (1985, 55–7); Miller on readers of nature (1970, 83) and readers of character (108–11) in Hardy.

by his schoolfellows ('Who dragged Whom round the walls of What?', 31) as a mockery of his social status, and answers it, ironically, by fragmenting the syntax of his daughter's life as mischievously as his schoolboy interlocutors did the body of the epic text. For Hardy, just as the ability to read Nature's message is a reflection of stability and moral worth, so the opportunistic manipulation of signs becomes an index of deracination.

It is the opportunistic readers, however, who survive, and the characters who are connected with the life of nature who are extinguished. Giles himself, king of the trees, ends up like a kind of fertility figure who is ritually put to death. Being master of trees does not ensure survival, apparently, but quite the reverse. Why this should be the case has something to do with Hardy's ambivalent feelings about nature and about women— feelings expressed in the motif of dismemberment and developed through the characters' relationships to this motif and to each other.

What is disconcerting about some of the most powerful and interesting details of this text is the somewhat incoherent way they are worked out and connected with the development of the plot. The business of Marty's hair, so forcefully introduced in the opening chapters, turns out to be somewhat anticlimactic. Barber Percomb, with his two-faced house and his Mephis-tophelean aura, is more fully developed at the beginning of the novel than seems necessary for his function as the narrative unfolds; and later on, although the revelation that Mrs Charmond's hair is not her own does in a very indirect and coincidental way contribute to her death, the end of the affair is so perfunctorily narrated that the expected impression of poetic justice is undercut rather than emphasized.[54] The other striking details likewise end up doing less work than might have been expected. Fitzpiers's ghoulish designs on Grammer turn out apparently to be mere character notation, used primarily to suggest that he is a callous experimenter whose interest in Grace has a cold-bloodedly theoretical motivation; after his

---

[54] Beach was one of the first to observe the 'altogether disproportionate' attention given to the sale of Marty's hair: 'it serves no purpose but to motivate the separation of Felice and Fitzpiers, which might so much better have been motivated—without machinery—by the natural decay of a selfish and sentimental love' (1922, 174).

marriage to her, no more is made of his passion for dissection. The account of John South's death has the power and suggestiveness of myth, but there seems to be no particular connection between the *manner* of the death and the result which follows from it—Giles's loss of his property. And finally, the mantrap affair seems badly managed—at once melodramatic and anticlimactic. It is disconcerting that the operative trap is not in fact one of Mrs Charmond's, since it is in her mansion that the device is first observed and discussed; it is anticlimactic when this elaborate 'machinery' merely consummates a reconciliation which was under way in any case; it is out of character for meek little Timothy Tangs to attempt such a bloodthirsty revenge, and then not even stay around to observe the result; it is peculiarly coincidental that this disembodied set of teeth is set by the cuckolded husband of a woman whose own teeth, strong enough to crack nuts, testify to her infidelity to him; and it is ironical that the device, designed to injure a rival, in fact does something for that rival's estranged wife—gives her a face-saving excuse for the repossession of her abandoned husband. Indeed, the final scene may leave us wondering just who has caught whom. Although Grace is the ultimate possession, the one everybody wants, it is not clear in the end whether there is anything there to get hold of: she seems in the last few pages to have turned into a different person, more worried about her hair than about her father's feelings or her reconciliation with her husband.[55]

Some displacement is taking place here—as if female power were being disguised as male. There seems to be a good deal of imaginative energy not fully harnessed to the vehicle Hardy has devised, the outline even of some submerged myth not fully brought to light or assimilated to the overt patterns of the plot. Another look at the novel's most powerful woman may clarify the outlines of this myth.

Mrs Charmond is the central figure in a mythic pattern which draws together a number of strands of the novel. Described as the 'divinity who shaped the ends' (103) of the people of Little Hintock, she dwells among trees—indeed, in a house almost

---

[55] Boumelha suggests that generic incoherence and shift in point of view account for the change in Grace: at the end of the novel we are no longer in her mind (1982, 112).

buried by them—in the middle of a large wooded estate, like some demonic nature-goddess, an unwitting Diana of the Grove.[56] Though the control she has over others is presented, especially in the opening chapters, as essentially economic— Barber Percomb pointing out to Marty that she can make good her threat to seize the hair because she owns the roof over Marty's head—the fact that she wants to buy a piece of someone else's body, to appropriate Marty's sexuality, suggests that Hardy is equally interested in other kinds of power. The mantrap, with its dual associations of class oppression and sexual rapacity, is her appropriate emblem, displaced though it later is on to Tim Tangs. Her type—the worldly interloper who disrupts a rural community—is familiar in Hardy's fiction, and we are prepared for her affiliation with the other interloper, Edred Fitzpiers. What are unexpected, however, are her apparent alliances with the 'good' characters—alliances (not openly recognized either by the characters themselves or by the narrator) which may suggest that her function as a demonic divinity is by no means irrelevant to the novel's fundamental structure.

Giles is a thoroughly sympathetic character, yet his relationship to Mrs Charmond is an ambiguous one, in that he contributes, usually definitively, to each of the episodes in which Mrs Charmond is implicated. Marty sells her hair in the end not because of Mrs Charmond's economic pressure, which her father informs her does not extend as far as Barber Percomb suggests, but because of Giles's preference for Grace: it is a symbolic gesture of despair not an economic surrender. Mrs Charmond owns John South's tree, but Giles cuts it down anyway, with the purest of motives but with fatal results. And, surprisingly, the anticipated repercussions do not materialize. Indeed Hardy has to invent another incident, the confrontation between Giles's lumber-wagon and Mrs Charmond's carriage, to account for the hostility which could have been more economically and powerfully motivated by the tree-cutting: a lesser motive to displace a greater. South's mania, though exacerbated by his tormented awareness of Mrs Charmond's economic power, is confirmed by Giles, who, by acting in

[56] On Hardy's knowledge of Frazer see Laird (1980).

accordance with South's delusion, actually strengthens it. Mrs Charmond evicts Giles, but only because he and his father have neglected to extend the lifehold. It is almost as if Giles, like Percomb himself, is acting as Mrs Charmond's agent; as if, though he is her principal victim, he is also, in a mysterious way, her puppet.

Peculiar also is Mrs Charmond's relationship to Grace Melbury. Grace's fascination with the wealthy newcomer is analogous to her fascination with Fitzpiers—indeed, Mrs Charmond is Giles's rival before Fitzpiers is. Mrs Charmond seems also drawn to Grace: she initially wants her as a companion, and it is only when Melbury appeals to her on the grounds of Grace's affection for her that she is moved by his plea to leave Fitzpiers alone. The bond between the two women is unexpectedly emphasized when, in the wood, Grace confronts Felice as her rival only to end up moments later wrapped in her arms; indeed, the wording as they draw apart— 'the cold lips of the wind kissed her where Mrs. Charmond's warm fur had been' (228)—unexpectedly suggests lesbian attraction.[57] And in the almost comic scene where Fitzpiers's three women, Grace, Felice, and Suke Damson, gather round his empty bed, there is some suggestion of a kind of ritual alliance of women drawn together by fundamental interests: we respond less to the social ironies of the situation (although it is those which Hardy himself underlines) than to the undercurrent of mythic meaning.[58]

Moreover, there is an alliance between Grace and Felice in terms of the deeper structure of the plot which is analogous to the relationship between Felice and Giles. The narrator underlines pointlessly the parallel between Felice's nursing of

[57] Millgate (1971*b*), 249, suggests that the scene is a 'muted echo' of the 'lesbian' episode in *Desperate Remedies*; Boumelha, who sees the women's alliance as positive, disputes this reading (1982, 109). The quoted sentence did not appear in the serial version of the novel but was added during revision, at a point when Hardy was strengthening the impression of Grace's sexuality: see Kramer (1981), 26–51, 228. The detail of the spontaneous kiss (229) was added in the final proof-reading for the Wessex Edition: see Kramer (1981), 50. The sexual suggestiveness of some of the passages in the novels proves to some readers that Hardy could *not* have known what he was doing: see for example Guerard (1949), 36, 105. See also p. 166 n. 27.

[58] Boumelha on the contrary sees the union of the three women at the bedside as supporting the novel's 'naturalistic undermining of monogamy' (1982, 110); see also Goode (1988), 104.

Fitzpiers and Grace's of Giles, almost as if to deflect attention from the more sinister parallel he does not mention: that both Felice and Grace evict Giles from his dwellings and thus combine to destroy him. Felice's repossession of Giles's house is the ultimate cause of the breaking-off of his engagement, his initial illness apparently resulting from his consequent demoralization; Grace's appropriation of Giles's cabin is probably the direct cause of his death (though Fitzpiers's theory, that the exposure merely completed the process begun by the earlier illness, makes the two women even more clearly collaborators). It is ironical that the first condition Grace lays down on returning to her father's house is that Fitzpiers shall leave it—that having killed her lover by evicting him, she immediately puts her husband, too, 'out in the cold'. Grace also insists that Fitzpiers eschew his esoteric studies and give up smoking. Indeed, although her father prophesies that her influence over her husband will be short-lived, it is her emasculating power rather than his mastery over her that is dramatized at the end of the novel. The 'chorus' characters, observing Grace's power over her father, comment sardonically on her ability to get what she wants. There is some suggestion that Fitzpiers, the erstwhile beheader, may, in agreeing to burn his books, find that he has broken his staff as well.

The subtext of *The Woodlanders*, then, seems to be a myth of the castrating woman who acts through male agents who may also be her victims, and whose influence, whether or not deliberately exercised, unmans and destroys. In a novel about possession, the ultimate possessors and dispossessors are women, who can cast out a man and cut him off from shelter and status—the submerged metaphor here being the comparison between the house and the woman's body. Felice Charmond is an overtly sinister type, but what is surprising is that the putative heroine Grace, without herself in the end being much damaged, causes just as much harm. The explicit moral of the narrative is that men victimize Grace, that her father's ambition and her husband's philandering blight her life; and Melbury perpetuates this theory about Fitzpiers.[59]

---

[59] Hardy apparently wanted to strengthen the impression that Grace's return to her unfaithful husband was a tragedy for her: see Kramer (1981), 43. His 1889 revisions to

But in fact Grace seems to have mastered both of them, and to have perversely destroyed the one man who has selflessly loved her.[60]

Two people die in the novel ('on-stage'—Felice Charmond's death is merely reported), and both of them in ways which reinforce the idea of an avenging female deity. Hardy's treatment of the two death-scenes confirms their essentially mythic nature.

Hardy works hard to provide motivation for the vigil in the hut, and indeed the scene is so powerful on its own terms that we willingly suspend our common sense for the interval, but the unanswered questions (why didn't Grace's father investigate her disappearance? why didn't Grace ascertain precisely where Giles was sleeping? why didn't she realize she simply had to move on when it became clear that the alternative was a three-day stay alone in the hut?) make clear that it is a mythic impulse which really shapes the narrative.[61] The martyrdom of Giles is a kind of Clarissa situation in reverse, not the locking in of a woman but the locking out of a man by the inhumanity of a sexual code which overvalues female inviolability. Though Grace's mortal power over Giles is camouflaged by the narrating of the episode from her point of view, the episode literalizes the conceit of the sonneteers: her inaccessibility actually kills him. When Grace finally lets Giles in and strips the clothes off his unconscious body, the scene is parodically analogous to all the scenes in narratives about female victimization where the woman has to be drugged or unconscious to be raped.

And a kind of rape it is, for Giles's body is violated by the female deities he trusted: his beloved Grace is apparently too stupid and self-centred to think about his welfare, and Nature, the Great Mother whom he has served, refuses to succour him. Grace's defiant assertion that she has proceeded with Giles to

---

the dramatized version of the novel make her future unhappiness explicit; see Millgate (1982), 299; Hardy (1928), 289.

[60] Howe (1967), 108, Johnson (1983), 84–94, and Williams (1972), 166, are among the few readers to take a strongly critical view of Grace. Rogers notes that she destroys Giles (1975, 253–4); see also Childers (1981).

[61] Readers who have drawn attention to the problems with this episode include Gregor (1974), 146–50; Johnson (1983), 91; Guerard (1949), 118; Howe (1967), 104.

the 'extremest' point has a sinister irony, the traditional equation of sexual violation and death (à la Clarissa) ironically reversed when the victim is male. Hardy characteristically demonstrates through passive female characters (like Fanny Robin in *Far from the Madding Crowd*) or enervated males (like Clym in his furze-cutting phase) what being absorbed into nature really means. Here, in the death of the emasculated protagonist, he dramatizes the darker side of Giles's involvement with nature. Giles is indeed, as has been suggested, a Keatsian figure—not only in his apotheosis as autumnal nature-god, but in his final willingness to fade far far away into the forest dim.[62]

John South's death-scene, less germane to the main plot, emerges even more clearly as myth.[63] South's tree—'Mrs. Charmond's tree' (100)—is a rich and enigmatic symbol. In Lacanian terms, the tree seems to combine the functions of mirror-stage imago and phallic signifier. It is an Other with which South has identified in a lunatic way: he imagines that the tree, 'exactly his own age . . . has got human sense, and sprouted up when he was born on purpose to rule him, and keep him as its slave' (100). Terrified though he is of it, as it is dismembered he too progressively disintegrates. At the same time, as it is systematically 'shrouded' by Giles, the tree becomes increasingly phallic, until at last its 'naked stem' stands 'like "the sword of the Lord and of Gideon"' (98) unsheathed to destroy. To read South's infantile terror of the tree as a refusal of the phallic signifier links this fatal obsession with Giles's father's ongoing neglect of paternal, and patriarchal, responsibility: his failure to renew the lease on his home. The two fathers' weaknesses combined—Winterborne's ongoing failure to renew the lease, and South's craven fear, which leads to his premature death—deliver Giles over into the power of Mrs Charmond. The more phallic the tree becomes, the more pathetic it is, and the more hysterically South, in his own

---

[62] See Lodge (1974*a*), 16, on the Keatsian ambiance of Giles as a wood-god. Brooks (1971), 228, observes that when Giles dies he dissolves into nature, moving down the evolutionary scale. Jacobus (1979*a*), 118, compares Arnold's Balder and Giles as males in whose death nature dies.

[63] Among those who have commented on this scene are Brown (1961), 81; Jacobus (1979*a*), 124–5; Williams (1972), 158; Peck (1981*b*), 147. Jacobus's sense that South 'dies from the idea of death' is closest to my own.

impotence, identifies with it—so that when it goes, he goes too. The fact that Giles, while victimized by paternal inertia, is also in collusion with it—for either he or his father could have renewed the lease—is in line with Hardy's sense of how the paternal blight customarily operates.

South's obsession realizes in a sinister way the implications of his daughter Marty's pleasingly fanciful analogy between a tree's life-span and a human being's, and brings into grisly focus the issue on which Fitzpiers likes to muse—the relationship between the 'Me' and the 'Not Me' (50).[64] The terror lies in the fact that nature's hieroglyph, Mrs Charmond's tree, is both the Me and the Not Me, and in the interchangeability of these identities it points to the illusory nature of the subject and the problematical process of its constitution. The two men who dare to defy Mrs Charmond and cut the tree down to save South's life, Fitzpiers and Giles, play into her hands, and give her the power to repossess Giles's dwelling and evict him; and Giles, in laying bare the tree's phallic shape, ultimately unmans himself. At issue in both scenes—South's death and the death of Giles—is the home which cannot protect, which cannot be retained—the female body which casts a man out, stripped and vulnerable, to be exposed to the Law of the Father and cut down like a 'felled tree' (315). At issue also in the fable of John South is the deceptiveness of the Great Mother, who, in the delusory sense she creates of the objectivity of her own images, hides her secret truth: that the seeds of dissolution and death are within the self.

Indeed, the central import of the novel's symbolism is that Giles, as master of trees, is master not of life but of death. The novel is filled with images of the tree which means death—from the uprooted apple tree which is Giles's emblem, and which, if it is read as an allusion to Genesis, guarantees his own fall, to the tree on which Absalom is hanged (200), to the 'executed' trees among whose branches Marty South stands like a bird in a cage, stripping off the bark with a tool made of a deer's leg-bone, to the many personified trees presented in terms of the 'Unfulfilled Intention'—like those in the 'wilder recesses' of Mrs Charmond's park, 'wrinkled like an old crone's face, and

---

[64] For a detailed discussion of this concern in Hardy, see Jones (1975), 507–25.

antlered with dead branches', 'where slimy streams of fresh moisture, exuding from decayed holes caused by old amputations, ran down the bark' (185); or like the half-dead oak, 'hollow, and disfigured with white tumours, its roots spreading out like claws grasping the ground' (199); or like the 'old beech, with vast arm-pits, and great pocket-holes in its sides, where branches had been removed in past times'; or like the 'Dead boughs . . . scattered about like ichthyosauri in a museum' (288); or like 'the rotting stumps of [trees] . . . that had been vanquished long ago, rising from their mossy setting like black teeth from green gums' (289). The potentially positive image of the tree is exploded into a demonic emblem of the intuition Hardy will not openly voice: that the body of the Great Mother is, for males at least, the body of death.

Two impulses in Hardy conflict with one another in *The Woodlanders*—his affection and respect for 'readers' like Giles and Marty whose patient, percipient observation of nature unites them with her, and his suspicion that the body of nature is a fragmented text whose ultimate message is disintegration. It is ironical that Giles and Marty's relationship with nature is celebrated just at the point when one of them is dead and the other ready to annihilate herself in fidelity to him. There is something disconcerting in the final image of Marty South deploring Grace's flight into 'the arms of another man than Giles' (338)—a strikingly graphic phrase in view of the fact that if Grace were in Giles's arms, she would be embracing a corpse—and exclaiming over his grave, in an unconscious echo of the predatory Fitzpiers a few pages earlier, 'you are mine, and only mine' (329, 338). Marty is evidently intended to be a pathetic and impressive figure—and is often read as if she were a kind of Isis, doggedly putting Giles, as well as the text, together again—but her determination to bind herself to a dead man can also be felt as morbid and fanatical.[65] It is significant that Hardy's real heroine is the only unthreatening woman in the novel, a girl with an androgynous name and an undeveloped

---

[65] For positive readings of Marty see Johnson (1894), 117–18, 267–8; Abercrombie (1912), 120–2; Brown (1961), 73–84; Guerard (1949), 141–2; Drake (1960), 257; Howe (1967), 107; Jacobus (1979a), 131; Wotton (1985), 58. Among those who have criticized Marty or seen her as an essentially sterile figure are Casagrande (1971), 113–17; Schwarz (1979), 29; Boumelha (1982), 107–8; and Gregor (1974), 145–7.

body, 'the contours of womanhood so undeveloped as to be scarcely perceptible in her', who had 'rejected with indifference the attribute of sex for the loftier quality of abstract humanism' (338), and who was originally introduced to the reader in the context of sexual self-mutilation. Those who read nature end up, apparently, in nature's embrace, their sexuality expunged, their desires thwarted, marked with mortality—while a novel-reader like Grace Melbury can slip out of death's iron jaws leaving only her skirt behind. The imagery of the exploded body which plays an increasingly insistent role in Hardy's fiction is connected with the eventual disappearance from it of characters like Oak, Clym Yeobright, and Giles Winterborne, nature's interpreters.

4

The Mayor of Casterbridge:
The Bounds of Propriety

The common impression that *The Mayor of Casterbridge* is the most controlled and shapely of Hardy's novels depends upon the reader's recognition of the conventions of classical and Shakespearian tragedy.[1] Henchard, who completely dominates the narrative, is brought down by a fatal flaw which is also the source of his greatness; the plot, depending as it does on the ill-timed disclosure of various secrets which were bound to come to light eventually, is a careful structure of plausible coincidences, and—with its relentless demonstration that 'Character is Fate'[2]—a perennially useful topic for examination questions.[3] The minor characters, rightly called 'choric' in this novel, are kept under firm control, intervening only to signal important transitions in the main narrative, and so are the female characters: although the way the plot unfolds suggests that a man cannot get away from women, the focus is kept firmly on the two principal men, Farfrae gaining what Henchard loses in a way which is as schematic as the contrast between them. The text incorporates a number of parallels to *Lear* and concludes with a resonant tribute both to the oldest who hath borne most and to the young Elizabeth-Jane who, though she will never see so

[1] Those who discuss the novel in terms of tragedy include Dike (1952); Paterson (1959*a*); Guerard (1949); Millgate (1971*b*); Brooks (1971); Edwards (1972); and Karl (1975). Starzyk (1972) and Peck (1981*a*) suggest that the conventional tragic paradigm is undercut; Howe (1967) and Levine (1981) see Henchard rather as a romantic overreacher. On what is repressed by the concept of 'the tragic', see Wotton (1985), 63–5.

[2] Thomas Hardy, *The Life and Death of the Mayor of Casterbridge: A Story of a Man of Character* (London: Macmillan, 1912), Wessex Edition, vol. v, 131. All subsequent quotations from the novel are from the same edition.

[3] See Widdowson (1989), 80–92, and Wotton (1985), 201–7, on the way the educational establishment has produced the novels by means of examination questions and study guides.

much, will see it steadily and see it whole through the smoke-coloured glasses of a peculiarly Hardyan pessimism. It is to the tragic shape of the narrative that we must first respond, whether or not we finally locate the novel's meaning in, or in divergence from, that paradigm.

If this way of describing the novel's sense of generic decorum makes it sound somewhat pompous and schematic, it should be added that some of the shrewdest and funniest moments in *The Mayor of Casterbridge* depend upon the reader's, and sometimes the characters', sense of the boundaries between discourses. When we first meet Farfrae singing at the Three Mariners, the class antagonism he evokes from Christopher Coney is dramatized as a clash of genres, Coney taking the singer's lyrics about 'yer own country' (60) as an expression of personal feeling, the 'literal' (278) Farfrae interpreting Coney's 'grim broad way of talking' (64) ('the best o' us hardly honest sometimes', 60) as sociological data ('None of ye has been stealing what didn't belong to him?', 60). And at the trial of the furmity woman, Stubberd's testimony, with its euphemistic Bs and Ds and its disrupted syntax, is an ironical contrast to Mrs Goodenough's own language. When she testifies against the mayor—'Twenty years ago or thereabout I was selling of furmity in a tent at Weydon Fair' (231)—her suddenly folkloric idiom restores to his life-story the inexorable continuity missing in Stubberd's narrative about her own; and when she objects to Stubberd's testimony on the grounds that 'I was not capable enough to hear what I said, and what is said out of my hearing is not evidence' (231), the joke—which turns on her blithely collapsing two speech-acts into one (her own words then and Stubberd's words now) while simultaneously splitting the subject into two (the 'I' who speaks and the 'I' who hears the speaking)—inverts and parodies legal discourse, with its unproblematic assumption of the identity of the subject and its obsessive focus on sequentiality. In *The Mayor of Casterbridge* the discourse of the 'minor' characters is often not merely a quaint contrast to that of the protagonists but a dialogical intervention in it.[4]

In other ways, too, this novel is unusually controlled. There is little of the melodrama which for some readers mars *Far from*

---

[4] See Wotton (1985), ch. 5, who cites Bakhtin; also p. 69 n. 27.

the Madding Crowd and Tess of the d'Urbervilles; few of the purple patches—like the narrator's descriptions of Eustacia and Tess —which evoke a questionable kind of pathos; little of the grotesque, or of that startling somatic imagery with which this study has been concerned. Potentially inflammable material— pregnancy, illicit sexual relationships, illegitimacy, and even the possibility of homoerotic attraction—is dealt with in terms so delicate and ambiguous that the text has traditionally been judged particularly appropriate for teaching to high-school students.[5] Unable, in the context of Victorian expectations, to do what Henchard urges Stubberd to do—'Say the words out like a man' (231)—Hardy handles the women's stories rather as Stubberd handles the furmity woman's or as Henchard handles Elizabeth-Jane's—with a discretion 'worthy of a better man' (140), as the narrator rather oddly remarks.

Lucetta in particular is a potentially scandalous figure.[6] But although the text has its own ways of signalling that she is a 'false woman' (243) who could be called 'something worse' (244)—indeed it makes her suggest in her own words what the 'something worse' might be (the 'woman you meet in the street', 283)—she is for the most part decorously enough dealt with in a somewhat stylized way for which she herself provides the cue. Content to be defined by her clothing (she will be 'the cherry-coloured person' for the season, 191) and to stage herself in a series of calculated vignettes, she is characterized by Hardy in the same way, by means of slightly theatrical encounters and elegant costume. The skimmity-ride, which reduces her to a 'piece of silk and wax-work' (297), might be read as either a fitting retribution for her triviality[7] or a parody of the method by which she has been constructed by the text.

Another way of putting this is to say that Lucetta has no body. Indeed all the bodies, male and female, in this text are cannily constructed, decorously self-contained, and carefully subordinated to their thematic function. Although Elizabeth-Jane and Henchard are presented as emotionally or spiritually

---

[5] Along with Far from the Madding Crowd and The Return of the Native: see Widdowson (1989), 80–2.

[6] Her illicit affair with Henchard, avoided in the serial version of the text, was made clear in the book version: see Winfield (1973), 57–8.

[7] See Vigar (1974), 163, and Bullen (1986), 149.

'deep'—she a 'dumb, deep-feeling, great-eyed creature' (152)
with 'an inner chamber of ideas' (109), he filled with 'volcanic
stuff beneath the rind' (129)—there is little of the *somatic* depth
and penetrability so characteristic of Hardy. The one body on
which the eye lingers for a moment is Farfrae's—on 'his cheek
. . . so truly curved as to be part of a globe', on 'the lids and
lashes which hid his bent eyes', on the 'velvet-pile or down . . .
on the skin at the back of his neck' (50)—but it is a female eye
and it stays on the surface. Indeed Farfrae, whether in his own
natty clothing or 'in the costume of a wild Highlander' (121), is
all surface—shallow where Henchard is deep—and the two
men are constructed as opposites in every way: Farfrae, 'slight
in build' (42), 'fair, fresh and slenderly handsome' (180),
something of a lady's man, Henchard, with his 'heavy frame,
large features, and commanding voice' (36), eminently male
('constructed upon too large a scale' to observe the minutiae of
female behaviour, 209); Farfrae graceful and flexible, Henchard
inflexibly erect—'stately and vertical' (44); Farfrae double if
not duplicitous—described in terms of 'second thoughts' (42)
and 'double strands' (183): 'warm or cold, passionate or
frigid', 'commercial and . . . romantic' (183)—Henchard
emphatically unitary: straightforward and single-minded. The
novel encodes Henchard as a real man by setting him against
the smaller, younger, more ambiguous figure. This somewhat
relentless schematization is perhaps why Farfrae does not really
seem to *inhabit* the body Elizabeth-Jane gazes at: the two men's
bodies are so contrapuntally moralized that they have little
erotic life of their own.

Surprisingly, the women's bodies are even more generalized
than the men's: Susan 'the pale, chastened mother' (104), 'a
mere skellinton' (96); 'subtle-souled' (135) Elizabeth-Jane
with her 'grey, thoughtful eyes' (100); Lucetta a phenomenon
of 'artistic perfection' (153). There is a good deal of emphasis
on clothing in this novel, but it is clothing as costume or as class
notation rather than as second skin. There is no sense here of
sexy texture, no rustling of silken skirts, no garments which
define the boundaries of the body, no textile which takes on a
life of its own. (Indeed, the one peculiarly Hardyan metaphor
in the narrator's description of clothing—his assertion that
Elizabeth-Jane's plumes are *not* Argus-eyed—deprives her

precisely of the kind of erotic self-consciousness which makes his more compelling heroines so memorable.) The most vivid image of female flesh we are given, the glimpse of the young Susan's face in the opening chapter, penetrated by the afternoon sun 'which made transparencies of her eyelids and nostrils and set fire on her lips' (2), precisely makes the point that her corporeal vitality depends upon what is outside herself. Although Lucetta is pregnant when she goes to meet Henchard in the Ring to beg the return of her letters, the narrator, intent though he is on emphasizing the pathos of her appearance and its power over Henchard's feelings, alludes to this fact only in the most decorous and ambiguous of phrases.[8] Female bodies in *The Mayor of Casterbridge* neither expand to decentre the man's story nor open up to expose male fantasy of penetration and control. Their containment is an aspect of the novel's tragic decorum and one of the reasons that *The Mayor of Casterbridge* has no compelling female character.

If there is a deeply imagined body in this text, it is the body of Casterbridge itself, rightly given equal emphasis, in the title, with the central human character. There is some contradiction in the way this body is presented. A rectilinear shape ('like a chess-board on a green table-cloth', 'a place deposited in the block upon a corn-field', 105, 'a plot of garden ground [with] box-edging', 30) with a firmly delineated border ('square earthworks', 72, 'a square wall of trees', 'a rectangular frame of deep green', 30), Casterbridge has seemed to readers analogous to the figure of the mayor himself with his solid 'frame' (36, 238).[9] Yet the town is also characterized in more organic terms as a 'nerve-knot of the surrounding country life' (70), and although 'Country and town met at a mathematical line' (30) its frame is nevertheless penetrable by the richness of the countryside.[10]

---

[8] He mentions 'a natural reason for her slightly drawn look'. In the serial 'nature' is displaced by 'artifice . . . the only practicable weapon left [Lucetta] as a woman': by the detailed description of the process by which, assisted by 'disfiguring ointments' from the druggist, she turns herself into a witch-like creature with 'a countenance withering, ageing, sickly'. See *Graphic*, 33 (1886), 421–2. The parallel passages are printed in Chase (1964), 36–8.

[9] See Paterson (1959*a*), 163; Brooks (1971), 205; Showalter (1979), 107.

[10] Readers who have discussed the interconnection between town and country include Brown (1961), 66–7; Brooks (1971), 205–7; Fussell (1979), 21–2; Bullen (1986), 164–6. Enstice (1979), 12–34, demonstrates that Hardy makes Casterbridge

Indeed, the central trope in this novel is the boundary which is stable and yet permeable—the body which retains its essential shape and yet merges with or is penetrated by other bodies.[11] An aural avatar of this idea is the series of clock-bells Elizabeth-Jane hears as she enters the town, each with its own particular tune but each overlapping the next, binding the town's hours each to each in charming technological obsolescence; and the single most memorable visual representation is what she sees her first morning in Casterbridge:

When Elizabeth-Jane opened the hinged casement next morning the mellow air brought in the feel of imminent autumn almost as distinctly as if she had been in the remotest hamlet. Casterbridge was the complement of the rural life around; not its urban opposite. Bees and butterflies in the cornfields at the top of the town, who desired to get to the meads at the bottom, took no circuitous course, but flew straight down High Street without any apparent consciousness that they were traversing strange latitudes. And in autumn airy spheres of thistledown floated into the same street, lodged upon the shop fronts, blew into drains; and innumerable tawny and yellow leaves skimmed along the pavement, and stole through people's doorways into their passages with a hesitating scratch on the floor, like the skirts of timid visitors. (65)

Doors and windows tend to be open in this novel; here they let the country in. The town is eroticized: the bees and the seeds which penetrate it pollinate it, and whispering skirts rustle here only in the timid leaves. Passageways are also important: the two women have entered the town along a 'road dark as a tunnel' to find 'a sense of great snugness and comfort inside' (31), and individual buildings in Casterbridge repeat on a smaller scale the same pattern of penetration via passageway and *copia* at the centre:

The front doors of the private houses were mostly left open at this warm autumn time . . . Hence, through the long, straight, entrance passages thus unclosed could be seen, as through tunnels, the mossy

---

more regular in shape, more unified, and more self-sufficient than the historic Dorchester. Bullen (1986), 159–68, discusses the town and its architecture in terms of the 19th-century notion of 'an intimate connection between society and building style'.

[11] Again Anzieu's (1989) insights seem relevant: cf. p. 38 n. 28.

gardens at the back, glowing with nasturtiums, fuchsias, scarlet geraniums, 'bloody warriors', snapdragons, and dahlias, this floral blaze being backed by crusted grey stone-work remaining from a yet remoter Casterbridge than the venerable one visible in the street. (68)

To look through these houses is to glimpse the past, and so is to dig into the earth: excavators in Casterbridge may come upon a Roman skeleton 'lying on his side, in an oval scoop in the chalk, like a chicken in its shell' (80)—or a foetus in the womb. Indeed once the town's framework has been firmly established and we move inside it, the square or rectangle gives way to ovoid or rounded shapes as walls bulge into picturesque irregularity.[12] The same houses which were pierced to reveal their secret gardens become bodies, 'bow-legged and knock-kneed' (68), which jut into the street. The Three Mariners, famous for its 'good stabling and . . . good ale', is entered through a 'long, narrow, dimly-lit passage' (46) but inside it is at once snug and bountiful: beer-making facilities obtrude into the rooms for guests and 'beams and rafters, partitions, passages, staircases, disused ovens, settles, and four-posters, [leave] comparatively small quarters for human beings' (50). Henchard's own house, with a passage through which Elizabeth-Jane can see 'to the end of the garden—nearly a quarter of a mile off' (71), is always entered in well-defined stages, 'through the tunnel-shaped passage into the garden, and thence by the back door towards the stores and granaries' (87) which are 'packed' and 'bursting' (71) with grain. The garden itself, 'silent, dewy, and full of perfume', can be reached from the yard through a 'private little door' (88)—the same 'green door' (312) which, when Henchard has become Farfrae's employee, shuts him out from what has become 'Farfrae's garden' and from Lucetta.

Architecture in Casterbridge, speaking 'cheerfully' of fertility, of social and economic integration, and 'of individual unrestraint as to boundaries' (68), has indeed become eroticized. Henchard's house, which reflects and endorses him at the

---

[12] Enstice (1979) points out that Hardy's portrait of Casterbridge is not only selective—excluding Dorchester's Georgian façades and its modern buildings—but inconsistent in its own terms: 'the long gardens of all the major houses might . . . seem strange in a town where the dwellings are "packed" together' (9).

height of his power,[13] also epitomizes the town itself, which is at once a city, a walled garden, and—with its stable 'frame' and rich vital centre—a splendidly androgynous body. Because, like the Great Barn in *Far from the Madding Crowd*, this body has a maternal aspect, it is paradoxical but consistent that the countryside is felt as enriching the town only as long as Henchard is *inside* Casterbridge. Whenever he is drawn out from the centre—to value the wheat in Durnover, to save the women from the bull on the road to Port-Bredy, to spy on Farfrae courting Elizabeth-Jane on the Budmouth Road—he learns something to his disadvantage; and on two occasions —when he holds his doomed entertainments on the ancient earthwork and when he consults Wide-Oh Fall about the weather—nature turns violently against him. Indeed, this last journey—a 'crooked and miry' way along a 'turnpike-road' which becomes successively 'a lane . . . a cart-track . . . a bridle-path . . . a foot-way overgrown with brambles' (212–23) to a cottage, 'which, with its garden, was surrounded with a high, dense hedge'—is a kind of demonic parody of the way into his own house. And when at the end of the novel he is exposed on the heath, the land—explicitly a maternal body, with the tumuli jutting 'roundly into the sky . . . as though they were the full breasts of Diana Multimammia supinely extended there' (381)—does not succour him and he dies of starvation.

Yet even as it expels him, the town endorses the man who represents what was best in it. Casterbridge, open to nature and just touched by technology but not yet penetrated by the railway, is not punctured, does not burst, sprawl, or dissolve. This, the text seems to suggest, is the body which produced Michael Henchard, even though he is born as a tragic hero precisely through his expulsion from it. Casterbridge as an erotic presence displaces and diminishes the individual female characters, all of whom contribute to Henchard's exile at the end of the novel.

---

[13] Casagrande and Lock (1978) have shown that Henchard gets his name from a Dorchester mansion the destruction of which Hardy regretted. Bullen (1986), 159, finds Henchard's house 'an apt visual metaphor for his solid, old-fashioned principles'.

Casterbridge is more than a physical entity; it is also a social organism. The notion of the border or boundary continues, however, to be important in its conceptualization. The various social groups which make up the town 'touch' at the very borders which mark them off.[14] Spatial boundaries often correspond to social boundaries in this novel. There is a precise distinction between the clientele of the Three Mariners and that of the King's Arms, between those who sit at 'the lower end of the table' and those who sit at the top, between those inside the building and those outside, between 'the west end of a church' and 'the leading spirits in the chancel' (40); there is a clear if subtle difference between the two bridges which mark at once 'the lower part of Casterbridge town' and 'the merging point of respectability and indigence' (257), and between the two classes of alienated men who frequent them. 'Merging points' are important: the novel deals with points of contact between social groups and with moments of penetration.

Boundaries and their breaching help to construct the figure of Henchard in his social and economic as well as in his personal relationships. The mayor's relationship to the town is adumbrated in the episode which introduces him, when he is seen at the King's Arms sitting in that 'spacious bow-window' which 'projected into the street' (35), exposed to the people on the pavement, who can enter the dialogue without entering the building.[15] The scene in fact punctually dramatizes the very situation which will bring about his downfall—his accountability to the ordinary people of the town and yet his distance from them—as well as the quality in him which will make him vulnerable. Henchard is an expansive character who eventually expands too far. Continually blundering across borders he ought to have respected, he expands—like the bow window he sits in, like the bad bread he is responsible for, which runs all over the ovens—until he falls flat, goes 'so far afield' (123) that he ends up on the heath. Yet the image of the mayor in the window, while ominous in the context of the plot, is also

[14] The various social groupings and the links between them have been discussed by Brown (1962), 56–7, and Fussell (1979), 23–5.

[15] Page (1977), 80, Brooks (1971), 200, and Goode (1988), 79, have discussed the way Henchard is framed in this scene. Millgate (1971*b*), 223, calls attention to the intimations of class hostility here.

ideologically and generically reassuring, endorsing as it does the basic institutions of a nation whose ordinary people are used to making their voices heard while at the same time making an easily readable distinction between those anonymous voices and the larger individualized figure who is being framed for his central role in the tragedy.

The novel seems to depict as a particularly English strength the mingling of classes and the crossing of boundaries. All but one of the novel's main characters move on a horizontal axis, entering the town on foot and mingling with its people as they become established. Farfrae succeeds because he is willing to move from Scotland to England and America and because his affability and competence soon commend him to the local people; Elizabeth-Jane is idealized at the Three Mariners for her 'willingness to sacrifice her personal comfort and dignity to the common weal' (49) and in Henchard's household for keeping the feelings of the servants in mind;[16] Henchard, on foot at the beginning and end of the novel, comes to grief when he loses contact with his customers and his fellow townsmen. Lucetta alone, with her 'ups and downs' (187), is defined from the beginning on a vertical axis and in terms of her 'great elevation' (309) above the community. Looking down from High-Place Hall on to a town square which serves as 'the regulation Open Place in spectacular dramas' (190), she is an observer of rather than a participant in the theatre of the town. Inevitably, it is when she hears the two housemaids identifying her effigy—' 'tis dressed just as *she* was dressed when she sat in the front seat at the time the play-actors came to the Town Hall!' (320)—and realizes that she is not part of the audience but part of the play that she is brought low.[17] Pride will have a fall, as we know from the moment we hear the name of her mansion.

It is perhaps worth noting however that the metaphor cuts both ways. The very imagery of the theatre which satirizes

[16] Elizabeth-Jane's association with the horizontal needs to be qualified: her tendency to look down on events has also been noticed (see Bullen 1986, 158). The text's ambivalence about her social position—the tension between the 'horizontal' and the 'vertical' in her construction—will be dealt with later in this argument.

[17] Brooks (1971), 201, makes essentially this point. Millgate (1971*b*) and Bair (1977) discuss the theatricality of the novel as a whole; Goode (1988), 79–83, shows how Henchard's theatricality is ironized by Elizabeth-Jane's 'awareness'.

Lucetta as a mere observer also focuses attention upon her and on those who come to visit her. It is the people in the box seats who are after all the protagonists in the drama *we* are watching. While endorsing the life of the common person by implicitly criticizing Lucetta for looking *down* on it, Hardy's fable at the same time unabashedly chooses as its central characters only individuals who are elevated by their uncommonness. Our sense of generic conventions reinforces the social distinctions which the narrative takes for granted even as it uses Lucetta and her mansion to moralize about them.

The novel handles criminality with a similar ambiguous tact. The group which destroys Lucetta is identified with a particular part of town, Mixen Lane—an area which, though quite distinct from Casterbridge proper, also has permeable boundaries. Though the clientele of Peter's Finger is quite different from the Three Mariners', 'the lowest fringe of the Mariners' party touched the crest of Peter's at points' (296). Mixen Lane itself has a mixed population—it is home not only to petty criminals but also to 'needy respectability' (295)—and in Peter's Finger 'ex-poachers and ex-gamekeepers, whom squires had persecuted without a cause' (296) consort amicably enough. Prostitutes standing in doorways invite border-crossing; Peter's Finger itself, with its unused front door and its well-used side door, functions as the town's back door, and much is made both of the river which separates it from the countryside and of the traditional process by which this border can be breached.

The Mixen-Lane mixin' is on the whole presented with sympathy and with humour. Yet the crossing of legal and social lines is cannily handled. While Hardy presents Mixen Lane's evasion of the police as a game and suggests that the solidarity of poacher and gamekeeper against an oppressive system has some legitimacy, at the same time he presents the pathos of 'needy respectability' precisely in terms of its being obliged to mix with genuinely low-life characters. The text suggests that the strength of English life is in the flexibility of its social borders, but its tolerance of Mixen Lane is made possible by the very borders, internal and external, which constitute it. Hardy can express a certain sympathy with the dispossessed within a fictional structure which keeps them firmly in their place.

The novel, then, has a powerful investment in the permeable boundary as a positive image. There is one passage, however, which violently reverses these established associations and also undercuts the essential verticality of Lucetta's home, High-Place Hall. This mansion is initially presented, with an almost Gothic intensity, as a border-point—a point at which the upper world and the underworld have met. Like Peter's Finger, the building has two doors and the back one is involved with criminal activity: it opens on to a sinister alley by which 'it had been possible to come unseen from all sorts of quarters in the town—the old play-house, the old bull-stake, the old cock-pit, the pool wherein nameless infants had been used to disappear' (161). It is at this point that the *corps morcelé* reappears: the mask on the *key*stone of the door, traditionally stoned by Casterbridge boys, has become almost as 'ghastly' as Troy's gargoyle, with its 'comic leer' and its lips and jaws 'chipped off . . . as if they had been eaten away by disease' (161). Perhaps because of the previous reference to unwanted pregnancy, the macabre image of the mouth decayed and gaping suggests sexual horror, syphilitic degeneration, and the mask above the door becomes itself a kind of door (or key*hole*?), a terrifying aperture which devours and contaminates.

We might expect truly corrupt dealings to take place in that lane, but they do not (the only time the door is actually used is when Henchard goes through it to visit Lucetta, narrowly missing Elizabeth-Jane). Just for this reason, it becomes clear, if only in retrospect, that the house asks to be read as emblematic. But emblematic of what, precisely? There seem to be three alternatives, which depend upon three unstated analogies with other figures in the text. If we see the house with its two doors as like Peter's Finger, the analogy is between the corruption of wealth and the corruption of poverty. By having the mansion announce that 'Blood built it, and Wealth enjoys it' (160), the text might seem to identify Lucetta with a social class whose economic exploitation and decadent pleasures have oppressed and even helped criminalize the underclass which destroys her.[18] (The language taints Lucetta not Mixen Lane, whose individual inhabitants are never involved in the vicious and

18 Brown (1962), 31, emphasizes the class associations of Lucetta's mansion.

depressing activities adumbrated here.) If on the other hand High-Place Hall is—as most readers assume and as the sexual imagery implies—like Lucetta herself, the mansion points to her duplicitous character and suppressed past, perhaps even to her 'ghastly' body, and hints at the kind of corruption Hardy cannot make explicit.[19] If, finally, Lucetta's house is—like Henchard's—seen as an epitome of the town of which it is a part, its ominous 'back door' is Mixen Lane itself, the *porta Esquilina* of Casterbridge.[20] These readings work in opposite directions: while the first two tend to imply that Lucetta deserves what she gets, the third casts a more sinister light on her victimizers than readers are accustomed to notice.

This last suggestion might be allowed to unfold. Unlike High-Place Hall's, Casterbridge's 'back door' does figure in the plot: it admits Newson, who not only intervenes to disastrous effect in Henchard's life but who also contributes to the skimmity-ride which kills the lady of High-Place Hall. Lucetta is a peculiarly disposable character,[21] discarded as easily as her effigy, which—unlike Henchard's—never turns up to haunt the story with a specular *frisson*. Perhaps because the skimmity-ride, as Henchard himself points out, kills her but saves his life, its organizers are dealt with complacently enough—their duping of the constables treated as essentially comic—and Newson's willingness to contribute to the fun seems merely an index of his rather thoughtless geniality.

Responding no doubt to the dominant tone of the narrative here, few readers take the criminality of the skimmity-ride very seriously, apparently assuming that Lucetta's miscarriage and death were not foreseen or intended by its organizers.[22] The

[19] See Paterson (1959*a*), 164; Brooks (1971), 201; Vigar (1974), 150; Grindle (1979), 97; Bullen (1986), 160–6.

[20] Millgate (1971*b*), 223, suggests this analogy. See Spenser, *The Faerie Queene*, II. ix. stanza 32, for a paradigmatic equation of the house, the city, and the human body.

[21] At an early stage of composition Hardy had Henchard burn Lucetta's photograph: 'there's an end of her and here goes her picture. Burns it up flame creeps up face etc.' See Winfield (1973), 37.

[22] Readers who do take it seriously tend to deal with it in rather general terms as a reflection of class enmity: see Brown (1962), 57, and Lerner (1975), 77–8. Kramer (1975), 175 n. 11, and Williams (1972), 154, do point out that the skimmity-ride is conceived by its organizers specifically as an attack upon Lucetta rather than upon Farfrae. Williams is the only one to observe that Lucetta's punishment is quite out of proportion to her 'crime'.

impression is facilitated by Victorian decorum—the decorum which forbids specific or repeated references to Lucetta's pregnancy. A reader who cannot be very aware of her condition as the skimmity-ride is being planned can be counted on not to raise the question of whether the people in Peter's Finger would have been aware of it (but surely they would?). Politics of class displace politics of gender: foregrounding Lucetta's power as a wealthy person—as Nance and the group do as they discuss bringing her down—obscures her vulnerability as a pregnant woman—which Hardy cannot in any case have them discussing—and allows the danger and malice of what they are doing to be underplayed.

The text, then, although it allows a 'political' reading of Lucetta's fate, also contains an excess of meaning which complicates such a reading. By treating the Mixen-Lane machinations as social comedy and by metaphorically displacing the less endearing kinds of criminality from Mixen Lane on to Lucetta, Hardy loads the narrative against her in ways which seem motivated as much by misogyny as by sympathy with the underclass. Because Hardy is making the town into a positive body which will be used to endorse Henchard, and because he is willing to taint with deeply sinister associations the woman who prefers Farfrae to his protagonist, he constructs Casterbridge's doubleness as social flexibility and displaces that doubleness on to the duplicitous woman. Permeability can be constructed as creative and comic on condition that the too-penetrable, too-flexible woman be cast out. Lucetta miscarries and dies: the expansive potential of the female body is decorously displaced to testify to masculine magnanimity and to the organic vitality of the community which has killed her.

The survivors in the novel have—like Hardy himself—a canny sense of boundaries. While intuitively aware of borders, Farfrae is untroubled by them; he can move from Scotland to England, from song to calculation, from one idiom to another, in a way which keeps all his options open. Master of many discourses, he not only has a 'special look when meeting women' (196) but also two distinct ways of talking: a simple, single, manly language with men and a coy, suggestive style with women—a pastiche of secondhand lyrics and sentiments. So firmly is this contrast established that Hardy can amusingly suggest a flash of real feeling in Farfrae simply by having him get his languages crossed—when during his first meeting with Lucetta he suddenly finds himself bursting into an unpremeditated paean to the joys of trading.

As Farfrae appropriates discourse, so too does he appropriate bodies. Farfrae *puts on* a role as he dons a Highland costume; he takes possession by getting inside—taking from Henchard his business, which Henchard insisted he enter, Lucetta, whom he impregnates, and his house, into the heart of which Henchard had originally conducted him. Emblematic of this facility is the image of Farfrae inside the agricultural machine—a grotesquely hybrid body, 'compound of hornet, grasshopper, and shrimp' (191)—humming one of his Scottish songs. Like the figures in a Jonsonian antimasque, who metamorphose into emblems of their ruling passions, Farfrae easily assumes the body of the horse-drill—the wooden horse by which technology is being smuggled into Casterbridge?—and speaks for it. His incorporation into a technology which will obviate the old pieties ('the romance of the sower is gone for good', 194) points not only to his identification with the modern but also to his power to enter and withdraw from whatever machinery he puts in motion.

With Elizabeth-Jane Farfrae is equally lithe and elusive. He stays 'on the border' with her until the very end of the novel, archly humming and whistling at her, hinting at deeper intentions or at the disappointments of his first marriage, advancing and retreating in a way which causes her considerable pain.[23] Perhaps the most touching encounter between them is the one which raises the issue of touching, and has everything to do with the sense of bodily boundaries: their meeting in the granary, with its emblematic ironies and the 'extreme delicacy' (108) of its imagery. Farfrae's closest approach to intimacy is the moment when he blows the dust and chaff off Elizabeth-Jane's clothing. The gesture is like a caress which moves over the surface of her body—though here it is her clothing which is of concern, and *as* clothing, not as a kind of second skin (he is afraid that rain will spoil the fabric). There is a charming decorum both in his solution, which suggests his sense both of

[23] Kramer (1975), 70–80, analyses Farfrae's inadequacies in some detail, arguing that his character degenerates.

the boundaries of her body and of the social boundaries he cannot cross, and in the solution of Hardy, who hints so deftly at what cannot be written. Indeed, the scene invites comparison with Oak's sheep-shearing and Troy's sword exercise, though such a comparison generates its own ironies: if Oak is all tender touch and Troy all blazing brand, Farfrae is all hot air.

There is a level of course on which he himself recognizes this and the very recognition helps make him invulnerable. Although Farfrae owes much of his popularity to his singing and to the romantic Highland persona which the songs construct, he is quite willing to admit that his nostalgia lasts only as long as the songs. Farfrae's 'literalness' and 'simplicity' (114, 187)—the very frankness with which he owns up to what might be considered somewhat factitious emotions in this particular case—protect him from wider-ranging criticism.[24]

And they protect the text at the same time. For the way Farfrae characterizes himself is merely an extension of the way the novel characterizes him. As allusions to Sir Walter Scott remind us, Farfrae's famous two-stranded nature has a textual basis.[25] Generated as a 'character' not only in binary opposition to Henchard but in terms of a paradigm worked out in the Waverley novels, Farfrae, when he creates a persona from borrowed bits of speech and song, at once collaborates in and parodies his own construction. Hardy has delineated in Farfrae both the charm and the limitations of the 'literal' mind, and the instinctive shrewdness of its exploitive strategies. But if Farfrae is too 'literal' to scrutinize what he is doing, so perhaps is the text which has cannily constructed him for its own purposes.

One of these purposes is the simultaneous expression and disguise of homoerotic feeling.[26] There is a sense in which Farfrae's flirtation with Elizabeth-Jane at once doubles and blurs his relationship with her stepfather. Hardy manages, while making perfectly clear that the relationship between the two men means much more to Henchard than it does to Farfrae, to make us sympathize deeply with Henchard when Farfrae

---

[24] See Brown (1962), 27, who is thus disarmed.

[25] See *The Mayor of Casterbridge*, 69, 237, 296. Brown (1962), 44–8, who sees not Farfrae but Henchard as a typical Scott hero, identifies Farfrae rather as 'the Canny Scot of tradition' (16). Elliott (1984), 40, suggests the music-hall Scot as a source for Farfrae.

[26] See Kramer (1975), 86–7, and Showalter (1979), 106–7.

becomes indifferent to him. Because Farfrae cannot justly be accused of leading Henchard on, the text can demonstrate how the break between them proceeds from the hero's own nature, as a properly tragic plot should. But because we have seen him leading Elizabeth-Jane on, we are ready to *feel* with Henchard that Farfrae has indeed been a tease, even if we are unable to pinpoint precisely where his behaviour has been unreasonable.

The text represses this analogy, however; and it does it by encouraging the reader to take for granted an absolute distinction between male–male and male–female relationships. While Farfrae's relentless archness where Elizabeth-Jane is concerned might call into question the 'simplicity' he displays with Henchard, the text naturalizes the discrepancy by consistently suggesting that, although women evoke double-talk, transactions between men can be simple and straightforward. Henchard feels a frank, spontaneous, true-hearted affection for Farfrae— an affection we are not invited to question. Though it is possible to feel that there is an erotic dimension to Henchard's attraction for the younger man, Farfrae's failure to recognize the intensity of Henchard's emotion facilitates the repression of this dimension. Farfrae's unselfconsciousness keeps *Henchard* 'simple' and single, and the nature of his feeling for Farfrae undefined and unexaminable. Lawrence in *Women in Love* will rewrite the wrestling match to release its erotic potential, but Hardy's text depends upon the reader not questioning Farfrae's 'natural' tendency to draw a firm line between male friendship and heterosexual flirtation.

Farfrae's facility in drawing lines comes increasingly to the fore at the end of the novel, when pity for Henchard's poignant situation is being demanded of the reader. Under these circumstances the narrator lets Farfrae speak for himself. When he lumps Henchard, as his employee, in with ' "the rest of the men" ' (313); when, after Newson has taken Henchard's place as prospective father-in-law, he concludes that ' "all is as it should be, and we will have no more deefficulties at all" ' (362); when during the final search for Henchard Farfrae demurs about going further because he does not want to stay out overnight and ' "make a hole in a sovereign" ' (381)—Farfrae's words are given in direct discourse, and the narrator, who perhaps feels he can count on the reader's appalled sympathy for Henchard at this point, makes no comment on them.[27] On the other hand, when Farfrae, having shed wife and child so much more easily than Henchard was able to do, concludes that 'by the death of Lucetta he had exchanged a looming misery for a simple sorrow' (348), the somewhat ambiguous handling of the free indirect discourse implies that the narrator endorses his judgement. Farfrae's compartmentalizing is essential to the economy of the text. His 'simplicity' contains the erotic reverberations of male friendship; his equanimity as a widower keeps the fallen woman in her place. The novel needs the lines Farfrae draws to keep itself in line.

Repellent though Farfrae's canniness may appear to the reader at the end of the story, it evokes no objection from Farfrae's wife, who seems to have aligned herself unproblematically with his proprieties. Farfrae's and Elizabeth-Jane's common concern for the 'respectable' (43, 49), though it keeps them apart until all the bloom is off their romance, makes it inevitable that they should end up together. But whereas Farfrae's propriety is handled with restraint by the narrator, who leaves us, moved by affection for his victims, to draw our own conclusions, Elizabeth-Jane's is foregrounded in ways which are more ambiguous.

Readers, while not vitally interested in Elizabeth-Jane, tend to idealize and simplify her, responding to emphatic cues from the text. What is rarely commented on is that it is her terrible sense of propriety which kills Henchard.[28] When Elizabeth-

[27] The narrator's irony about Farfrae's 'dear native country that he loved so well as never to have revisited it' (373) and the detail about making a hole in a sovereign were added in late revision: see Chase (1964), 52.

[28] Gregor's treatment of Elizabeth-Jane as a 'developed consciousness' (1974, 125) is typical. Lerner (1975), 78, Brown (1962), 24, and Butler (1978), 71, note her excessive interest in gentility, though Brown argues she outgrows it; Hartveit (1977) rationalizes it in a somewhat circular fashion. Duffin (1937), 40, who realizes that she is 'but an instrument' of the plot—'the old bull is to be killed and she is the weapon chosen: no other would have served'—and Karl (1975), 427, who suggests that Hardy's women tend to be 'furies or fates, temptresses, hostile creatures struggling to free themselves while entrapping males', confront her cruelty most directly. Goode, analysing the novel's two 'conflicting modes of narrative totalization' (1988, 90), the masculine/theatrical and the feminine/analytical, sees 'respectability' as the limitedness of the latter. For me Goode's impressive argument is somewhat vitiated by his own binary oppositions which construct femininity as awareness and thus obscure the woman's body and the text's exploitation of it.

Jane primly announces to Newson that she really 'ought to forget him now' (364), when she addresses him with chilling propriety as 'Mr.' Henchard (376) and berates him for having 'cruelly' sent 'my warm-hearted real father' away 'with a wicked invention of my death, which nearly broke his heart' (a 'wicked invention' of her own), her ruthless prissiness breaks *his* heart in a way that would seem difficult to ignore. Yet the narrator seems to ignore it and the text almost forces us to ignore it too in the long run, because Elizabeth-Jane is rehabilitated in the last pages to generate its philosophic ending. Our desire for generic decorum—our insistence that character shall be coherent in a realistic novel—invites us to repress or downplay evidence which seems contradictory. I propose to read Elizabeth-Jane more sceptically as a construction of the text and to look particularly at the gaps and discontinuities in the treatment of her propriety.

On the whole the text seems to approve of Elizabeth-Jane's sense of decorum, for it is in terms of this that her sensitivity, refinement, and maturity are constantly defined. It is her almost paranoid sobriety, her very moderate estimate of life's possibilities, which is the basis of her judgement of what is fitting, and that sobriety seems usually to be presented as wisdom. Her humility, as well as her conviction that mental cultivation is more important than physical, make her uncomfortable with showy clothing; her sense of the seriousness of life makes her dislike jokes and indeed any kind of premature or excessive celebration—even dancing at her own wedding. The coda of the novel ('happiness was but the occasional episode in a general drama of pain', 386) seems generated equally by Elizabeth-Jane and by the narrator, who endorses, by expressing it in his own idiom, the attitude he describes. It seems clear that some of her authorial father's own attitude to life has gone into the construction of Elizabeth-Jane and that she is to be seen as decidedly superior to the ordinary woman precisely because of her greater seriousness of mind.

The treatment of Elizabeth-Jane's various excellences remains however somewhat blurred and ambiguous. Take for example the issue of her self-improvement—so vital an aspect of *Jude the Obscure* and presumably so meaningful to Hardy himself. We keep being told that she is improving her mind and that her main interest, when she achieves a degree of middle-class security, is to rectify those inadequacies of education and culture of which she is so conscious. Henchard, when he visits her room after her departure, is touched and impressed to find it full of 'books, sketches, maps, and little arrangements for tasteful effects' (1966). But it is hard to believe in those books she reads so 'omnivorously' (149), hard to imagine them actually being consumed,[29] for these are books without *bodies*, without print or binding or titles. (Henchard's own token library, with its three titled volumes, is more fully realized.) It is hard, too, to believe that Elizabeth-Jane gains in wisdom and understanding as her education progresses, for she is already level-headed and wise and temperate when we first meet her. She is also well spoken. It is not the articulate young woman we meet in Chapter 2 but young Thomas Hardy who calls wild hyacinths greggles;[30] the only time Elizabeth-Jane uses dialect words is when Henchard chastises her for it, and the only way we know which specific words she learns to avoid is in the paragraph where the narrator tells us she used them no more.

We must believe, on the other hand, in her sartorial transformation. When Elizabeth-Jane first meets Farfrae, her 'plain dress' is in accord with her 'earnestness and soberness of mien' (63) and he appreciates the harmony. When her adoption by Henchard has enabled her to improve her wardrobe, Elizabeth-Jane resolves not to 'blossom gaudily' and suddenly, feeling that to do so would be 'inconsistent with her past life' (109). The narrator's florid characterization of the attitude she does *not* take—'she refrained from bursting out like a water-flower that spring, and clothing herself in puffings and knick-knacks, as most of the Casterbridge girls would have done in her circumstances' (100)—is presumably to be read as praise of her moderation. But because each item she purchases demands something else to 'go with' it, to 'harmonize' (109), she ends up remade from top to toe. The metamorphosis is oddly enough effected by the same principle of decorum which had kept her plainly dressed before. The fact that she is then said to be distressed by the discrepancy between her improved

---

[29] See Gregor (1974), 116, and Lerner (1975), 15.
[30] Elliott (1984), 31, cites the *Life*.

appearance and her unimproved intellect is (so to speak) window dressing. What has been dramatized is the change in her appearance, and if we are impressed by her it has to be at least in part by the same phenomenon which impresses the worldly observers of Casterbridge, if not for the same reason.

'We now see her in a black silk bonnet, velvet mantle or silk spencer, dark dress, and carrying a sunshade' (101). The change in her wardrobe marks the change in her social status. The sunshade is to protect her skin, to keep it white. Pale skin is a mark of beauty because it is a mark of social class, a sign which differentiates the middle class from the working woman. How we are to read Elizabeth-Jane's attitude to such differentiation remains undecidable.

Elizabeth-Jane will be blamed by her father for not drawing the line clearly enough. Though from the time she is adopted by Henchard she earnestly desires to fulfil his expectations and is terrified of the possibility that 'her tastes were not good enough for her position, and would bring her into disgrace' (125), Elizabeth-Jane keeps making mistakes, apparently because of her natural, artless humility. Hardy enlists our sympathy for her in a series of episodes which cast Henchard as the heavy father and Elizabeth-Jane as his innocent victim. When he berates his stepdaughter for dancing with Farfrae, using dialect words, failing to write lady's-hand, and thanking the housemaid, Henchard is brutal, arbitrary, and clearly wrong. But the longer the sequence goes on the more questionable it becomes, and its climax—the scene when she carries bread and cider to Nance Mockridge—undercuts the very pattern it seems to complete.

By this time one might expect Elizabeth-Jane—so 'thoughtful' (100), 'reflective', and 'observant' (196)—to think twice before serving the servants: it is equally hard to believe, after four previous warnings, either that she would believe such a gesture appropriate or that she would do it if she did not. The way Nance is described—standing, like the prostitutes in Mixen Lane, 'with her hands on her hips, easefully looking at the preparations on her behalf' (151)—and the way she behaves complicate the situation. While Nance's instinct to snap back at Henchard is understandable, her exposure of Elizabeth—at best impulsive, at worst gratuitously spiteful—displays her as inferior in moral as well as in social qualities to the mistress who serves her.[31] The more deeply we sympathize with Elizabeth-Jane, the more strongly we register the misdirected malice of Nance's retort.

Accordingly Elizabeth-Jane's implausible gesture marks the point at which too much deference to the working classes becomes indecorous. Even while we recoil from the *manner* in which Henchard attacks her and Nance, his *judgement* seems to be confirmed by Nance's vengeful reflex, and his *motive* may evoke our sympathy: his baffled rage can be read as a defence against the affectionate pride he had begun to develop in her, a pride based partly on his sense of her social superiority to himself. Hardy seems to be implicated with Henchard in his attraction to the refinement of their 'daughter' and in the sense of her (specifically class-based) superiority to the working people from whom she has risen.

The anomalies here invite a rereading of the episode to which Nance refers—the scene in the Three Mariners where Elizabeth-Jane worked to help pay for their room. They might even remind us that the narrator's praise of her as willing 'to sacrifice her personal comfort and dignity to the common weal' (49) is illogical. It is because she herself insists on being 'respectable' that she and her mother are in the Three Mariners in the first place; working for the room is not sacrificing her dignity but preserving it, and she is doing it for herself as much as for 'the common weal'. And her demeanour in the inn manifests quite a sharp awareness of class distinctions (she will serve in the private but not in the public rooms, she does not mind waiting on Farfrae because 'He's so respectable, and educated—far above the rest of 'em in the inn', 64). The attempt to read her as caught in a double bind—forced to offend against a tyrannical bourgeois standard of gentility in order to finance it—is actually undermined by the specious tribute, which blurs her motivation. What seems to be happening here is that the narrator himself has enough of a stake in the

---

[31] Robert Barnes's illustration of this episode for the serial emphasizes the class difference between Nance, boldly facing the reader and scratching her elbows, and Elizabeth-Jane, daintily dressed, head deferentially bowed towards Henchard. See *Graphic*, 33 (1886), 241.

notion of respectability to feel that her gesture needs to be defended.

The issue of the sunshade compounds the ambiguities. The narrator's language attributes an almost moral dimension to Elizabeth-Jane in her care of her skin ('deeming spotlessness part of womanliness', 101). Spotlessness is an excellent thing in a woman just because it is anomalous. The prostitutes in Mixen Lane also keep themselves curiously pristine—a quality which is noteworthy precisely because it is an exception to the rule: 'A white apron is a suspicious vesture in situations where spotlessness is difficult' (295). Like the prostitutes, the furmity woman, too, is distinguished by a 'white apron, which, as it threw an air of respectability over her as far as it extended, was made so wide as to reach nearly round her waist' (5) and which even at her trial contrasts 'visibly with the rest of her clothes' (229). An apron throws an 'air of respectability' over a woman by concealing and displacing what the furmity woman exposes when she is caught committing a 'nuisance' (230) in the gutter by the church.[32] Mrs Goodenough is the novel's witch—she is repeatedly described as a 'hag' (6, 23, 24) and a 'haggish creature' (5)—and the narrator also describes Elizabeth-Jane, in her prescience, as a 'discerning silent witch' (197).[33] The very language which differentiates Elizabeth-Jane not only from the working woman but from the fallen women and the witch links her, as a woman, with them as well.

Indeed, although she is schematically contrasted to Lucetta and at key moments opposes her, Elizabeth-Jane becomes defined for us to some extent as Lucetta is defined, in terms of her clothing and her image in the mirror. Although Lucetta speaks of herself *as* clothing, the narrator actually tells us as much about Elizabeth-Jane's wardrobe as about hers. Lucetta is introduced as Elizabeth's 'wraith or double' (153) and the women—both of whom have occasion to examine themselves in the glass and predict, ruefully, the coolness of male response to their physical charms—are constructed by and in mirrors. Lucetta's experience of the skimmity-ride is a specular epiphany: hearing the voices of 'scandal' in the excited conjectures of the

---

[32] It also connotes the concealment of pregnancy: 'aprons-up' means pregnant (Partridge 1984, 24).

[33] See also p. 98 n. 8.

housemaids, seeing herself as others see her ('Tis me!'), and as her husband will see her from now on, she suddenly understands that her world is a hall of mirrors and the revelation kills her. But this violent event is foreshadowed not only by the scene in which Lucetta searches her glass for signs of ageing but also by the moment when Elizabeth-Jane looks at her carefully adorned self as she would be looked at by Farfrae and 'luminously' comprehends that her appearance is '"just enough to make him silly, and not enough to keep him so"' (128). It is because Elizabeth-Jane is aware of the specular nature of the subject—more aware, perhaps, than any of Hardy's other characters—that she is so stoical and self-controlled; but she is ineluctably linked with Lucetta nevertheless, defined, like all of Hardy's women, by the male gaze which alone can fulfil her.

The two women are most sharply contrasted in their notions of propriety—notably at the moment when Lucetta, broaching the subject of her marriage to Farfrae, invites Elizabeth-Jane to condone a woman's breaking her engagement to a man she no longer loves. Elizabeth's judgement—'there is only one course left to honesty. You must remain a single woman' (248)—itself evokes explicit judgement. On the one hand the narrator draws attention to her rigidity, pointing out that her 'craving for correctness of procedure was . . . almost vicious' and that 'Any suspicion of impropriety was to Elizabeth-Jane like a red rag to a bull' (an interesting simile in context: to the bull which 'viciously' threatened Lucetta only pages earlier?). On the other hand he apparently agrees that Lucetta ought to have fulfilled her engagement to Henchard regardless of her changed feelings (he later takes care parenthetically to gloss her dying confession to her husband, the exact words of which we are never allowed to hear, 332). Indeed the narrator's very intervention here functions—despite its suggestive echo—as much to explain and excuse Elizabeth-Jane's rigour as to condemn it.

This should not be surprising, since Elizabeth-Jane always lines up with the Father—whoever he happens to be at the moment—and with the patriarchal order, and that order is always endorsed by the narrator as long as Henchard is the patriarch. It is important to remember the sequence here: that

Lucetta's marriage was hastened by the furmity woman's revelation and that the interview between Elizabeth-Jane and Lucetta takes place shortly after both women have learned Henchard's secret. Elaine Showalter points out a curious gap in the text when she observes that Elizabeth is never shown confronting Henchard with his offence against her mother: Hardy, she says, seems to have forgotten to write the scene.[34] Apparently the knowledge that Henchard had lied to her in asserting that he and Susan 'thought each other dead—and—Newson became her husband' (140) and that he had sold her mother and, she believes, her own infant self spurs Elizabeth-Jane not to confront Henchard, not to question her own paternity, not to mourn the stain which this publicity might cast upon her own reputation but instead to urge the Father's claim to Lucetta!

The omission noted by Showalter is not the only gap in Elizabeth's story. Consider the text's account of her 'vicious' propriety. The narrator attributes it in this episode to 'her early troubles with regard to her mother' (248)—evidently the wife-sale (Elizabeth-Jane admits to Lucetta that Henchard 'did treat my mother badly once, it seems, in a moment of intoxication', 249). But when, six chapters earlier, Elizabeth-Jane laments to Lucetta in very similar language that her mother's separation from her father had cast 'shadows' (195) upon her life, she cannot *there* be referring to the wife-sale. Is she troubled by her mother's supposed involuntary bigamy? But this is a 'shadow' of which the townspeople (and presumably Lucetta herself) could know nothing, and which Elizabeth-Jane—who had transferred her loyalty to her new 'father' with some initial reluctance but with no apparent sense of *shame*—is never shown to ponder. In any case, Elizabeth's anxiety about 'respectability' antedates all such revelations: it is one of the first things we hear about her at the beginning of the novel when she can know of no 'shadow' on her reputation. Henchard, with his nagging about social decorum, plays on the anxiety—it is an irony the text does not particularly draw attention to that he helps strengthen the very propriety which leads her to reject him—but he does not create it.

---

[34] Showalter (1979), 109.

The text has forgotten a lot about the inner life of Elizabeth-Jane, whose rage for order is at once overdetermined and underexplained. It is as if what Hardy knows about her—the fact that she is illegitimate—has shaped her own responses. Since we have learned to know Elizabeth as the text knows her, in terms of its needs and priorities rather than her own, we may not even register the incongruity of her reaction when the truth about her parentage does emerge. Although Henchard had plausibly believed that he could damage Elizabeth-Jane in Farfrae's eyes by revealing that she was 'legally, nobody's child' (354), neither she nor Farfrae seems particularly to take in the awful fact when it is finally disclosed. Instead of the complicated dismay she might be expected to feel about Newson's exploitation of her 'simple' (17, 83) mother (dismay complicated by the realization that it is to this exploitation that she owes her existence [35])—instead of distress at her own illegitimacy (or does it not matter now that she has acquired a stable surname from her husband?)—Elizabeth-Jane sympathizes with the 'real father' (376) in *his* simplicity ('you were always so trusting, father; I've heard my mother say so hundreds of times', 365). The one issue which would adequately have motivated her vicious sense of propriety—her shame at her own illegitimacy—is repressed at the very moment when that propriety comes most damagingly into play.

The text's forgetfulness serves its fable well. For his tragic ending, Hardy needs to have Elizabeth-Jane reject Henchard gratuitously and choose Newson over him. By having her ignore the circumstances of her birth, he can make his fictional daughter speak for the Father-as-biological-progenitor and the principle of patriarchy, and he can have her at the same time create, by means of her very rejection, the Father-as-tragic-hero she will pay tribute to at the end of the novel.

The question of Elizabeth-Jane's paternity is of course a literary trick on the reader. It is not only Henchard but the reader who is fooled by the narrator's carefully ambiguous language into thinking that the lost daughter has been found. When we discover the sleight of hand, it is a little disconcerting, perhaps because of the ease with which a girl-child can be

---

[35] Goode (1988), 92–3, who deals with the theme of joking, makes this point; on practical jokes in *The Mayor of Casterbridge*, see also Welsh (1975), 26–7.

dropped out of the text—as into that 'pool wherein nameless infants had been used to disappear' (161). As Showalter suggests, Henchard would not have sold a son so easily,[36] nor could Hardy so easily have replaced one son with another. Because to his readers paternity would matter so much more in the case of a son than in the case of a daughter, one point the novel is making—that 'real' fatherhood is spiritual and emotional rather than biological—would have been unacceptable.

The whole question of the claims of paternity is, however, full of problems. If there is pathos in the fact that, though Henchard himself has finally risen above questions of biological relationship, has learned to be a father in a 'deeper' sense, he must lose the child he finally deserves, it is a pathos which blurs the real issue. The question is always about who gets the woman—whether she is Susan, Lucetta, or Elizabeth-Jane—and the pathos is that Henchard always loses to a male rival. Newson's *merely* biological fatherhood is played down only in the interests of Henchard's essential fatherhood. The conflict remains male rivalry over a disputed woman, and changing the basis of the claim from biological to spiritual fatherhood merely mystifies the notion of patriarchal possession. Though the novel can be read as a critique of patriarchal notions of ownership, I would argue that what it really expresses is the anxiety that such ownership is not possible. What happens to Henchard when his daughter turns brutally against him expresses as much the fear of a woman's 'vicious' propriety as compunction over patriarchal presumptuousness.

The focus on the rival claims of Elizabeth-Jane's two fictional fathers also blurs the paternal role of her authorial father. In her philosophy and in her deference to the claims of propriety Elizabeth-Jane is Hardy's own child. The problem is not only that she has too many parts to play in this text but that the parts are contradictory. She is the novel's 'poor only heroine' (356) whose romantic feelings for Farfrae evoke our sympathy, especially in the first part of the novel, which is largely told from her point of view. But she also has to function as Henchard's nemesis—the last of the 'infernal harpies' (145)

---

which snatch away his feast, the Delilah to his 'Samson shorn' (373), the tamer of the 'netted' (349) and 'fangless lion' (357)[37]—and thus in the final pages has to do heartless things. Yet too much cannot be made of her cruelty here, since she is going to be used in the last paragraphs of the novel to reflect a view of life very like that which Thomas Hardy in his own person has expressed in other texts. If Henchard is Lear and Whittle the Fool, Elizabeth-Jane is alternately Regan, Edgar, and Cordelia. She is indeed nothing but an image in a mirror.

For all its tragic decorum, then, the ending of the novel is somewhat muddled, both because Hardy's impulse to create Elizabeth-Jane in his own image is at odds with the functions she has to serve in the plot and because the text's more liberal and generous social notions are at odds with Hardy's instinctive terror of the woman who castrates and kills. Female characterization escapes the boundaries Hardy has drawn and deconstructs his carefully wrought parable. What the story illustrates is not so much that Henchard should have been a better father as that he should never have exposed himself to the power of a woman.

The novel indeed turns on the question of exposure. The text eroticizes the notion of exposure which it borrows from *Lear*: its central terror is not so much guilt as shame. Lucetta is exposed before the town and before her husband and dies of it. Elizabeth-Jane's indecorous past is exposed by Nance Mockridge and her real paternity is exposed when Henchard, as she sleeps, is able to trace Newson's features which 'come to the surface' (144) in her face. (We seem not meant to register the impropriety of his visit to her bedroom: the text focuses so firmly on the notion of establishing paternity that it does not notice its own exposure of the father.) Abel Whittle is exposed in the physical sense, and so is the furmity woman, when Stubberd shines his light on her as she urinates ('"Put away that dee lantern"', he reports she demands, 231). Henchard is exposed repeatedly—by Susan, who calls his bluff by going off with Newson in the first chapter and who, by first concealing and then revealing the truth about

---

[37] The suggestions of castration are obvious. While I agree with Showalter (1979) that Henchard is unmanned, I see the way the text's attitude to unmanning is handled as decidedly more ambivalent than her argument would suggest.

Elizabeth-Jane, dupes him into exposing his feelings in a way he will bitterly regret; by Mrs Goodenough, who sends Susan on to Casterbridge, reveals the wife-selling to the town, and asks Jopp about Lucetta's letters; by Lucetta, who marries Farfrae behind Henchard's back and leaves him exposed to his creditor Grower; by Newson, who reveals the lie which turns Elizabeth-Jane against Henchard; and finally by Elizabeth-Jane herself, whose repudiation of him exposes him literally to death on the heath.

Women are at the bottom of Henchard's exposure. Even a thoroughly good woman is likely to expose a man in complicated ways; even a thoroughly bad man—like Jopp, so transparently constructed as a plot device—is dangerous only when mixed up with women. Grossly mistreated as he has been by Henchard, Jopp does harm only when he gets involved in Lucetta's scheme to repossess her reckless correspondence, and when—improbably ignoring his implied threat of blackmail—she snubs him and piques his desire for revenge. And Newson's intentions, apparently, are quite innocent. Though his behaviour is perhaps somewhat crude and thoughtless, the ultimate result of his intervention could not reasonably have been predicted. How could Newson have guessed either that Henchard would care so much about Elizabeth-Jane or that Elizabeth-Jane would care so little about Henchard?

A real man does not expose people. Although Henchard regrets telling Farfrae 'the secret o' my life', it is made clear that he risked nothing in doing so: ' "I had forgot it," said Farfrae simply' (114). Henchard's desire to expose is examined more carefully but only to be denied. Twice he is shown wrestling with the temptation to avenge himself on the women who have hurt him by destroying their relationship with his rival—and conquering it. The moral struggle is foregrounded, the temptation is, quite precisely, dramatized ('he had quite intended to effect a grand catastrophe at the end of this drama', 284) and we register the moral victory.

Whenever he is not harassed beyond endurance, Henchard's chivalrous instinct is to protect women, however exasperating they may be. He marries Susan and does in fact succeed in protecting her (she is the only person with a 'past' who is not exposed during her lifetime)—even if his gesture of sending her back the five guineas, which 'tacitly . . . said to her that he bought her back again' (79), is somewhat problematic in a text which deals explicitly if coyly with prostitution. And he fully intends to do as much for Lucetta—'the double of the first' (289)—if only in the sense that he no longer feels great personal warmth for either of them. He embraces Elizabeth-Jane with real feeling, hoping and waiting to endow her with his name; he saves Lucetta and Elizabeth-Jane from the bull without a second thought; he is easily persuaded to abandon any thoughts of revenge against Lucetta ('his heart smote him for having attempted reprisals on one of a sex so weak', 288).

Unfortunately, however, he just cannot seem to cope with the 'finnikin details' (87) of the written word. Because he opens Susan's letter, Elizabeth-Jane is exposed to his wrath and emotionally, if not literally, expelled from the household. Because he leaves the packet of Lucetta's incriminating correspondence in his dining-room safe, he risks Farfrae's access to it. Because he fails properly to seal the packet Jopp carries, Lucetta is exposed and destroyed. 'Constructed upon too large a scale' to attend to the 'minutiae' (209) of print or women, Henchard suffers disproportionately for what must be taken as involuntary errors. Yet the figurative language associated with him is ambiguous. Is he the 'bull breaking fence' (311) driven back by Farfrae during the royal visit? the bull tormented in 'the old bull-stake' (161) to which Lucetta's back door gives access? Or is he—'by nature something of a woman-hater' (89) as he admits to Farfrae—the bull who hunts down and fatally gores the woman he rescued?

The one incident which implicates Henchard directly in the process of exposure seems at the same time to make the point that man-to-man encounters are simple and straightforward. Henchard insists on Abel Whittle's coming to work without his trousers on, and Whittle is distraught at the prospect of specifically sexual shame. Though he has people pulling through the window on his great toe, he dreads 'the women-folk . . . looking out of their winders at my mortification' (113). However, nothing of the sort takes place, and by the reader who takes the episode, in context, as another step in the deterioration of the friendship between Henchard and Farfrae, nothing of the sort is expected. What is going on here is apparently between

Henchard and Farfrae not between Henchard and Whittle, and it has to do with justice and with managerial tact not with sexual curiosity. In retaliation for ordering Whittle to expose himself, Henchard is immediately exposed by Farfrae, who countermands his order 'before them' all instead of waiting 'till we were alone' (114). Disagreement between men is open and straightforward and leads quickly to poetic justice—Henchard is obliged on the spot 'to feel what wretches feel'; forgiveness between men is equally straightforward—on the heath, exposed to the elements, Henchard is sheltered by the very man he would have stripped. The text does not encourage us to meditate on the erotic implications of Whittle's projected exposure or to connect it to a curiosity about what a Scotsman wears under his kilt—not even when the motif is repeated, when the witch who exposes Henchard turns out to have been herself exposed by Stubberd's lantern. Our sense not only of social decorum but of generic decorum works against Henchard's exposure here: it encourages us to see the protagonist's blunder merely as an expression of his tragically flawed nature, Whittle's loyalty as a moving corroboration of Henchard's essential good-heartedness and integrity.

Integrity is the impression we are left with. Although the scene on the heath invites comparison with *King Lear*, there is a sense in which the ending of the novel denies the very exposure it seems to dramatize. Unlike Shakespeare's protagonist, Hardy's is not stripped bare, nor is he reduced to incoherence. Rather— given as many words in the last few pages of the novel as he mobilizes at a stretch anywhere else—he is clothed to the end in tendentious rhetoric which asserts the very ego-integrity it pretends to deny.[38] Precisely because his ordeal *is* modelled so self-consciously on Lear's, we can never forget that, unlike Lear, Henchard is always, as he realizes when he sees his effigy in the water, ' "in Somebody's hand" ' (345)—in the hand of the author who insists at the end of his story on endowing him with a factitious unity and wholeness.

That moment when Henchard confronts '*himself* . . . his counterpart, his actual double' (342) is a telling contrast to the

---

[38] Brown (1962), 62, and Lerner (1975), 68, suggest that we seem to hear his voice speaking.

mirroring of the women. When Elizabeth and Lucetta look into a mirror, they see themselves through the eys of man. When Henchard on the other hand looks (*more* narcissistically?) into the *water*, he sees himself as seen by Somebody else. This, the text suggests, is how the genders are constructed: he for Somebody only, she for Somebody in him. Lucetta's last cry expresses her utter dependence on her husband's regard: ' "he will never love me any more—and O, it will kill me—kill me!" ' (321). But—despite the fact that her lament could serve, both with and without a change of pronoun, for Henchard himself— the way the protagonist's death is handled suggests that things are otherwise with a man.

The emotional effect of the novel's ending depends on its success in imposing various kinds of unity on Henchard and his story. The return of Abel Whittle links the middle of the tale to its end and testifies to the essential unity of Henchard's life and character. His long speech is a flashback which recuperates events not focalized by Elizabeth-Jane and re-establishes the flow of the narrative. The episode reaches its emotional climax with Henchard's will, which, as 'a piece of the same stuff that his whole life was made of' (384–5), stands as a testimony to his essential integrity.

But the 'piece' is a piece of paper—the will is, as Whittle says, 'writing' (384)—and there are paradoxes in a written document which solicits oblivion.[39] Henchard's will is a self-contradictory project, endlessly deferring the extinction it invokes. The writer ineluctably refers to his dead self by means of pronouns like 'I' and 'my' which imply that the 'I' continues to exist: it is 'behind *me*' that mourners will or will not walk 'at my funeral', it is 'I' who will or will not be buried in consecrated ground, '*my* dead body' which will or will not be looked at. The language implies the immortality of the essential Henchard, the man who lives on in Hardy's words as well as in his own. Yet if the will is 'a piece of the same stuff that his whole life was made of', it becomes (as indeed it literally is) a page in a volume called *The Life and Death of the Mayor of Casterbridge*—the *Life* becomes text and '*my* dead body' an illusion.

---

[39] See Levine (1981), 249: 'Henchard's last written words are the name he is asking to obliterate—and boldly imprinted . . . It is as though Henchard has stumbled onto the modernist criticism that reminds us of the peculiar status of language.'

Mrs Goodenough, in making clear that the 'I' is always split and always an effect of language, has already exposed the fantasy which shapes Henchard's rhetoric.

The body is not in fact looked at. With proper tragic decorum, the protagonist dies off-stage:[40] we never get inside the hut and Henchard as a corporeal being vaporizes into past tenses which testify to his permanent, essential qualities ('He was kind-like to mother', 383). Indeed, the illusion of Henchard's immortality seems to have infected the very tenses of the narrative voice, which, though it begins by distinguishing between the past and the past perfect ('What Henchard *had written* in the anguish of his dying *was respected* as far as practicable by Elizabeth-Jane') goes on to refer to 'her independent knowledge that the man who *wrote* them *meant* what he *said*' (384)—as though the writing, the meaning, and the saying were all contemporaneous with the respecting. (The qualification—'as far as practicable' —is a nice touch, deferring to the end to the claims of propriety: will the mayor's wife actually have her stepfather, the late mayor, buried in *un*consecrated ground?)

But whatever common-sense problems she presents, the text needs Elizabeth-Jane to perceive this writing, this meaning, this unity: it is her consciousness which generates the statement that his will is a piece of the same stuff as his whole life. Rehabilitated for the occasion and realigned with the *sententiae* of the narrative voice in the last two paragraphs of the novel, the woman who killed Henchard must be there to *know* him. But just because it is so conspicuous a piece of ventriloquism, Elizabeth-Jane's meditation deconstructs itself. Henchard is exposed not only by her rejection of him, which condemns him to death on the heath, but by her very tribute to him, which reinstalls the specularity it is constructed to repress.

A woman's death is different. When Susan and Lucetta die, not only do the other fictional characters quickly forget them (no need for a special request!) but, since their deaths lead directly to interesting plot developments, the reader forgets them too. As individuals they are nugatory; the rhetoric with which their dying is surrounded emphasizes precisely the

---

[40] Butler (1978), 72, suggests that the treatment of Henchard's death is 'a masterpiece of tragic reported action'.

pathos of the representative and the continuity of life which goes on without them. Lucetta dies on the border—between bride and mother, between night and morning. As the sun rises and the birds stir, the housemaid comes to take the muffler off the door-knocker, 'Because they may knock as loud as they will; she will never hear it any more' (333). There is more sense of Lucetta's inner life in these words than in all the scenes which 'characterize' her, but it is an inner life which is not at all individualized or morally shaped: simply sensation at its most random and ordinary.

Susan's death is also treated with great rhetorical power, though with little sense of her as an individual character. In death 'Mrs Henchard's dust mingled with the dust of women who lay ornamented with glass hair-pins and amber necklaces, and men who held in their mouths coins of Hadrian, Post-humus, and the Constantines' (153). On the one hand this is a kind of dignity—on the other it is annihilation indeed (the point has already been made that the skeletons people find when they dig in Casterbridge do not even unnerve them, so remote do they seem from the present life of the town). Negligible as a personality, Susan nevertheless becomes the focus of some local attention when Mother Cuxsom reports her dying monologue and voices on her behalf the stylized lament so often quoted by Hardy's readers: 'And all her shining keys will be took from her, and her cupboards opened; and little things 'a didn't wish seen, anybody will see; and her wishes and ways will all be as nothing' (138). Her eloquent words impose a slightly studied closure not only on her life but on the chapter and clearly signal that the novel is finished with Susan.[41]

Yet the figurative suggestions of the language speak not of closure but of opening up, of exposure. In her last words, Susan, like Henchard, describes the way she wants her burial to be handled. Like Henchard, too, she refers to her deceased self with the first-person pronoun:

' "Yes," says she, "when I'm gone, and my last breath's blowed, look in the top drawer o' the chest in the back room by the window, and

---

[41] See Stevick (1970), 43–5, 78–9, on the tension between finality and continuity in Hardy's chapter endings.

you'll find all my coffin clothes; a piece of flannel—that's to put under me, and the little piece is to put under my head; and my new stockings for my feet—they are folded alongside, and all my other things. And there's four ounce pennies, the heaviest I could find, a-tied up in bits of linen, for weights—two for my right eyes and two for my left . . ." ' (137)

But unlike Henchard's, Susan's 'me' is a dead body in all its corporeality, a body whose eyelids have to be closed with some force (with 'pennies, the heaviest I could find') until they stiffen, and her concern with how it is to be handled is practical, concrete, housewifely. Susan envisages not the cemetery and the funeral service but the house and the life which will go on in it after her death and she makes no claims for the dead body but only for those who continue to live in the house ('And open the windows as soon as I am carried out, and make it as cheerful as you can for poor Elizabeth-Jane').

She does make one modest request on her own behalf— ' "bury the pennies, good souls, and don't ye go spending 'em" '—but her will, unlike Henchard's, is ignored, and Coney spends the money at the Three Mariners. The meta-phorical language with which this act is described (' " 'Twas a cannibal deed" ') associates it not only with digging up the body itself but also with digging *into* it. The women are on the side of decorum—the men, truculently pragmatic, on the side of 'life' (' "why should death rob life o' fourpence?" '). But Solomon Longways, defending his crony (' "I wouldn't sell skellintons" '), picks up the suggestion of penetration and exposure and, even as he contrasts Coney's act with grave-robbery, helps establish the parallel. Susan had requested that things be opened up—the back room, the top drawer, the windows—but she will not be able to arrest the process her death has initiated: her closets will be opened by the servants, her body by the coffin-worm, and the 'things a' didn't want seen' (her underwear? her bones?) 'anybody will see'—as coolly and promiscuously as they gaze at the Roman skeletons exposed as the life of the town unfolds.

The final impropriety, the last dirty secret, is the extinction of the subject. Sex and death are linked in the too-penetrable body of the woman, the woman with a 'past', the woman with the skeleton in her closet. Daughter or doll, witch or skeleton, prude or prostitute, woman cannot after all endow a man with the integrity and stability he desires. The intuitions about personal dissolution expressed in the narrative of Susan's death deconstruct the fantasies of moral and spiritual integrity expressed in the narrative of Henchard's. *The Mayor of Casterbridge* is about exposure, and what is finally exposed is the text's own dream of phallic unity embodied in the tragic hero.

5

Tess of the d'Urbervilles:
The Word in Nature

Tess of the d'Urbervilles teaches us to read it in terms of its ending. From the opening pages, the novel's effect depends upon a strong sense of sequence, on Hardy's ability to suggest that Tess is caught in time and doomed to be destroyed as certain temporal patterns unfold. The kinds of devices upon which critics used to focus so heavily—ironies of timing, coincidences—suggest Tess's entrapment in a number of inexorable sequences. Her fate seems predetermined both by heredity (the narrator emphasizes that she has her mother's nubility and sensitivity to music, and implies she shares her father's quixotic pride) and by a historically specific environment. The cycle of nature is presented as analogous to her own experience: as her fatal love for Angel develops, the sequence of Tess's emotions is echoed, and exacerbated, by the waxing summer heat, so that the unfolding season itself seems to announce her fall. Then, too, as the novel's title suggests, Tess is mysteriously fated to expiate the crimes of her aristocratic ancestors. Finally, the motif of Druidical sacrifice locates Tess's fate within a still more distant English past and implies that there is some ancient mythic pattern which she is doomed to repeat, some demonic sequence in which she is doomed to be yet another term.[1]

From the opening pages, then, Tess's doom is overdetermined, not by one but by several chronologies, all of which point to the same end.[2] We read the novel in terms of its

[1] On repetition in the novel, see Miller (1970), 102–5; (1982), 116–46. On Hardy's presentation of Stonehenge, see Bullen (1986), 219–22.

[2] Jacobus (1976a) observes, 'Of all Hardy's novels, Tess is the one which most arouses emotional commitment in its readers, yet most risks alienating them by belabouring its effects' (403).

aspirations to tragedy and in anticipation of the inevitable destruction of the heroine, who is borne down, we may feel, less by the President of the Immortals than by the sequences upon which Hardy has constructed his plot.[3]

In his prefatory remarks about *Tess*, Hardy describes his intentions in terms of sequence. The Explanatory Note to the First Edition describes the narrative as an 'attempt to give artistic form to a true sequence of things';[4] and the Preface to the fifth edition defends the novel for its unconventional sequence. His story, Hardy says, is

one wherein the great campaign of the heroine begins after an event in her experience which has usually been treated as fatal to her part of protagonist, or at least as the virtual ending of her enterprises and hopes. (4)

Hardy implies that by choosing to *begin* at what conventional society would consider the *end* of Tess's story, he is following natural, not social law—that by inverting a novelistic convention he is challenging a social prejudice. In the author's mind, then, sequence itself carries moral and thematic weight in *Tess of the d'Urbervilles*, and reflects the distinction between the natural and the social points of view.

Given this emphasis on the author's part, we might wish to look closely at this beginning which is an ending, and at the message which it carries. But if we turn to page 1, we discover that the novel does not begin exactly where the Preface says it does.[5] Instead, it begins with Parson Tringham announcing to Jack Durbeyfield, Tess's father, that he is in reality 'Sir John'. It begins, in fact, not where the life of a ruined woman ends, but where the plot of a foundling romance ends: with a kind of

---

[3] In the *Graphic* version, this was 'Time the Arch-satirist': see Laird (1975), 76.

[4] *Tess of the d'Urbervilles*, ed. Juliet Grindle and Simon Gatrell (Oxford: Oxford University Press, 1983), 3. All subsequent quotations from the novel are from the same edition.

[5] Laird's researches have made clear that the d'Urberville connection was added at a relatively late stage of composition: see Laird (1975), 84–6, 109–17. The novel in its first stages of composition did not begin with discovery of Tess's parentage. The version Mowbray Morris saw, when he complained that 'It is obvious from the first page what is to be Tess's fate at Trantridge', must have been an early version in which the heroine had been aware of her noble ancestry ever since infancy. The notion of sending Tess to claim kin was added in L3. See Laird (1975), 33; Grindle and Gatrell (1983), *8, 27*.

displaced recognition scene which establishes the true (aristocratic) identity of the heroine. If we are reading the opening
chapter in terms of Hardy's prefatory remarks, there is a kind
of structural parallelism established in the very first pages
between Tess's parentage and her parenthood, between her
aristocratic blood and her ruin.

This relationship is presented as metonymic, even causal—
Tess's pregnancy follows, and follows from, the discovery of
her lineage. But it is also metaphoric: in the narrative of her
own life, the two facts can be substituted one for another. Tess
is a woman with a past: the statement has two different meanings, and it is from the gap between these meanings that some
of the ironies of the plot emerge.[6] When Tess, on the verge of
telling Angel the secret of her pregnancy, loses her nerve at the
last moment, she pretends that what she was going to confess
was her aristocratic background. Angel responds to both
secrets, when he knows them, in ways which are inappropriate,
given his advanced and freethinking pretensions. He ought not
to have been impressed by Tess's lineage, but he was; he ought
to have forgiven Tess her mistake, but he did not. The two
secrets both function as tests which Angel fails to pass, and
their structural identity is thus underscored.

Angel's self-contradictory reactions point, indeed, to the
fundamental dichotomy between the two different kinds of
narrative which Hardy is combining in this novel. The foundling romance is a form which endorses the existing social order,
in that the transcendent virtue of the apparently lower-class
heroine is explained when she turns out to be the daughter of a
king, or of a rich man. The novel Hardy is claiming to write is
one which challenges the existing social order: a defence of the
fallen woman as a victim of social prejudice. There seem to be
two impulses here which are at odds with one another, and
some of the contradictions in the novel may be illuminated by
an awareness of the conflict.

To see Tess as the heroine of a foundling romance makes
sense of some of the details of her nature which are less realistic
than Hardy tries to make them sound. Tess seems not really to
be her parents' child. Despite a perfunctory attempt to establish

---

[6] Beach observes that *Tess* belongs to a popular genre of novels and plays about a
woman with a secret (1922, 200–2)—which however usually end happily.

traits which she shares especially with her mother, Hardy does not convince us that the sensitive, introspective, flower-like maiden owes very much to her biological connection with Joan and Jack Durbeyfield. Tess is characterized by fine and subtle intuitions, which seem not to have been learned in Marlott; by a highly articulate world-weariness, which owes more to her creator's own pessimism than to concepts aired in the Durbeyfield household; and by articulate, indeed eloquent, language, which seems scarcely to have been marked by a local accent.[7] And most important of all, perhaps, she is distinguished from her fellows by the exceptional beauty for which jewels and fine clothes are the natural complement. The special pathos of her victimization by Farmer Grobie and his demonic machinery derives not only from Hardy's generalized indignation at the sexual and economic vulnerability of rural women, but from his particular and erotic sense of Tess's unique fineness and fragility.[8]

I would argue, indeed, that the figure of Tess reflects some of the contradictions in Hardy's own feelings about social class.[9]

[7] The gap between Tess and her parents broadened in subsequent editions: see Laird (1975), 184. In August 1889 Hardy says in a letter that the fact that his heroine is 'of Norman blood and name' is only 'by the way'. However, the heredity theme is strengthened in the final stages of the pre-publication of the novel: see Grindle and Gatrell (1983), 3–4. Jacobus sees the gentrification of Tess as a betrayal of 'the humane and egalitarian impulse at the heart of the novel' (1976*b*, 323–4).

[8] On this point, see Snell (1985), 378, 387, 393–4. Laird (1975), 78, points out that most of the comments on rural decay were added quite late in the revisions and argues that Hardy makes no attempt to explore the economic causes of decay. Tess's story is a variation of a popular melodramatic archetype—the tale of the working-class woman betrayed by an aristocratic man; Clark (1986) argues that this middle-class myth served to disguise both the *economic* exploitation of the poor by the rich and the vulnerability of working-class women to rape by men of their own class.

[9] Hardy's diary entry for 30 Sept. 1888 reads: 'The decline and fall of the Hardys much in evidence hereabouts . . . so we go down, down, down' (Hardy 1928, 281). In the novel Richard Crickmay mentions the Hardys in his list of decayed local families. Hardy liked to think he was descended from the le Hardys—a 'county family'—and once said he could have called the novel *Tess of the Hardys* if it had not seemed too personal: see Millgate (1982), 4, 293–4. One of Hardy's names for the Tess-figure in the early stages of composition was 'Sue': see Grindle and Gatrell (1983), *25*. Millgate suggests that one reason for the name's appeal was Hardy's interest in Lady Susan Fox-Strangways (1982, 353). Hardy's account of Lady Susan's elopement with the actor William O'Brien focuses on the question of who is doing the stooping when an artist marries the daughter of an earl (Hardy 1928, 11; 1930, 13). Hardy was completing *A Group of Noble Dames* while he was writing Tess: see Grindle and Gatrell (1983), *11*. His Preface to this collection of short stories suggests Hardy's fascination with aristocratic women of both past and present: he pays tribute to 'several bright-

There are two principles or sets of values expressed in the novel which are important to Hardy's own sense of identity and which can only with difficulty be brought into alignment: 'nature' and 'aristocracy'. There is a tension between Hardy's loyalty to nature, to the countryman's life, and to his working-class roots and, on the other hand, his fascination with the upper classes, with genealogy and blood-lines. Following Fredric Jameson, I see the narrative as a symbolic resolution to a real problem: Hardy's own 'ressentiment' about his class affiliation, especially as experienced in relation to women and to the aristo-cracy—his feeling of being an outsider whose real worth is not given its due because of his 'past'—and at the same time his pride in that very past, in the regional and traditional values which such people underestimate.

In *The Political Unconscious* Fredric Jameson is using struc-turalist means to a Marxist end, looking at the novels of, for example, Balzac, Conrad, and Stendhal by charting their characters on to Greimas's 'semiotic rectangle'. Jameson calls Greimas's system an 'ontological structuralism', one which Greimas himself believes gives insight into the logical struc-ture of reality.[10] Jameson, eschewing metaphysics, finds the rectangle useful instead as an emblem of the ideology which generates it. He argues that narrative is an attempt to resolve contradictions in ideology—that these contradictions actually generate characters or groups of characters. The conflicts which I have seen in Hardy, then, would be charted as in Fig. 1. It can be argued that the novel does indeed take shape around character-positions which fulfil the requirements of the rectangle (see Fig. 2). I see Tess's family as non-aristocratic, despite their family name and their silver spoon, for reasons already discussed: their manifest inferiority to Tess herself. I locate Angel within the category of aristocracy because he is

---

eyed Noble Dames' who have discussed the stories with him and responded open-mindedly when the stories touched family scandals (Orel 1966, 25). See also Hardy (1928), 255–6, where Hardy records his interest in the families of the doges in Venice, and in the Contessa Mocenigo, whom he describes, in terms reminiscent of *Tess*, as 'the symbol and relic of the bygone and ancient families' and who he hints was a model for one of the characters in *A Group of Noble Dames*; also Hardy (1930), 6, where he mentions discussing Tess with 'another noble dame'.

[10] Jameson (1981), 166–8.

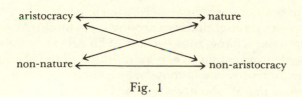

Fig. 1

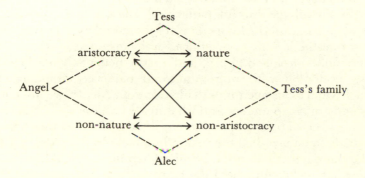

Fig. 2

distinguished by an alienating superiority to everyone with whom he associates: he is more intelligent than his family, and so is undervalued by them; and he is set apart from the rural people—like the prince in disguise—or as Tess herself says like Peter the Great inspecting the shipyards—during his pastoral idyll at Talbothays Dairy.[11] Furthermore, his plain-living and high-thinking family turn out, rather unexpectedly, to be in possession of jewels which make Tess look like *her* ancestors' portraits.[12]

This view of the novel explains a number of its aspects which seem to call for comment. For one thing, it clarifies some anomalies in Hardy's treatment of Angel and Alec. It is clear that the two men are carefully set up by Hardy in terms of their

[11] Millgate (1982), 68, 295, 205, suggests that Angel was probably based on Horace Moule and on Hardy's father's story of a parson's son who became a miller.

[12] This incident with the jewels was apparently suggested by Emma Hardy: see Millgate (1982), 324. Hardy imagined the reverse metamorphosis, from society lady into field worker: see Hardy (1928), 293–4.

binary opposition—schematically, even alliteratively, paired.[13] Alec appears through flames carrying a pitchfork; Angel plays the harp. One is dangerous because of his excessive sensuality, the other because of his excessive spirituality; the two together combine to destroy the heroine. The contrast generates banal, if apposite, moral conclusions: it is less an illegitimate pregnancy which destroys a woman than the self-righteousness of an attenuated and misapplied Christianity.

Yet for all the careful patterning, there is an asymmetry between Angel and Alec as they are presented by Hardy which raises aesthetic and even ethical problems. Angel is a much more fully developed figure, and a more believable one. He is also presented with more authorial balance: although his cruelty to Tess is even more culpable than Alec's, we are consistently made to understand what made him the way he is and how he feels about what he is doing.[14] Alec, on the other hand, is made to behave like the villain in a melodrama. Alec has to be a thorough villain if the idealized heroine is to kill him, and Tess has to kill him because Hardy has to have society kill her[15]—but the melodramatic treatment of the character nevertheless impoverishes the novel to some extent.

Greimas's semiotic rectangle helps explain the imbalance between these apparent binary opposites. Alec is, from this perspective, not Angel's opposite but Tess's. Angel, on the other hand, is aligned with Tess,[16] precisely in terms of the qualities they both share with Hardy. He is characterized by an innate pessimism and religious scepticism; he is intellectually superior to his own family; and he is dispossessed of the status which ought rightfully to have been his—like Tess, and like Hardy, who also never went to university. Indeed, the recognition of the parallels between Angel and Hardy himself make clearer what readers may instinctively feel: that Alec is a scape-

[13] Hardy probably took the name 'Angel' from a church monument: see Millgate (1982), 38. The doubling of Alec and Angel and their switching of roles have often been noted: see Howe (1967), 122–3; Millgate (1971*b*), 275–6; Brooks (1971), 236; Gordon (1987); Daleski (1980); Boumelha (1982), 43, 131–2.

[14] See Heilman (1970); also Claridge (1986), who defends Alec.

[15] Auerbach (1980), 41, makes this point.

[16] Gordon notes the structural similarities between the Durbeyfield and the Clare families (1987, 131).

goat, and that Hardy has some personal stake in his condemnatory and yet empathetic portrait of Angel.

Angel's putative dislike of old families is worth mentioning in this connection.[17] It is interesting that Angel himself never says that he despises them, until his fit of temper after Tess's confession. Up to this point he disclaims and qualifies the republican sentiments attributed to him by others. The effect is curiously double-edged, allowing Hardy to create the impression that Angel's delight in Tess's lineage is a betrayal of his own principles, without having his intelligent and thoughtful protagonist go on record as voicing, in the rather crude way his interpreters do, an automatic contempt for blood-lines.

But the most important feature of the text which this reading helps explain is the curious atemporality of the heroine.[18] Although Tess is associated with cyclical nature, and perceived as caught in a series of chronological patterns, she herself exhibits an odd blankness about sequence. She is improbably incompetent, for example at predicting chains of cause and effect. It is hard to believe that an adolescent girl brought up by Joan Durbeyfield would be as ignorant as Tess seems to be of the nature of the threat posed by Alec, yet Tess reluctantly surrenders to a number of overtures without any apparent sense of where they are leading. Then, too, despite her obsessive fear of Angel's learning her history, Tess is unrealistically unable to predict his response when he does—improbably naïve in her jubilation that her transgression is 'just the same' (318) as his. What has been called her passivity is often an unwillingness or inability to stop chains of consequences once they have begun to unroll. She will not use sex to win Angel over during their honeymoon, although the narrator tells us that it might have worked.[19] She decides not to ask her in-laws for money because her feelings are hurt when Mercy Chant

---

[17] Hardy said in an interview that Angel 'always professed to despise ancient lineage, and yet as a matter of fact he was delighted that Tess was a d'Urberville': *Black and White*, 27 Aug. 1892; cited by Laird (1975), 132. See also Johnson (1894), 63, who reiterates this story.

[18] See Morrell (1965), 29–34. For another reading of Tess's relationship with time and history and her detachment from the physical world, see Gordon (1987).

[19] See Boumelha's fine analysis of the narrator's uneasy tone at this point (1982, 124–5).

mocks her boots.[20] (The ultimate consequence of this decision is her vulnerability to Alec's overtures—a consequence to which Hardy himself seems blind, as he does nothing to rationalize her responsibility for this particular chain of events.)

Tess's peculiar relationship to time can be read by assuming that she is a coherent 'character' and by attempting to set up a paradigm into which such reactions will fit. Recently it has been read as the result—irritating or impressive, depending on one's point of view—of the polemical project revealed by Laird's study of Hardy's revisions: his desire to make Tess more innocent than she was in the first drafts of the narrative, more purely and pathetically a victim.[21] I see Tess's relationship to time in terms of a larger project: that dehistoricizing of her which is necessary if she is to serve as a resolution of the tension between nature and aristocracy which I believe underlies the narrative.

Tess can be loved for her aristocracy only if she is felt as innocent of it—innocent of and indeed the victim of history

---

[20] See Morrell (1965), 40, 98.

[21] Hardy's personal emotional involvement with his heroine has long been recognized. In a letter to Thomas Macquoid, Hardy said 'I am glad you like Tess—though I have not been able to put on paper all that she is, or was, to me' (Grindle and Gatrell 1983, *14*). The impression of a member of the Garrick Theatre company who performed *Tess* at Max Gate in 1925—that 'He talked of Tess as if she was someone real whom he had known and liked tremendously'—is recorded in the *Life* (Hardy 1930, 244). Details from the *Life* and the Notebooks suggest that Hardy projected on to Tess emotions and perceptions of his own. Compare his childish fantasy of rescue from a harvest supper with Tess's situation after the dance at Chaseborough (Hardy 1928, 19–20; *Tess*, ch. 10). See also Hardy's enigmatic comments on 'Souls outside Bodies' (Hardy 1928, 263, 270–1; cf. *Tess*, ch. 18). Ebbatson notices the similarity between Tess's 'blighted world' sermonette and a quotation about the relatively 'abortive' and 'imperfect' status of this world recorded in Hardy's notebook: see Björk (1985), i. item 1311; Ebbatson (1982), 11. See Millgate (1982), 91, on the fatalism of Tess and of Hardy. Abercrombie (1912), 144–5, was one of the first to suggest that the 'intense and personal regard on the part of the author for his own creation' causes problems; see also Paris (1969) and Claridge (1986). Howe (1967), 130–1, on the other hand suggests that the novel gains power from Hardy's commitment to his heroine, as do Miller (1982), 119–20, and Bayley (1978), 234–6. Laird (1975), 118–31, believes that Hardy's identification with Tess developed as he wrote, and changed the course of the narrative. He points out that the first edition is sometimes less frank than the *Graphic* serial version in depicting the feelings of Angel and Tess at Talbothays, and argues that the function of Hardy's successive revisions was to desexualize Tess and her relationship with Angel, and to idealize her. See Jacobus (1976*a*, 1976*b*) on Hardy's rehabilitation of Tess and his 'character assassination' of Alec and Angel. Poole (1981) challenges the assertion that Hardy was simply downplaying Tess's sexuality, as does Brady (1986).

itself. It is, I think, her innocence of history which makes readers feel she has a mythic dimension. Her epithet—'of the d'Urbervilles'—expresses precisely that connection in separation which links Tess with her aristocratic forebears, in such a way as to skip over her actual parents and erase all local, specific identities and allegiances. Tess inherits aristocratic glamour without being implicated in aristocratic guilt.[22] She is like her mother but not like her father, from whom she nevertheless inherits a superiority he himself does not have. She is linked in a mystified synchronic way with her remote ancestors and condemned to suffer for their crimes; the doom does not make very much moral sense and has to be handled in a slightly unreal Gothic fashion—through winking portraits, sinister omens, and local legends.[23] Hardy seems to be suggesting, by his discussion of Tess's rapacious ancestors, that the aristocracy of the past condemned the poor to suffer in the present; but since the figure of Tess contains both the contemporary victim and the historical victimizer, it short-circuits any serious social criticism of the contemporary class structure.

It is interesting that Tess is harassed by new social forces: by a man whose family has bought its title with new money; by the brutal technology—exemplified by the threshing machine—which bends human life to its inhuman rhythm. But precisely how this newness is connected to history is blurred. Clearly Alec's family's interest in adopting an ancient family name derives from the value such a name has acquired in a process which is not delineated. Again Alec serves as a scapegoat—mocked precisely for his newness, while the 'oldness' on which alone this newness could be parasitical is exonerated (in the figure of Tess herself) from any responsibility for creating him. The class from which Tess descends creates Alec as surely as it destroys Tess (or, one might also say, as surely as Tess destroys him)—but is not in the novel to receive the blame. It is significant that Tess is not harmed by any contemporary 'real' aristocrat: she herself usurps that position, and precludes the presentation of an old family with *contemporary* power.

[22] Bayley (1978), 167, noting the fusion in Tess of peasant and aristocratic qualities, observes that 'Tess, for Hardy, was an apotheosis of having it both ways'.

[23] The detail of the portraits was not added until after MS revisions: see Laird (1975), 116.

Tess has value for Hardy because she is associated with the glamour of the real aristocracy; but she must not be implicated in its crimes. She must expiate them with her death, but without ever having been besmirched by them. She must retain, in the context of an implicating history, the 'purity' Hardy insists on in the subtitle. She must not operate in time—she must not operate time—but be operated upon. She must be destroyed, and yet not destroyed—victimized, and yet preserved intact. The ways in which Tess is disconnected from her past are necessary if she is to figure the unity he desires.

Hardy has set up his narrative in terms of the dangers of misreading his heroine. The novel as a whole is a plea for a specific reading of Tess: Alec and Angel destroy her because they read her wrongly, and Hardy's purpose is to analyse and expose their misreadings, place these misreadings, culturally and historically, and dramatize their destructiveness.

Implicit in the notion of misreading is the concept of a real Tess who must be differentiated from the false images which Alec and Angel have of her. Both men are presented as insensitive to this Tess, the inner Tess, the Tess as she herself experiences herself, to which we as readers are apparently given a privileged insight. This is not the only Hardy novel in which the problem of personal identity, the question of the relationship between subject and object, the 'Me' and the 'Not Me', becomes a subject of speculation, nor is Tess the only character of whom the narrator says things like:

Upon her sensations the whole world depended, to Tess: through her existence all her fellow creatures existed, to her. The universe itself only came into being for Tess on the particular day in the particular year in which she was born. (221)

But the question of subjectivity becomes an especially crucial one in the structure of this novel.[24] Hardy makes Tess's selfhood a central issue, allows his heroine to protest passionately

[24] Critics who deal with the dichotomy between Tess as subject and Tess as object include Tanner (1968); Eagleton (1971); Silverman (1984), who suggests that since Tess is constituted by being looked at there is no 'inner' Tess to set in opposition to the outer one; Freeman, who argues that Hardy, himself 'relentlessly' watching Tess, turns her into 'the sign of his own sensitivity and merit' (1982, 323); Wotton (1985), 89–94.

against being misconstrued, and encourages us to feel that she has been systematically violated and victimized by not being recognized for what she really is. The question remains, however, to what extent he himself is implicated in the very attitudes he exposes in his male characters—particularly Angel's.

Alec apparently treats Tess simply as an object. Angel is more complicated. While struggling to keep in mind that Tess has a life of her own, Angel consistently objectifies her—but in two different ways, which makes his character inconsistent. On the one hand he apparently responds with some enthusiasm to her body. Everyone remembers the details—though in fact they are few enough—in which Angel muses over Tess's lips (212) in terms reminiscent of those already used by the narrator (23, 127–8); looks down into her snake-like red mouth as she yawns (242), and plumbs the depths of her bottomless eyes (243), as did the narrator in his turn before Angel came along (127–8). Indeed, in the dairy 'the ardour of his affection [was] so palpable that [Tess] seemed to flinch under it like a plant in too burning a sun' (244). It seems odd that all of these perceptions are given to Angel, not Alec; for while Alec is overtly predatory, Angel's love is *said* to be lacking in sexual warmth. Directly after Angel and Tess become engaged, and Tess has kissed him passionately to mark her acceptance of him, we are informed that 'there was hardly a touch of earth in her love for Clare' (276), and that Angel was constitutionally 'less Byronic than Shelleyan' (277). By 'Shelleyanizing' Angel Hardy has made sure that the blame for Angel's penetrating gaze will devolve upon him—as indeed it has, particularly in some fine recent feminist criticism of the novel.[25] There does seem to be something of self-exploration and self-expiation in Hardy's portrait of Angel.[26]

Hardy implicates himself also, however, in Angel's idealization of Tess as a 'fresh and virginal daughter of Nature' (172). There are no virgins in nature; and Hardy shows clearly how destructive to Tess this idealizing will be—makes Tess protest

[25] See Escuret (1980); Freeman (1982); Silverman (1984); Boumelha (1982), 120–1.

[26] Bayley (1978), 182, remarks, of Angel's repudiation of Tess, that 'Hardy knew that he—and most of his male readers—would have behaved in a similar situation much as Clare does'.

against it—has her recognize that 'she you love is not my real self, but one in my image; the one I might have been' (304). And he makes clear that Angel is deceiving himself—that he is attracted to Tess precisely because she is *not* a child of nature in any simple way, because she is so much superior to the other milkmaids. Indeed it is Tess's felt alienation from nature which draws Angel to her in the first place: her musings deeply appeal to him, because they express in naïve terms precisely his own overbred pessimism. Angel exploits Tess by using her to confirm the Romantic vision of a natural life which he believes that he himself, in withdrawing from the public arena, has chosen. His outrageous treatment of her is itself a comment on the irresponsibility of the dream of pastoral innocence.

Yet Hardy, even while criticizing Angel for what he does to Tess, is at the same time using Angel to do the same thing on his own behalf.[27] Through Angel, Tess is endowed by the text with some of the very attributes which she herself explicitly disowns. By attributing to Angel an idealized vision of Tess as nature-goddess which Tess herself repudiates, Hardy is able to have it both ways. In those early mornings when the couple feel like Adam and Eve (185), and Angel insists on addressing Tess as Artemis and Demeter, when she becomes for him 'a visionary essence of woman—a whole sex condensed into one typical form' (186), Hardy establishes a vision of Tess, which does not fade merely because Tess protests against it.[28] Indeed, her protest confirms her status: what better proof that she is indeed nature's child than her uneasiness with Angel's culture-bound metaphors? The text, aware that 'nature' is itself a cultural construct, nevertheless allows the figure of Tess to draw power from the Romantic illusion.

Hardy originally thought of calling the novel 'The Body and

[27] On the 'idealizing vision' by which lovers constitute one another in Hardy's fiction, see Wotton (1985), chs. 9 and 10. Gregor (1974), 185–90, argues that both Tess and Angel idealize each other, and that Hardy intends us to realize that they are both wrong. Johnson (1983), 107–9, attributes the 'etherealizing process' that Tess undergoes to Angel. To my mind both ignore the narrator's complicity with Angel's point of view.
[28] Critics discussing the mythic dimension of Tess include Brooks (1971), 233–53; Wickens (1983); Laird (1980), who presents evidence that Hardy's reading of Frazer's *The Golden Bough* may have shaped the characterization of Tess, strengthening the impression of her alignment with the forces of fertility.

Soul of Sue', and the novel we have is still structured around that dichotomy.[29] Evidently Alec has possessed Tess's body but not her soul. Angel's sin against Tess is his failure to realize this. His repudiation of her causes—or deepens—a radical split in Tess, makes her separate herself from her body; it constrains Tess to define herself—while it *enables* the narrator to redefine her—along the lines of pure spirit. It is Angel's very rejection of her, in other words, which allows the text—or the narrator, or Hardy—to expiate the fascination with Tess's body expressed in the first half of the novel, and this is what it proceeds to do. Tess is increasingly spiritualized as the novel goes on. The narrator emphasizes her growing dissociation from her own body, so that by the time she gives herself to Alec she has 'ceased to recognize the body before him as hers—allowing it to drift, like a corpse upon the current, in a direction dissociated from its living will' (515).[30] But the imaginative effect of this theoretical *division* is actually to *unify* Tess, who becomes pure spirit, pure voice.[31] Her final speech to Alec, a disembodied 'soliloquy' heard through the door by Mrs Brooks, is almost operatic in its stylization;[32] and her final statement—'I am ready'—seems intended to have the resonance of Shakespearian tragedy. It is as if the 'real' Tess, Tess as she herself experiences herself, has become identical with soul: her body has virtually become invisible before her execution.

For Tess to be essentialized in this way, however, some of

---

[29] Hardy also considered 'Too Late Beloved' and 'A Daughter of the d'Urbervilles' before arriving at the final title. See Millgate (1982), 295, on the body–soul opposition in Hardy.

[30] This statement was added in 1892, after Hardy had formulated it in response to an interviewer who challenged Tess's purity: see Laird (1975), 99. On the significance of the change, see Grindle and Gatrell (1983), *48*.

[31] Some readers respond intensely to these cues: see for example Howe on Tess's 'radiant wholeness': 'She dies three times, to live again' (1967, 110–11; see also 130–1). Others feel that Tess fades out at the end of the novel: George Meredith complained that in the final chapters she becomes 'a smudge in vapour—she at one time so real to me' (1970, ii. letter 1396).

[32] Hardy enjoyed opera: see Millgate (1982), 79, 99; also Hardy (1928), 57, 296, where Hardy observes that the manner of the singers in *Carmen* is 'possessed, maudlin, distraught'; also Captain Northbrook's sardonic comment in 'The Honourable Laura': 'Recitativo—the rhythm excellent, and the tone well sustained' (*A Group of Noble Dames*, 220). See also Hardy (1930), 77, 117, 118, 260–1. *Tess* was made into an opera (Hardy 1930, 139, 143).

her history has to be repressed. The seduction scene calls attention to its own omissions and ambiguities;[33] equally significant
are the less visible gaps in the final chapters of the novel. We do
not see the scene in which Alec wins Tess back to him, but only
the scenes in which she defies him; we do not see their life
together—nor, indeed, very much of the idyll between Tess
and Angel in the mansion in the New Forest; we do not see the
murder, but only the spreading blood-stain which is its emblem;
we do not see the execution, but only the black flag.[34] Such
omissions, which can certainly be justified by criteria of decorum, function nevertheless further to spiritualize Tess, to
raise her above the world she leaves desolate by her absence.

In defining self as soul, however, Hardy leaves a surplus of
body, and that surplus gets back into the novel through the
natural imagery for which it is so celebrated. Hardy uses
'nature' in this novel in two ways: as a brooding physical
presence and as a polemical principle, an abstraction or norm
invoked again and again to the same end: to persuade the
reader that Tess is indeed what he calls her in his subtitle:
'A Pure Woman'. Both these methods, however, self-destruct.
When Hardy, defending his subtitle, complains in his 1892
Preface that Tess's critics ignore 'the meaning of the word in

---

[33] The question of whether Tess was raped or seduced has been raised repeatedly
by critics. See Howe ('surely no rape', 1967, 116); Gregor ('both a seduction *and* a
rape', 1974, 182); Laird (1975), 72; Daleski (1980), 331–3; and Brady (1986). Miller
(1982), 117, objects to the question on the grounds that 'immanent repetition' in the
text functions precisely to frustrate our desire for a single explanatory paradigm.
Rooney (1983) insists that to pose the question in these binary terms is to surrender to
the dichotomies of phallocentric discourse. A version of the seduction scene omitted
from the serial version of Tess was published separately as 'Saturday Night in Arcady'
in the *National Observer*, 14 Nov. 1891. In this narrative the Tess figure is called 'Big
Beauty' and does not refuse her wooer's arm; the actual seduction is omitted entirely
—the couple is last seen by a passer-by at the top of a hill and the next day the woman
is pale and thoughtful. This sequence was not restored until the Wessex Edition of
1912: see Grindle and Gatrell (1983), 15.

[34] Those who have commented on gaps in the text include Millgate (1971*b*), 280;
Gregor (1974), 199; Bayley (1978), 183; Miller (1982), 118; Boumelha (1982), 126–7;
Anderson (1985), 64. Bayley and Barrell deal in different ways with the element of
fantasy and self-delusion in the construction of Tess. Bayley suggests that 'the oneness
of Tess' (1978, 189) who becomes 'ultimately and absolutely a visionary figure' is a
'male fantasy' (181); Barrell, comparing Tess with the landscape, suggests that the
myth of violation paradoxically establishes an (equally mythic) purity: 'she, and the
Vale, if they can be violated, must certainly once have been intact; and if they can't
be, still are' (1982, 360).

Nature' (5), the epistemological naïveté of the phrase points to some of the problems he gets himself into.

By insisting that Tess, in surrendering to Alec, is only behaving naturally, Hardy establishes the principle upon which he repeatedly defends her: that those who condemn her do so on the basis of 'an arbitrary law of society which had no foundation in Nature' (386). When, for example, the narrator insists that the evening woodland does not (as Tess imagines) condemn her, when he emphasizes that emotional regeneration is natural to a 'fallen woman' and that therefore social regeneration ought also to be possible, when he implies that Tess's natural impulse to praise nature is a lot saner and more truly religious than the Christian impulse to insist on her damnation, when he sets up the pathetic analogy between his victimized heroine and the murdered pheasants—in all these instances he implies that Tess is a natural creature and should not be condemned by society's 'arbitrary law'.

But, as many critics have pointed out, this argument is self-contradictory.[35] The text makes clear that specifically human excellence involves more than a surrender to 'nature'. If Tess's behaviour is merely natural, and to be defended on that ground, why should Alec's be condemned? If nature is the norm, what about the dairymaids, natural creatures right enough, who in their lovesick misery 'writhed feverishly under the oppressiveness of an emotion thrust on them by cruel Nature's law' (207)? It is precisely because Hardy, more consciously than any of his characters, posits 'nature' as inanimate, indifferent, and amoral that we are disconcerted when he puts his narrator's argument into the mouths of characters whose point of view he disavows—when he has Joan Durbeyfield conclude complacently that Tess's pregnancy is 'nater, after all, and what do please God' (117) and Angel

---

[35] The theme of nature as a norm was part of Hardy's conception of the novel from the beginning: see Laird (1975), 38–45. On the inconsistencies in Hardy's concept of 'nature', see Johnson (1894, 249–58); Schweik (1962), 14–18; Paris (1969); Lodge (1966), 175; Bayley (1978), 177; Miller (1982), 130–1. Gregor (1974), 175–6, 203, sums up the case against Hardy and attempts to answer it. The contradictions in Hardy's concept of 'natural law' are examined in detail in the articles by Goetz (1983) and Saldivar (1983) on *Jude the Obscure*. On the Darwinism in the novel, see the exchange in the *Southern Review* (Adelaide): Morton (1974, 1975); Ebbatson (1975); also Johnson (1983), Beer (1983), and Robinson (1980).

insist that Alec is Tess's husband 'in Nature' (342).[36] Their facile use of the abstraction as polemical counter parodies the narrator's, and reveals the theoreticalness and arbitrariness of his reasoning as well as of theirs.

Hardy's use of nature as setting is equally problematical. The most impressive and memorable natural scenes in the novel are those which mirror the growing love of Tess and Angel at Talbothays—notably the celebrated description of the 'rank' garden (175) through which Tess moves towards the sound of Angel's harp in Chapter 19. The detail in this passage is as rich and circumstantial as the purpose is transparent: to suggest that since Tess, in particular, is part of nature, her desire for life and love will be irresistible, her surrender to Angel inevitable. The heavy, sticky ripeness of the garden suggests the pressure on her of sheer sexuality—as, indeed, do all of the other evocations of growing summer heat in Phase Three of the novel.[37] However, what makes this particular scene stand out from the others is that there is a gap between the narrator's and the character's points of view here so sharp as to be slightly disconcerting, and to seem to call for interpretative commentary. Tess moves through this very sensuous and even threatening garden apparently oblivious to it, 'conscious of neither time nor space' (175). She has, indeed, recently been criticized for this unconsciousness, which is seen as a symptom of her culpable idealism, her dangerous attempt to rise above the body, and is linked with her uncritical awe of Angel's sexual purity as well as with her irresponsible desire for incorporeality.[38] Yet such a reading does not account for the peculiar intensity of the description itself, the note of fascinated disgust which informs the tone of the narrator (a note which Hardy strengthened in revisions).

I see the gap, rather, as revealing what most of the time remains concealed—that *all* the natural imagery mirroring the

[36] See Laird (1975), 46–7, on Hardy's revisions of Joan's phrase: ' 'tis all in the course of nature'—'all what pleases God'—''Tis nater, after all, and what pleases God'. Angel's statement was added in 1895: see Grindle and Gatrell (1983), 342.

[37] Among the many critics who have discussed this scene are Van Ghent (1953), 200–1; Lodge (1966), 182; Tanner (1968), 224; Jacobus (1976*b*), 329; Gregor (1974), 185–8; Daleski (1980), 336–8; Ebbatson (1982), 33–5; Silverman (1984), 17–18; Johnson (1983), 104–5; Beer (1983), 256; Wotton (1985), 91–2. For Hardy's revisions, see Grindle and Gatrell (1983), *33*, *44*, 175.

[38] See Daleski (1980); Gregor (1974), 185–8; Brooks (1971), 245–6.

relationship between Tess and Angel is displaced. It is precisely because Tess does not define her attraction for Angel as sexual that the sultry weather 'tells': the imagery would lose its point if the overt relationship between them were as sultry as the weather. It is the repression of the sexual nature of the attraction between them that makes the natural imagery so powerfully metaphorical. (I want to remain ambiguous about who is doing the repressing.) And it is also, perhaps, the suppression of the whole story of the relationship between Tess and Alec, which as it were gets told for the first time, in a kind of ponderous slow-motion, through the Talbothays imagery— as if Tess, though Alec's mistress and the mother of a child, had never been through this process before. Indeed, she declares she has not: Tess defends herself to Angel (and constitutes herself to herself) through a myth of plenitude and presence, which depends, however, on a radical dehistoricization: 'What was the past to me as soon as I met you? It was a dead thing altogether. I became another woman, filled full of new life from you. How could I be the early one?' (459).

Natural imagery, I would argue, bears so much weight in the novel because, while apparently mirroring Tess's experience, it in fact restores the sequence, the temporality, the physicality, repressed in the figure of Tess herself. The suggestion that Tess *should* have acknowledged the reality figured by the garden seems from this perspective irrelevant: Tess cannot 'see' the fissures which she herself is created to close. But there is a paradox here: Tess can be read as a pure child of nature not in spite of but *because* of her alienation from it. It is precisely because she *does not* feel what nature figures that she deserves the epithet. Attempting to constitute a 'real' Tess, a Tess who will exist to herself, Hardy has got her caught in an explicable relation with an Other which mirrors the 'body' which this 'self' represses. 'Nature' reveals the inadequacy of Tess as a figure of unity, and perhaps reflects less the relationship between the main characters than the anxieties and concerns of the author which these characters are invented to resolve.

Such concerns emerge also in the famous description of the landscape around Flintcomb-Ash, the demonic anti-Wordsworthian vision of earth and sky as 'upper and nether visages'

(393) mirroring each other, 'the white face looking down on the brown face, and the brown face looking up at the white face' (394)—and neither looking at the human figures who crawl like flies between. The threat to Tess has consistently been expressed in terms of looking—both figuratively (as in the penetrating rays of the sun, to which Tess is symbolically sacrificed at Stonehenge) and literally, so that Tess has become obsessed with repelling the male gaze. Apparently, however, while to look at Tess is to violate her, not to look is worse still. The grotesque vision of the human face as featureless—as 'only an expanse of skin' (393)—suggests the worst threat of all: the utter extinction of the subject.[39] It is into this context that Hardy introduces the paragraph about the Arctic birds, the most glaring and unqualified example of pathetic fallacy on the narrator's part in the novel. The attribution of human consciousness to the birds, their inexpressible 'memory' of Arctic wastelands never otherwise to be perceived, foregrounds the question of the relationship between being and perception, and suggests the anxieties of a subject dependent for sustenance on an Other which will not look, and thus vulnerable to dissolution and fragmentation.

The vision is that of a defaced or deformed or scattered body. The land around Flintcomb-Ash is imaged as an immense recumbent female, 'bosomed with semi-globular tumuli—as if Cybele the Many-breasted were supinely extended there' (389). Upon this gigantic but sterile mother lie scattered and relatively tiny fragments of the male body, the phallic stones which are mentioned in two different contexts by the narrator, and which Tess, characteristically, does not recognize (396).[40] At Flintcomb-Ash the anxiety evoked by the idea of looking is revealed as having less to do with a female object than with a male subject.

The character who really has become invisible—who really is not being looked at in this section of the novel—is not Tess, whom we are still watching, but Angel. His departure for

[39] Grindle and Gatrell's edition (1983, 393) records the revisions to these lines: 'only an expanse of skin' was 'a level expanse of muddy skin', 'of tawny skin'; 'visages' was originally 'blanks'. For a discussion of this passage in terms of 'subjective geography', see Barrell (1982), 354–6.

[40] The word 'phallic' was 'nondescript animal'; 'nondescript phallic': see Grindle and Gatrell (1983), 393.

Brazil means his extinction as well as Tess's, for when he returns it is as an emasculated figure, prematurely aged and withered. Indeed, Angel after his illness is described in much the same terms as Clym Yeobright, another world-weary intellectual who seems to embody certain aspects of Hardy's own self-image. Angel's punishment, though less absolute and melodramatic than Alec's, is also a kind of death, a state of emotional and even physical attenuation and emasculation.

The pairing-off of Angel and Liza-Lu is interesting in this connection. As retribution for essentializing Tess, the text leaves Angel with an essentialized Tess, a girl who embodies, as Tess says, 'the best of me without the bad of me' (536). The very fact that Tess wishes this sterile pairing to be an actual marriage underscores its antierotic character and makes the compensatory pattern ironic, Tess's dying wish into a kind of curse.[41]

Indeed, both Alec and Angel pay a heavy price for their misreading of the heroine. Alec is treated as a cardboard villain at the end even more than at the beginning of the novel. In one curious incident, however, the text does at least raise the question of whether Alec is not Tess's victim as surely as she is his. When Alec forces Tess to swear on Cross-in-Hand that she will never again tempt him, Hardy seems to be using the encounter primarily for some rather heavy-handed foreboding (' 'Tis a thing of ill-omen', 429). But his language imbues the image with more specific associations.

Cross-in-Hand is not really a cross, but 'the stump' of what the narrator says may once have been a more 'complete erection' (426). To anyone who has seen the not very impressive marker—which still stands—this seems unlikely, for the top is gently cupped rather than broken off. (The outline of the hand incised upon it is now completely obscured by lichen.) The 'rude monolith' (326) is more phallic in shape than the text, with its emphasis on a broken cross, makes it sound; yet at the same time Hardy's loaded language subliminally suggests

---

[41] Laird (1975), 99, sees the idea of the marriage as sentimental emphasis on Tess's self-sacrificial nature. Gregor (1974), 201–2, feels it reflects Tess's spiritual development. Other readers have found the pairing problematical in one way or another: see Miller (1970), 155; Boumelha (1982), 125–6. Jemima Hardy was distressed when Hardy's father refused to promise to marry her sister Mary if Jemima died: see Millgate (1982), 21 n.

castration.[42] Alec, who fears surrender to Tess, makes her reassure him with an ambiguous gesture—'put your hand upon that stone hand, and swear that you will never tempt me' (427)—which seems to invite the very involvement he apparently wishes to avoid. The incident may seem odd to the reader as well as to Tess; but while it suggests Alec's complicity in his own destruction, it also reminds us what the exclusive emphasis on Tess's victimization at the end of the novel may make us forget—that fascination with Tess kills Alec.[43]

In her discussion of the figure of the fallen woman in Victorian literature and painting, Nina Auerbach points out that the stature and power the fallen woman acquires—even though she suffers for it—involves a certain triumph over the men who seduced her, renders them invisible and irrelevant.[44] By including Tess in her discussion of this mythic pattern, Auerbach restores a meaning of the text from which we are conventionally distracted. Tess emerges a victimizer as well as a victim, and Hardy's fable turns reflexively against itself, revealing even as it attempts to unify Tess her genesis in dissolution and fragmentation.

My theme, then, is Hardy's necessary failure to construct an aesthetic whole not subject to such dissolution. The figures of Tess and of nature, set up to supplement one another, instead subvert one another, and mirror back, to the subject attempting to constitute itself through their reflection, a fragmented body. Hardy's desire, aimed with disconcerting directness at an

---

[42] None of the traditions about the monument which I have been able to find have anything to do with death or bodily dissolution. Harper (1911), 174, says the shaft has been thought to be the remains of a wayside cross or a property marker for the Abbey of Cerne—also possibly a meeting place of the tenants of that abbey, the hollow in the stone serving as a receptacle for their tribute. Lea (1969), 273–4, records that a gipsy-woman told him to put his hand upon the stone and wish. Kay-Robinson (1972), 139, records a number of these traditions and refers to its 'many conjectural purposes—more even than cited by Hardy': the ambiguous wording could suggest that Hardy's gruesome version is based on a local legend also known to Kay-Robinson but not listed by him, but does not definitely say so. See Hardy's poem 'The Lost Pyx'. Hardy's original version of this description even more strongly suggested that the landscape was like a dead body: 'those bleached and desolate uplands' originally read 'those desolate and cadaverous uplands' (Grindle and Gatrell 1983, 428).

[43] See Claridge (1986), 335: '*Alec does not deserve to be killed*'.

[44] Auerbach (1980), 34–5, 40–6. On the power of the fallen woman, see also Hardy's poem 'The Ruined Maid'.

unresponsive 'nature', opens up the fissures in the Romantic project, and deconstructs a subject tenuously constituted in words.

6

Jude the Obscure:
What Does a Man Want?

Jude Fawley wants; Jude Fawley is wanting. We know Jude through the rhythm of desire, repulsion, and renunciation which constitutes his inner life; we know him through those he wants, through Sue and Arabella and Christminster; and we know *them* in terms of their ability or inability to fulfil his desires. Jude is wanting: he is constituted in lack, defined from the first pages of the novel as 'a hungry soul in pursuit of a full soul'.[1] His emptiness is dramatized in the action—even in the part-titles—of the novel, as he moves from place to place in search of the fulfilment which continually eludes him. Jude's wanting provides the plot, the characters, and the emotional tone of the novel.

Jude wants Sue, and he wants a university education. Examination of Hardy's manuscripts has shown that the marriage problem was part of his conception of the novel from the very beginning, and that in his first draft it was Sue who was to have been the motivation for Jude's desire to visit Christminster.[2] Though Phillotson later replaced Sue in this capacity, there remain in the novel as it stands strong links between Jude's desire for Sue and his desire for Christminster. Sue is living in the city of his dreams, and reaching it involves discovering her. Desiring in her not only the woman but the cultivation she embodies—the kind of culture which exposure to Christminster has apparently already given to her—Jude attributes to her many of the values which he has attributed to the city, imagin-

---

[1] *Jude the Obscure* (London: Macmillan, 1912), Wessex Edition, vol. iii, 156. All subsequent quotations are from the same edition.

[2] Ingham (1976) demonstrates that the marriage question was always central and that the education theme was repeatedly expanded in revision. Bayley (1978), 203, argues that the two subjects are not convincingly related.

ing them both as bodiless, visionary presences, as shining forms encircled by haloes of light.[3] Jude is temperamentally logocentric: he naïvely believes in the reality of the idealized images he has constructed from inherited materials. Christminster is to be the heavenly Jerusalem of Revelation, Sue is to be the haloed apparition in his aunt's photograph. However, both will remain hauntingly elusive: despite his obsession about staying close to the university and to Sue, Jude discovers that it does not necessarily help to be 'on the spot' (100). For the truth is that both the desired woman and the desired city exist in their luminous purity only in Jude's imagination: by the very nature of his dreams, he is doomed to disappointment.

What particularly marks this novel, indeed, is the tone of what might be called 'logocentric wistfulness'. Like many of Hardy's heroes, Jude is a reader, but a reader of printed texts rather than of the signs of nature. The fact that it is the Bible which lies behind the language and imagery of the novel seems related to the stubbornness with which he insists upon a transcendent reality behind words and signs. And Jude's author shares his logocentric desire.[4] When Hardy presents his protagonist as a Christ-figure, there may be a degree of irony in the identification; but he treats Jude's analogous fantasies without disabling irony. Though we know from the beginning that Jude is going to be mistaken about Christminster and about Sue, we are to think more of him for his idealism, and less of those beings which fail to live up to his image of them. Christminster ought to be the City of Light, and if it is not, it is the city which is to blame; Sue ought to be 'worthy' of Jude's devotion. Both equally deserve his suggestively worded reproach to Sue: 'you are . . . not so nice in your real presence as you are in your letters' (197).

[3] For the parallel between Sue and Christminster, see Alvarez (1963), 114; also Saldivar (1983), 611. Miller (1970), 185, traces the image of the halo or nimbus in Hardy's poetry and fiction.

[4] I am assuming a degree of identification between Hardy and his protagonist. Hardy himself repeatedly denied that the novel was autobiographical (Hardy 1930, 44, 196), referring oddly to Jude on one occasion as 'that fictitious person. If there ever was such a person' (1930, 233). But the novel contains an episode also recorded in the *Life*: see Gregor's fine analysis of the moment in which young Jude looks through his straw hat and is 'seized by a sort of shuddering' (1974, 1–2; cf. Hardy 1928, 19–20). On the link between narrator and author see also Bayley (1978), 195, and Morgan (1986), 3.

Indeed, what Jude wants is implicit in his view of language. As a child, Jude imagines that there is a key which will render the whole of language transparent—undo Babel.[5] When he finds that no such key exists, that he cannot master the whole, he starts to plug away at the parts. But his vision of identity is rather endorsed than otherwise, and the fantasy of wholeness underlies the text: the desire for magical translation into a state of pure presence, the desire to be lifted above competing voices, absorbed into a unified community. This dream seems to be presented as a legitimate desire, a vision betrayed by the social organization of contemporary Oxford and by Victorian views of marriage.

Jude's Christminster is created for him by words, by printed books. Although the notion of a blessed place is suggested by Phillotson, the shape that place takes in his imagination derives from images which are essentially literary. Jude knows Christminster through the Bible, as the heavenly Jerusalem; through his study of Latin, as his 'Alma Mater' (41); and through the written words of her sons, who speak to him of 'her ineffable charm' (95) more kindly and clearly than Christminster ever speaks in person. These patriarchal texts testify with an authority which implies the reality of what they describe. But it is clear from the opening pages of the novel that the very terms in which Jude has conceived his desire preclude its fulfilment.

The famous opening to the second part of the novel, which has Jude listening to the 'ghostly presences' (92) of Christminster, suggests why this is so. These voices of Oxford seem stilted, 'got up' by Hardy, but the very awkwardness of the passage is part of its meaning.[6] The episode raises in paradigmatic form some of the issues of autobiographical fiction, since the quotations Jude remembers have of course been culled from Hardy's own reading.[7] Hardy's awareness of their miscellaneous, even arbitrary character is reflected in the

---

[5] For a discussion of this fantasy see Saldivar's (1983) analysis of 'natural law' as an illusory construct.

[6] Ingham notes that 'At the proof stage of the first book edition the Christminster voices were still being added to' for the purpose of expanding the education theme (1976, 169).

[7] Millgate (1982), 68, suggests, as an influence on the structure of this passage, Horace Moule's 1858 lecture for the Working Man's Mutual Improvement Society of Dorset on 'Oxford and the Middle Class Examinations'.

way the narrator accounts for them: they are supposed to be from 'a book or two [Jude] had brought with him concerning the sons of the University' (94), evidently tourist-guide anthologies of 'purple passages'. The attribution suggests that Jude is not as well read as Hardy (the quotations are not collected by *him*) but on the other hand absolves Jude of the kind of jejune self-satisfaction implied by their assemblage. The passage dramatizes the alienation it presents, its uneasy tone a perfectly accurate register of both the pride and the defensiveness of the autodidact. Its ironies make clear that print can provide no unmediated, unproblematical contact with culture as a whole or with the mind or spirit of the writers of the past.

Indeed, the episode raises the question of the relationship between the written and the spoken word, for though their resonant words seem 'spoken by them in muttering utterances' (94), Jude has been introduced to the 'voices' through the printed pages 'he had just been conning' (94), and their rhetoric (even that of Sir Robert Peel's Corn Law speech) is very much *écriture*. Jude dreams of appropriating what these voices represent, but they undo him even as they address him: as he listens to them, he begins to feel more ghostly, less substantial, than they. Each of these writers uses the first person pronoun; each one has a powerful ego and a confident, totalizing vision of human experience. Yet, speaking together, the voices depict a Christminster which must remain incoherent, not only because (as Jude himself realizes) it has always generated a wide range of conflicting opinions but also because it is constituted by the (inevitably) fragmentary reading of an (inevitably) partially educated individual. Jude seeks to be made whole, but it is clear that his very vision of Christminster must preclude the consummation he desires.

What Jude does for a living is relevant to these issues. A country stonemason who practises his craft 'holistically', he can turn his hand to a number of tasks, in contrast to the urban workers, who master one technique only. Jude's versatility recalls while it parodies Ruskin's vision of Gothic.[8] The values

---

[8] For Hardy's interest in Ruskin, see Björk (1985), i. *passim*; Orel (1966), 154, 274 n.; Bullen (1986), *passim*. Millgate (1982), 346, observes that Hardy's involvement in the restoration of a local church coincided with the writing of *Jude* and notes the relevance of the poem which came out of this experience: the lament of 'The

Ruskin imputes to the old architecture are seen as illusory, yet the presence in the novel of bastardized Victorian Gothic nevertheless implies *degrees* of authenticity and hints at a nostalgia for origin which the text at other times seems to debunk. (At times Hardy seems to suggest that Jude, in desiring a university education, is betraying a kind of Ruskinian vision of honest craftsmanship.) It is emblematic of this contradiction that Sue should dismiss the Gothic style as 'barbaric' (369), and yet at the same time be 'sentimentally opposed to the horrors of over-restoration' (361); it is not entirely clear whether this is supposed to be one of her many contradictions (as the narrator's adverb 'sentimentally' would seem to suggest) or whether the inconsistencies in Hardy's feelings shape her 'character' (for the noun 'horrors' may not be Sue's but the narrator's).[9]

For Hardy seems to endorse Jude's impulses by showing them as instinctively directed towards wholeness, while at the same time presenting that wholeness as an impossible dream. Is it because Jude is a working man, or simply because he is a human being, that he has to begin his apprenticeship laboriously and fragmentedly, by learning to shape one letter at a time? The process is analogous to the way he has to struggle with the heavy medium of the classical languages, alone and without help. The dream is of a whole which will at some moment add up to more than the sum of its parts, which will become monumental, permanent, resonant with interconnected meaning; which will make the individual whole, and unite him creatively with an organic community. But I would argue that the text is not entirely clear about whether it is Jude's class

---

Young Glass-Stainer', who, 'loving the Hellenic norm', is obliged to work in the 'crude', 'abnormal' Gothic style.

[9] In his suggestive reading of the novel, Goode seems to eliminate these ambiguities, asserting that Jude himself realizes that the 'mechanistic bits of reproduced masonry are probably no more factitious than the weather-worn originals' (1979*a*, 122). I feel that the text is more ambivalent than Goode allows about some of its 'decadent' enthusiasms, including the taste for the Gothic. Hardy in his non-fiction prose continued to make a sharp distinction between restored or imitation Gothic and the original. See Hardy (1928), 40–1, 145; (1930), 71, 78–9, 145 (where an old building is compared to 'a unique manuscript'), 150–1, and 'Memories of Church Restoration', 1906 (Orel 1966, 203–27); Björk (1985), i. item 809. Bullen (1986), 126–8, summarizes the evidence about Hardy's growing disenchantment with Gothic revival and restoration.

position which victimizes him, or whether this dream is by definition a hopeless one.[10]

In my reading, the text is shaped even more radically by Hardy's feelings about the body than by his feelings about social class. It seems to me that Jude's desire—for a wholeness of a quasi-spiritual type, a wholeness which completely transcends the body, does not depend upon the body—is intrinsically unrealizable, and that the class theme in the novel is as much 'vehicle' as it is 'tenor'. Take for example Jude's occupation. The facts that he, like Hardy's father, is a stonemason and that his dusty working clothes make him invisible to the upper-class undergraduates who pass him on the street suggest that it is his class position which is decisive. On the other hand, there is something idiosyncratically Hardyan about the way Jude's craft is presented. It is suggestive that Jude is a worker in stone, the deadest and most intractable of materials, and that he sees himself as in the business of supplying dead bodies, helping to provide 'the carcases that contained the scholar souls' (37)—for while this ought to be a perfectly legitimate aim, and would be in Ruskin's terms, it is one which, in Hardy's world, cannot be achieved with impunity.

Embodiment means death; stone itself means death. His work chills Jude and makes him vulnerable to the lung infection which eventually kills him; the dust marks him and makes him invisible to those who look through his body as through a pane of glass. But these literal details only mask the deeper, figurative import of the stonemasonry. Its implications are crystallized in the famous moment when Jude cuts into a stone the word THITHER (85)—an inscription which, we know, will remain to mock him. The act of embodying an aim in a word, and cutting that word in stone, is perfectly emblematic of Jude's logocentric desire. His aim is to make the word real—to ensure its fulfilment—by giving it a body. But in Hardy's world the opposite happens. When the word falls into matter, becomes incarnate in paper or stone, it partakes of the exigencies of material existence, and becomes sinister, mocking, dangerous. The common ('touch-wood') superstition that expressing satisfaction at a situation can reverse it is given an

10 Hassett (1971) sees Jude and Sue as Romantics whose imaginative vision of life is intrinsically unrealizable; see also Lodge (1979).

idiosyncratic slant by Hardy, who suggests that the real danger lies in inscribing the word, giving it a material body. The incarnate word takes the place of what it signifies, precludes its fulfilment. Incarnation means betrayal in this novel: to give or to take a body is to fall away from reality, to be involved in death.

Women give a man body; women betray the word and the spirit and lock a man into the flesh. The women in this novel thwart Jude by drawing him down into the body and then dismembering him—and this is as true of Sue as it is of Arabella. Though Mrs Oliphant's reaction to the novel is extreme, one of her sarcasms is well taken: 'it is the women who are the active agents . . . the story is carried on, and life is represented as carried on, entirely by their means'.[11] This statement not only confirms a reader's impression of Jude's behaviour, as he dances to Sue's tune, but also echoes certain judgements of the narrator—'if God disposed not, woman did' (249)—and of Jude himself: 'strange that his first aspiration—towards academical proficiency—had been checked by a woman, and that his second aspiration—towards apostleship—had also been checked by a woman' (261). Jude goes on to wonder whether 'the women are to blame; or is it the artificial system of things . . . ?' (261)—unable to imagine, evidently, any third alternative, assuming with Mrs Oliphant that 'men . . . are quite incapable of holding their own against these remorseless ministers of destiny'.[12] For all its comments about the various weaknesses of woman (and there are a good many), the novel dramatizes rather her fearsome strength. Even fragile Sue survives her male victims, while indestructible Arabella triumphs. There is an obvious structural similarity between *Jude* and *Tess*: in both novels, seduction by a sensual lover leaves the innocent protagonist vulnerable in a subsequent relationship with a 'spiritual' one.[13] In this novel, however, the victim is a man, and the destructive collaborators are women.

   Through Arabella, Jude thinks he will achieve a new kind of wholeness:

[11] Oliphant (1896), 140.
[12] Ibid.
[13] Lawrence (1961), 488, points out the structural parallel between Tess–Angel–Alec and Jude–Sue–Arabella.

He had just inhaled a single breath from a new atmosphere, which had evidently been hanging round him everywhere he went, for he knew not how long, but had somehow been divided from his actual breathing as by a sheet of glass. (45)

The pane-of-glass figure occurs three times in the novel, always to describe actual or potential alienation.[14] Here it is a fine and precise expression of the illusion of transfiguration by erotic love.[15] Jude translates himself instead of the Bible, and we know how he feels when he says that it is 'better to love a woman than to be a graduate, or a parson; ay, or a pope!' (53). But we are never for a moment allowed to forget that he is wrong, and that this repossession of his body will lead to dispossession and dismemberment.

That Arabella is a castrating woman is all too obvious: Hardy relentlessly signals that she will dismember Jude as efficiently as she dismembers the pig—will cut up his schedule, derail his career, and disrupt his subsequent relationship with Sue. Though Jude cannot 'read' the overdetermined signs which characterize his mistress, Arabella—of the detachable pizzle and the detachable hair-piece—is presented as a fearsomely phallic figure. (There is an apparently unconscious aptness in the terms Jude uses to describe her—'there was something lacking, and still more obviously something redundant, in the nature of this girl', 45.) The link between Arabella's hair and her castrating power is made clear in the allusion to Samson and Delilah: Arabella will chop a man off and chop him up if she is given the chance. And she will do the same thing to the patriarchal text. Arabella is jealous of Jude's involvement with books. She has no use for his ambition, and resents the time he spends on study. The scene in which she mishandles his books, smearing them with pig-fat and finally flinging them about the room, dramatizes her feeling of rivalrous contempt. As embodied male voices, books tend to

[14] In the schoolroom episode, Phillotson literally watches Sue through a pane of glass (271); Jude feels separated from the undergraduates at Christminster, who 'saw through him as through a pane of glass' (100). The same image is used in the *Life*, where Hardy is described as 'seeing through' individuals who condescended to him 'as though they were glass' (Hardy 1930, 179).

[15] Bayley (1978), 211, points out that 'Jude's courtship of Arabella is more essentially Shelleyan than his relation with Sue'.

become male bodies in this text—bodies which here are polluted and assaulted by the female touch.

But in the very act of assaulting the Word, Arabella also actualizes it, for as Delilah, she is the word made flesh—a kind of incarnation. And this very fact qualifies Hardy's point. While the moral of the biblical allusion is clear—Arabella is the last of a long line of wicked temptresses, and Jude should have known better than to fall for her—the fact that it *is* an allusion also works against this moral, suggesting that the word has to stay word, remain on the page, remain a translation exercise, an exercise in culture, or a moral emblem reinforcing patriarchal prejudice, for Jude (and Hardy) to be satisfied with it. When Jude returns to his books and 'the capital letters on the title-page [regard] him with fixed reproach . . . like the unclosed eyes of a dead man' (53), we are meant to feel that Jude has betrayed male words, betrayed culture and religion, for a woman; indeed that he is a kind of murderer, and that Arabella is his accomplice. But this metaphor, too, has an excess of meaning which cuts against its moral: it evokes a male body so lifeless, so ghoulish, that its superiority to woman's body does not make itself felt as fully as it seems intended to do.[16] The paradoxical power of Hardy's figurative style lies in its tendency to deconstruct itself—here, to suggest that Arabella is a scapegoat even as it scapegoats her.

And it is clear that Arabella *is* a scapegoat.[17] We seem intended to see her as a kind of sensual monster and hold her responsible for much of Jude's bad luck. But an examination of the actual causality of the plot reveals that Arabella does less damage than the novel's rhetoric seems to suggest. It becomes increasingly clear that, even if he had never met Arabella, Jude could not have achieved his dream.[18] His premature marriage is not the decisive barrier to university entrance, which would have required a more thoroughgoing and pragmatic campaign

[16] Slack notes that the 1895 edition of the novel has Jude closing his book before he goes out; for the 1903 Macmillan edition, Hardy eliminates this inconsistency and saves the simile (1957, 268).

[17] Lawrence (1961), 488–95, complains that Hardy inartistically vilifies both Alec d'Urberville and Arabella, who actually strengthens rather than harms Jude; see also Alvarez (1963), 116–17.

[18] This point is made by Eagleton (1987), 61–71. See also Bayley (1978), 214, on the 'false causal link' which vitiates the novel.

than he could ever have mounted, even if he had remained single. Indeed, blaming Arabella dilutes the social criticism: *Jude the Obscure* is *not* really a coherent critique of the class system, because it conflates its condemnation of that system with condemnation of her.

Nor, even without Arabella, could Jude have mastered Sue. Jude shapes our interpretation of his story when he remarks that it is Arabella who has blighted his relationship with Sue; yet, although the way Arabella keeps turning up at crucial moments does suggest that she is some kind of avenging fury, pursuing her doomed victim, her influence is not as definitive as it seems to be. Sue apparently gives herself to Jude on the first occasion out of jealousy of Arabella; but are we to assume she would never otherwise have done so, or that Jude would have been better off if she had not? It is true that it is Jude's involvement with Arabella which apparently precipitates Sue's marriage to Phillotson; but Sue was already engaged to Phillotson before she ever heard of Arabella, and Jude cannot fully possess her even when both he and Sue are legally free of their respective spouses. Shedding Arabella is, indeed, anticlimactically easy: the novel is not a very good analysis of the divorce issue, if only because the divorces it depicts are so readily obtained. When the neighbours shun Jude and Sue, it is less because they were married to others than because they are suspected (quite correctly) of not being married to one another.[19] Although Hardy does what he can to implicate Arabella in Sue's return to Phillotson—by having her inform Phillotson that his divorce was obtained on grounds which were invalid at the time, and thus apparently preparing his mind to take his wife back—Sue's motives for fleeing Jude have nothing to do with her rival. What happens is that Arabella is often used to trigger, or to make seem fated, a course of action which was implicit in Sue's nature—to give Sue an excuse for administering pain which she was bound to administer eventually in any case. It is as though the two women, antipathetic to one another

[19] Ingham, noting the 'remarkable ease' with which the divorces are obtained, decides that by 'the marriage question' Hardy must have meant 'whether marriage is a satisfactory and rational institution rather than "the stringency of the marriage laws"' (1976, 164). See also Lodge (1979), 194, and Bayley (1978), 208–9, who argues that it is not marriage which is the problem, but simply 'a free and emancipated sexual relation' after the glamour has worn off.

though they are, are at some level working together to destroy the protagonist.

I do not propose to deal in any detail with the question of Sue's sexual frigidity. It seems to me that her double nature is constituted by the male fantasies which shape her. Sue mirrors Jude—as the many references to their twinning and doubling make clear[20]—and she is what she has to be in order to arouse Jude and to thwart him. Jude creates her as a spiritual being before he ever sees her, and then expects her to satisfy him physically as well. Hardy creates her to play her part in the 'constant internal warfare between flesh and spirit' (232) by which Jude will be defined and destroyed. My approach is not to treat her as a real person with an internal consistency which analysis can uncover, but frankly as a production of the text, a place where its needs intersect. For the purposes of this discussion, what is interesting is her relationship to the patriarchal Word.

Like Arabella, Sue sets herself up as a rival to the male texts Jude loves. If Arabella is a Delilah, Sue is an Eve who entices Jude from the realm of innocent logocentrism into experience, by manipulating sign-systems which are sacred to him.[21] In contrast to Jude, Sue works in design rather than construction, in paint and chalk rather than stone. Her cleverness consists in moving lightly among signs sacred to the dominant culture, in 'colouring' and manipulating words which have real value to other people. Jude's first glimpse of his cousin colouring 𝔄𝔏𝔏𝔈𝔏𝔘𝔍𝔄 (103) suggests to a reader her frankly opportunistic stance—though Jude sentimentally imagines an organic, Ruskinian relationship between what she is and what she does.

[20] For example, the episode in which Sue puts on Jude's clothing (172–84). Lacan's insights about 'hommosexual' love are relevant here: see Lacan (1982), 155; MacCannell (1986), 44, 71–2, 107. Readers who see Sue's sexual attitudes as a projection of Hardy's and/or Jude's attitudes or conflicts include Steig (1975), 167; Goode (1979*b*), 102–4; Alvarez (1963), 115–17; Saldivar (1983), 611–12. Those on the other hand who treat her as a coherent character include Lawrence (1961), whose 'strong misreading' of the novel is brilliantly suggestive; Heilman (1966); Steig (1968); Guerard (1949), 109–14; Alvarez (1963), 118–19; Howe (1967), 141–3; Gregor (1974), 215–22; Jacobus (1975); and Boumelha (1982). Sue's link with feminism and with the New Woman of the 1890s is explored by Cunningham (1973), Boumelha (1982, 63–97), and Blake (1978); see also p. 165 n. 26. For biographical material which contributed to the figure of Sue, see Millgate (1982), 350–5.

[21] Lawrence's (1961) discussion of Sue's need for the Male and for the Word is suggestive in relation to her greedy appropriation of these texts (496).

Having the word printed in Gothic characters emphasizes its archaic visual decorativeness and recalls, while at the same time parodying, Jude's deeply felt THITHER.[22] It is characteristic of Sue that after making fun of the model of the city of Jerusalem, she is able to reproduce it exactly on the blackboard, for she is presented as a mere replicator and exploiter of discourse, echoing and playing with signs and concepts rather than internalizing them.

The female voice is a sinister power in the novel. Male voices are spiritual, ghostly; they speak through print, are the pure 'presence' to which the written word points; they come out of the past as history, religion, culture; they are univocal, unequivocal, stand-taking, ordered, formally rhetorical; they project a sure sense of self. Female voicing is more complex: it is oral rather than *écriture* (this is true even of Sue's notes, which are in the same distracting accents as her spoken word); it is of the body (involving clothing, gesture, body-language as well as actual speech); it is double, deceptive, contradictory; it involves mimicry, parroting, parody, role-playing; it is interactive, demanding and positing a response; it comes out of the past as legend, rumour, curse, or spell. None of these qualities is necessarily bad—indeed, they are the kind of things feminists are saying about women's language in general—but in this novel they are devastatingly and consistently destructive.[23]

Sue's dialogue has been criticized as stilted and unrealistic, but that is part of its point.[24] Her alienated, formal wording conveys perfectly the pert theoreticalness of everything she says. Like Jude, Sue is self-educated and half-educated: but where Jude's intellectual incoherence is seen as pathetic, Sue's seems wilful and aggressive: she uses her reading to rationalize her instinctual needs and desires. Her androgynous nature is relevant here: she 'tries on' male styles of thought as opportunistically as she dons Jude's clothing, or as she uses the arguments of the dead student whose lover she refused to become. Sue uses men against one another, and she uses men's

---

[22] Hardy's use of unusual typography is discussed by Harmon (1988), 309.

[23] See Spacks (1985); Irigaray (1985), 134–7, 111–13, and *passim*; Moi (1985), 140–7.

[24] See Alvarez (1963), 119; Stewart (1971), 190; Bayley (1978), 201–2; Pickrel (1988), 248.

ideas the same way. Less crudely but even more devastatingly than Arabella, she turns into 'missiles' the chopped-up bits and pieces of a male 'body'. There are two fragmenting processes which operate through Sue's words: female inconsequence and male analysis. Sue voices the conclusions of contemporary (male) criticism so as to undermine Jude's convictions intellectually, while her maddening ('female') inconsistency undoes him emotionally. The way Hardy describes Sue's behaviour during her last breakfast with Phillotson—'she talked vaguely and indiscriminately to prevent his talking pertinently' (271)— neatly captures the aggressively scatterbrained quality of her chatter throughout the novel, even when what she is saying seems to have some intellectual content. The moment when she quotes Mill against Phillotson is untypically comic, but it otherwise epitomizes her technique throughout.

Jude wants Sue to help him preserve his logocentric virginity: he flees to her in horror after reciting the creed in Latin on a bet. But she does the opposite. In Sue's nervous chatter, the patriarchal Word becomes text, and the text falls apart. When Sue quotes Swinburne to the effect that the Christian saints are 'dead limbs of gibbeted Gods' (180), when her Higher-Critical stance dissolves the biblical text into separable headings, chapters, and editions, when she offers to prepare Jude a new New Testament by dismembering the traditional one and reassembling its parts in 'chronological order as written' (182), we are in the presence of an antisacramental *sparagmos*: the metaphor acquires shocking force in the context of Hardy's imagery, and prefigures the scene in which Jude dismembers and burns his own books, 'the leaves, covers, and binding of Jeremy Taylor, Butler, Doddridge, Paley, Pusey, Newman' (262): a mass-murder, as well as suicide. Sue's irresponsible babble dismantles the text and undoes Jude.[25]

This is not to say, of course, that Hardy is consciously hostile to most of Sue's opinions, or even to the way she expresses them. Like Jude's 'voices', Sue's quotations are really Hardy's, gleanings from his own reading, often quotations from his favourite authors. But by reproducing 'familiar quotations' in two modes—the Jude-mode of phenomenological reverence

---

[25] Childers (1981), 322, comments on meekness, silence, and irrelevant chatter as women's weapons in Hardy's fiction.

and the Sue-mode of opportunistic *bricolage*—the text suspends their message somewhere in the gap between, relativizes it. And by making Sue both an intellectual mentor and a sexual tease, Hardy problematizes Jude's conversion to her 'modern' point of view.

Jude loses his faith for emotional as much as intellectual reasons, as he becomes more depressed and less hopeful in his private life; and since Sue is responsible for his hopelessness, she is also responsible not only for his scepticism but for the link between scepticism and hopelessness.[26] It is paradoxical that even though Jude *progresses* towards the beliefs which Hardy himself holds and towards an apparently liberating unconventionality which the text endorses, his maturing point of view seems to reflect not so much intellectual energy and independence as lassitude and collapse. A Jude who can ask Sue what edition of the Apocrypha she recommends (244) is a man who has surrendered, been at once seduced and emasculated by her opinions.

I would argue, however, that Hardy is scapegoating Sue just as he is scapegoating Arabella. Sue uses signs the only way one can in the post-Christian age posited by Hardy—to define, express, and defend herself rather than to transcend herself—and because she does this she is made to bear the weight of the ontological crisis. The novel knows that there is no truth behind signs, yet makes Woman culpable for pointing this out: it dramatizes as female scattiness the breakdown of logocentric security. Hardy's characterization of Sue enables him at once to depict woman as unable to 'master' male thought, and to blur male responsibility for the fragmenting force of that thought by having its *content* voiced by a woman.

Sue's scepticism makes her into the rival of the male 'voices' Jude has loved. Indeed, she effectually destroys his relationship with the voices of the patriarchy, which she mocks, undercuts, and dismembers. She emasculates him not only by denying him her body but by destroying his dream of cultural solidarity with the great men of the past and present. Though it is clearly not in any literal sense Sue's fault that a Christminster education

---

[26] For the historical placing of their clash of opinion, see Gittings (1975), 93–5, who argues that Sue's loss of religious faith and her Positivism are anachronistic for the New Woman of the 1890s and that she is rather 'The Girl of the Period' of the 1860s.

is beyond Jude, her mockery of what such an education would have stood for implicates her in his bitter disappointment. The collapse of his university dreams makes Jude pathetically dependent upon Sue. Her ghost replaces the ghosts of Christminster; indeed, when Jude declares that he will not be divided from her by 'things present nor things to come' (290), he implies that she has replaced God himself.

Indeed, Jude's obsession with Sue—or is it his obsession with Christminster?—isolates him from all his fellow *men*. Although Jude works with men, drinks with them, and apparently feels a vocation to teach them (he is even said to have led a working-men's reading group, which is, however, mentioned only at the moment when it expels him!), the narrative never dramatizes his putative capacity for male comradeship. There are indeed only two male friendships in the novel: Jude's original passion for Phillotson, and Phillotson's friendship with Gillingham: these two, and the relationship between them, I shall return to in a moment. There is no group of tolerant rustics in this novel to provide a sense of male community; Jude feels only justified contempt for the group represented by Tinker Taylor, with whom he occasionally drowns his sorrows —and whose generic name suggests a dismissiveness on the part of the author himself. The dream of inclusion in an idyllic community of scholars seems to have stood in the way of ordinary friendships with ordinary men, the relationship with Sue to have absorbed Jude's emotional energy when that dream falls apart. There is something downright claustrophobic about Hardy's picture of Jude's life with Sue.[27] While it seems

---

[27] Sue, too, is curiously isolated, without friends of her own sex. Millgate (1982), 351–2, notes the oddness of this, considering that Sue attends a training college and that her experience there is to some extent based on that of Hardy's sisters Kate and Mary, who did have warm friendships. The idea of such friendships, moreover, intrigued Hardy: see his journal entry on the 'mother–daughter' pairings at Stockwell Training College (Hardy 1928, 310). Hardy was anxious to protect Sue against the suspicion of lesbianism: he insisted to Gosse that there was 'nothing perverted or depraved in Sue's nature. The abnormalism consists in disproportion, not in inversion': see Millgate (1982), 354. (Hardy alludes to Sappho in his epigraph to Part III of the novel: see Björk (1985), i. items 522, 524, for other references to Sappho.) Bayley (1978), 205, comments on the 'judicious' tone of the letter—'as if Hardy had just learned to talk like that (perhaps from Gosse and Ibsen)'. Dellamora (1989), 215, notes the lack of same-sex bonding for both Jude and Sue. Analysing the formalization of gender roles in the 1890s, Dellamora also points out where Hardy 'learned to talk like that', noting that the word 'inversion' is the language of the new

appealing that their relationship is conceived as a friendship as well as a love affair, that Sue is his 'comrade' and companion as well as his life-partner, it also points to a vacuum in Jude's life. Sue fills the gap left by the dream of male fellowship, and that dream—not Arabella—is her real rival.

It is worth noting how the rivalry between Sue and Christminster contributes to the startling conclusion of the novel. The despair which causes Little Father Time to kill himself and murder his little siblings can be traced directly to Jude's behaviour on Remembrance Day—behaviour which by any ordinary standards can only be described as self-indulgent and irresponsible.[28] By insisting on standing in the rain until he has seen the procession, Jude not only makes himself ill, he makes it impossible to get an adequate room for the night. In effect, he deserts Sue, leaving her alone with the children. Her singularly ill-timed frankness to the landlady, when she admits that, although visibly pregnant, she has no husband, is so gratuitous that it might seem to be a bitter reflection on Jude's behaviour —if any such motive could be attributed to Sue, who at this point in the novel has become almost saintly in her endurance and uncritical devotion. In any event, the end result of Jude's fecklessness is the death of the children, and Sue's return to Phillotson. Jude sacrifices Sue's welfare to his obsession with Christminster, and then—though the novel establishes no *direct* link between the events—loses her to the rival who had imbued him with that obsession.

Why are women presented as rivals to the dream? Why are Christminster and Sue conceived as in some way interchangeable? How is the question of education connected with the marriage question? Indeed, what precisely is it that Jude wants in wanting Christminster?

---

sexology, and that Hardy's defensiveness about Sue's 'abnormalism' lines him up with the sexologists in an essentially conservative view of 'natural' sexuality. My feeling is that the emphatic foregrounding of Sue's problems with sexuality and gender may serve to repress similar problems of Jude's. Sue's and Jude's isolation from the community is discussed by Heilman (1966), 322–3, and Gregor (1974), 219–28. On the theoreticalness of their 'comradeship' see Bayley (1978), 212.

[28] Millgate (1971*b*), 329, and Bayley (1978), 210, note Jude's responsibility for the deaths of the children.

The evidence is inconsistent, even somewhat contradictory. There is the sense that the bookish life is a last resort, since Jude is no good for anything else.[29] Yet it is never entirely clear whether Jude loves reading as an end in itself. Certain passages seem to suggest that he does: that he has been inspired by the hymn to Diana, or the passages from the Christminster writers which are apparently supposed to be lodged in his memory. But most of his study seems to be less joyful discovery than painful toil; and reading loses some of its charm for him when every working man is doing it.

Indeed, it is also suggested that Jude's main motive is ambition, a wish to distinguish himself from other people. The young Jude dreams of becoming 'even a bishop' (40) and looking 'down on the world' through the windows of 'those palaces of light and leading' (100–1). He remembers Phillotson telling him that 'a degree was the necessary hall-mark of one who wanted to do anything as a theologian or teacher' (119), and later admits, in renouncing it, that his motive had been 'social success' (148). It is only when he realizes that he can never be an ordained clergyman that Jude lights on the 'new idea': to 'preach and do good to his fellow-creatures' (153). At that point he confesses that his former scheme had been motivated by 'mundane ambition', 'a social unrest which had no foundation in the nobler instincts' (153); but he is in a penitential mood, and part of the appeal of the new scheme is that it is a properly 'purgatorial course worthy of being followed by a remorseful man' (153).

Jude's desire, then, is overdetermined: none of these motives is fully dramatized in the novel, and the very fact that all of them can be invoked makes all of them seem somewhat theoretical. Something deeper and more consistent is needed to account for Jude's fanatic and ultimately suicidal obsession. What about the positive reasons, the details which convey the depth of his desire—the erotic motives for Jude's fascination with Christminster?

---

[29] Hardy makes a similar point about himself: 'Everybody said that Tommy would have to be a parson, being obviously no good for any practical pursuit' (Hardy 1928, 19). The emphasis is changed in a later statement: 'As a child, to be a parson had been his dream' (Hardy 1930, 176). The two statements, taken together, seem to register an ambivalence similar to the novel's.

His first impulse towards Christminster is simply presented as a yearning to join Phillotson. The power of this motive is startlingly suggested by the intensity with which Jude '[parts] his lips as he [faces] the north-east, and [draws] in the wind as if it were a sweet liquor' when he realizes that it was 'in Christminster city between one and two hours ago . . . touching Mr. Phillotson's face, being breathed by him' (21–2). The wind is the spirit not of God but of the only other Father he has known. Yet this father is described with lover-like intensity—even in a topos borrowed from Petrarchan love-poetry. And for good reason: this passage was originally written to describe Jude's feelings not for Phillotson, who was added at a later stage of the composition to bolster the education theme, but for Sue herself.[30] That Hardy felt able to retain the paragraph, essentially changing only the pronouns, is a remarkable testimony to the ambiguity of the erotic impulse of this fable.

As Jude grows older his desire becomes less personal but no less intense. His desire for Christminster is a desire for a transfigured state of being. Outside the walls of Christminster, experience is fragmented, he is alienated from his fellow man, and the world is brown, grey, dark, and gloomy (the word 'gloom' recurs frequently, to denote both emotional and physical states). He wants transfiguration, he wants to be swept out of this fallen world, translated, illuminated, penetrated, 'imbued with the *genius loci*' (136). The transformation involves being contained within the walls of the mystical city. 'Only a wall' divides him from the communion he desires— 'Only a wall—but what a wall!' (100). Christminster the cultural centre is a kind of Great Barn of English thought,[31] 'the intellectual and spiritual granary of this country' (133), and, like the Great Barn in *Far from the Madding Crowd*, a metaphorically female body. Christminster the university is the

---

[30] See Ingham (1976), 166. Paterson (1960*a*), 90, prints the passage with its revisions. Millgate (1982), 351, suggests that one of the models for Phillotson was Horace Moule. Hardy's journal entry for 20 June 1873 describes his last visit to Moule, in a context which recalls the imagery of *Jude*: 'we could see Ely Cathedral gleaming in the distant sunlight. A never-to-be forgotten morning. H. M. M. saw me off for London. His last smile' (Hardy 1928, 123). On Hardy's relationship with Moule, see Millgate (1982), 155–6 and *passim*.

[31] For another comparison between Christminster and the Great Barn, see Wotton (1985), 105. Brown (1962), 13, and Enstice (1979), 6, have noted the similarity between Christminster and Casterbridge.

welcoming mother, and Jude 'her beloved son, in whom she shall be well pleased' (41);[32] Christminster the city is Jerusalem the heavenly bride—before whose image, for a moment, he forgets Bridehead (126). Seduced by her 'romantic charms' (37), Jude longs 'to reach the heart of the place' (91), to '[penetrate] to dark corners which no lamplight reached' (91), 'to be encircled as it were with the breath and sentiment of the venerable city' (91). But in her 'ineffable charm' (95), 'so lovely, so unravaged' (94), Christminster remains, like Sue, tantalizing but inaccessible; and the gates are shut against him. It is a premonitory image, for Jude's fate is to remain 'outside the gates of everything' (100). Hardy's protagonist is always being denied access to a female body which would make him whole, and it is always the fault of a woman.

The misquotation of Matthew 3: 17 is significant: in imagining himself 'her beloved son, in whom she shall be well pleased', Jude has changed the pronoun of the biblical text and the gender of the complacent parent. Father becomes Mother: the fusion is significant, for there is a paradoxical element to Jude's desire. The sheltering body is metaphorically female, but the community contained within her walls is a community of men, of spiritual fathers and brothers; a dream-world where there are no distracting Arabellas and Sues, except as 'gorgeous nosegays of feminine beauty' rendered harmless by distance, 'fashionably arrayed in green, pink, blue, and white' (490); an enclosed community where Jude could be at one with 'those happy young contemporaries of his with whom he shared a common mental life' (100). Jude wants to be taken into the body of a woman who can make him a man among men. The problem is that this wholeness is a fiction in the first place, 'a very imaginary production' (125), as Sue says of the model of Jerusalem. Instead of acknowledging this, and condemning Jude for his wishful thinking, the novel blames the various female figures who fail to fulfil his impossible desires.

Jude's grievances against women go back a generation. His mother deserted his father—and Jude. His foster-mother, Aunt Drusilla, is a cold, rejecting woman who transforms family accidents into family myth: she displaces his mother, and then

---

[32] See Lodge (1979), 200, on the parodic baptism which follows this statement.

tells him he can never have a wife. Indeed Drusilla, 'opposed to marriage, from first to last' (251), is a kind of witch. Though the text allows the myth of the family curse to be understood as an ignorant woman's primitive superstition, whatever Drusilla predicts comes true, as if, in repeating it, she had willed it. Drusilla tells Jude on the day of his marriage to Arabella that it would have been better if he had died at birth, and he eventually comes to feel the same way. It is significant that her 'good' counterpart, Mrs Edlin, who professes to be more positive about marriage, has an equally negative impact on Jude's marital career. It does seem somewhat grotesque for her to relate, on the eve of Jude's planned marriage to Sue, the (possibly untrue) story of his and Sue's ancestor, gibbeted in a sort of corpse custody case. Since Sue has consented to the wedding because of her desire to provide an orthodox home for Arabella's child, the anecdote has a peculiar relevance to their situation; and although she herself is not shown taking account of this relevance, the effect of the gruesome tale is to make her call off the marriage. It is interesting that when she does, Mrs Edlin expresses her disappointment by complaining that they have 'spoiled' the saying 'marry in haste and repent at leisure' (346)! The doubling of Drusilla and Mrs Edlin reveals the deep structure of the mythic subtext. Women tend to work together in Hardy, however far apart they believe themselves to be.

Sue and Arabella also work with Drusilla to make her curses come true.[33] Even though Drusilla as a character is steadfastly opposed to Jude's relationship with both women, they both play into her script and actualize her dire and spiteful predictions, taking over her role of demonic mother and completing the destruction she has foretold. The text knows that because what Jude seeks is given in an illusory way by the (m)Other, no actual woman can ever provide it. So it creates a dual mother

---

[33] Abercrombie (1912), 160–1, observes the two women's 'kinship in Jude's destruction'. The doubling of characters is noted by Fischler (1981, 1984); Eagleton (1987), 69; Pickrel (1988), 246–50. A number of discussions of Hardy's misogyny deal with this novel: see Rogers (1975), Childers (1981), Langland (1980). Jacobus (1975), on the other hand, argues that Hardy presents Sue sympathetically, allowing us to see her side of the story. Eagleton (1987), 68, who sums up the case against Sue, suggests that she is a ' "representative" character in the great tradition of nineteenth century realism . . . and her elusive complexity points beyond herself, to a confused and ambiguous structure of feeling which belongs to the period in general'.

in Sue and Arabella, both of whom go through the motions of nurturing him but who really kill him.

Arabella is a mother out of nightmare. Her sheer size and physical vigour are intimidating, her immense bosom particularly threatening. She first appears less than a page after Jude's fantasy of the Alma Mater; she seduces him by playing games with the egg she is hatching between her prodigious breasts, and traps him into marriage by pretended maternity. She tends to reduce Jude to infantile helplessness, her presence in the bar at one point destroying 'his momentary taste for strong liquor as completely as if it had whisked him back to his milk-fed infancy' (217). In the final sequence, as Jude lies dying, Arabella denies him the care he needs to survive.

Sue is the very opposite physically: the narrator explicitly contrasts 'the small, tight, apple-like convexities of her bodice' with 'Arabella's amplitudes' (225). But the mother's curse nevertheless also operates through Sue, whose own mother was a shrew and who, unlike Jude, re-enacts the role of her abusive parent. Jude flees to Sue in the first place for maternal comfort and guidance, 'under the influence of a childlike yearning for the one being in the world to whom it seemed possible to fly' (145). His visionary image of her as haloed guide, counsellor, comforter, and friend makes it appropriate that one of her names is Mary.[34] And Hardy assigns to her at the end of the novel a speech which rewords the fatalistic conception of his own mother: 'There is something external to us which says "You shan't"' (407).[35] But what definitively places Sue in the position of a mother to Jude is that she marries, and eventually deserts Jude for, the man who initially served as a father to him —and that the children she mothers indirectly send her into this man's arms.

On the other hand, Sue's role as a mother and a stepmother to these real children is not entirely plausible. Her instant interest in and sympathy with young Jude—even in the face of her distress that 'half' of him 'is' Arabella—seems no more credible than her repeated pregnancies, which in view of her

---

[34] Millgate (1982), 350–3, suggests biographical sources for Sue's names. 'Bridehead' is also the name of one of the 'old-fashioned psalm-tunes associated with Dorsetshire' (Hardy 1930, 127).

[35] See Millgate (1982), 21.

sexual skittishness and her intact and immaculate body-image are hard to visualize. Sue has some peculiar ideas about procreation which might seem to militate against successful maternity. Her fantasy, expressed in her complaint to Phillotson, that, if Eve had not fallen, 'some harmless mode of vegetation might have peopled Paradise' (271), is more startling, not to say unorthodox, than it seems intended to be in context. The text apparently sympathizes with Sue's objection to marrying, on the grounds that marriage involves bringing forth, in Shelley's words, 'Shapes like our own selves hideously multiplied' (345)—even though the context makes the argument illogical, since Sue and Jude find themselves quite able to bring forth such shapes even in an unmarried state. And yet the narrator endorses as one of 'man's finer emotions' (212) Jude's wish that Sue's children should be her clones, containing nothing of Phillotson—'shapes like her own self', precisely.[36]

Such fantasies might suggest that the children in the novel are less likely to be believable individuals, characters in their own right, than figures for or mirrors of the main characters—'shapes like their own selves' in one way or another. And indeed this turns out to be the case. The children are more vivid as the grotesquely undifferentiated trail of corpses, or as the little bundles of empty clothing hanging on the pegs, than they are when alive; and Sue as a mother and stepmother turns out to be as grotesquely destructive as they are unreal.

The figure through whom Sue operates is Little Father Time, less a child than 'an enslaved and dwarfed Divinity' (332)—a *deus ex machina*, that is, enslaved to the exigencies of Hardy's plot.[37] It is impossible to respond to him as to a real child, a character in his own right: the only way of getting at his function in the novel is to look at the connections he forms among the other characters.

Through this child, Sue and Arabella are linked in motherhood. The two women's relationship to young Jude parodies their relationship to his father: Arabella's connection is physical only; Sue expresses idealized affection for both Judes, but she lets them both down in the end, so that they die of

---

[36] Cf. the central fantasy of *The Well-Beloved*.

[37] Dissatisfaction with this figure has been general: see Abercrombie (1912), 164–6; Guerard (1949), 69; Alvarez (1963), 121; Howe (1967), 145–6; Bayley (1978), 203–4.

despair. It takes the two women to finish the child off—as it takes both of them to kill Jude, and both Alec and Angel to destroy Tess. As in *Tess*, it is the more 'spiritual' and idealistic one of the pair who does the more damage. Like Drusilla, Sue gives her foster son the message that it would have been better for him to die young; and Little Father Time, already predisposed to agree, acts out her suggestion.[38] What precisely he brings about when he does so is made clear by looking at his relationship with his 'mother' and father, and with the other 'mothers' and 'fathers' in the novel.

Jude's father is dead before the book begins, and seems to have left his son no legacy—indeed to have made no impression upon him at all.[39] Although it was his abusive behaviour which drove Jude's mother away, Jude's feelings about him are never mentioned, except in a generalized way, as an aspect of the family problem with marriage. It is perhaps worth noting that Jude, when he deals with women, takes the very opposite tack: far from abusing his women, he allows them to abuse him—yet he loses them all the same. There is no suggestion that Jude's behaviour is a deliberate response to his father's, that (like Joe for example in *Great Expectations*) Jude has chosen to abjure his father's bullying stance; but there is a sense that the father, for whatever reason, has left his son wounded and defenceless. The novel opens with Jude's loss of a substitute father. Jude's first love, apparently, is Phillotson, but Christminster and then Sue take this father/lover away from him. Seeing Phillotson as occupying the place of the father makes some patterns in the novel emerge more clearly. The shape of the plot—with the four main characters changing partners—releases meanings which go beyond facile irony.

The romantic plot of the novel emphasizes how Phillotson takes Sue away from Jude, but it is equally true that Sue takes Phillotson away from Jude. Indeed, Sue meets Jude precisely at the point when it is made clear to Jude that Phillotson never had the emotional investment in Jude that Jude had in him. The

[38] Heilman (1966), 313, 318, suggests that Sue 'provides the psychological occasion, if not the cause' of the deaths and also comes 'close to husband murder'. See also Gregor (1974), 226.

[39] The process of designing a tombstone for his own father, who died in July 1892, perhaps suggested to Hardy the trade of his protagonist (Hardy 1930, 15).

older man's brutally insensitive remark—'I don't remember you in the least' (118)—is underemphasized by the narrative: Jude scarcely seems to notice it. In view of the place Phillotson had held in Jude's imagination, Jude's obliviousness to the rudeness is as disconcerting as the remark itself. Indeed, there seems to be a 'loop' in the sequence at this point: Phillotson loses his 'halo' (118) for Jude just *before* he speaks, because of his unimpressive physical appearance. But Phillotson's callous comment is a much more plausible trigger for Jude's sudden disenchantment than his faded looks, which might have depressed an ardent idealist like Jude but should scarcely have lessened his interest and sympathy. Once again, as in the motivation of Mrs Charmond's hostility in *The Woodlanders*, a lesser motive seems to be substituted for a greater, and the substitution alerts the reader to a covert level of meaning. It is important that it is at this moment in the novel that Phillotson suddenly becomes physically unattractive, that his repulsive exterior is from this point on a constant feature of his character notation, and that this unattractiveness acquires a specifically sexual dimension. There seems to be some displacement going on here, and the ground shifts under the reader's feet as the characters, not only of Phillotson but of Jude himself, suddenly seem to change.

Sue replaces Phillotson as the focus of Jude's interest in Christminster; she also replaces Jude as Phillotson's student and protégée. It is more than just a neat 'ironical clinch' (129) that Jude hastens to introduce Sue to the man who will take her from him: it is a clue to their structural interchangeability. The loss Jude suffers in Phillotson is re-enacted again and again in various parodic and sometimes gratuitous ways. Jude's idealism is betrayed by Tetuphenay and later by the composer Highridge. Even Vilbert becomes involved in the pattern. When Arabella marries him at the end of the novel, Vilbert becomes linked structurally to Phillotson (a parallel reinforced by Vilbert's lie, when he refers to Jude as 'a pupil of mine, you know', 355), in that Jude has finally lost both his women to the two men who seemed to father him in the opening pages. The text makes clear that Jude will never get what he wants from a man. Indeed, he could say of any of the men in his life what he says of Sue: 'you are not worth a man's love' (470).

Jude's relationship to his son is no more fruitful than his relationship to his 'fathers'. In a naturalistic novel the root of their alienation might well be biological: Jude could easily be shown as unable to sympathize with the 'half' of young Jude which comes from Arabella. What Hardy actually does with the figure shows that his method is less naturalistic than symbolic. For in spite of the fact that Sue's words foreground the question of genetic connection, Little Father Time is not like his mother at all. He is, indeed, the little clone Sue and Jude have both desired, a parodic epitome of both the authors of his being—both Jude and Hardy. A precocious infant, he seems to have possessed from birth the secret they did not glimpse until the age of 11.[40] Jude names the 'little hungry heart' (335) after himself, identifies with him, and projects on to him his own ambitions and his own reflections, imputing to him the sentiment—'Let the day perish . . .' (330)—which he later uses as his own epitaph (488). Little Father Time is less Jude's child than his dwarfish double—a parodic mirror-image, created to punish him. One's sense of what sin Jude is being punished for depends upon one's reading of what it is that the child accomplishes.

Little Father Time is less a character than an awkward plot device, but one which reveals the *origin* of the plot itself. Or rather, of one of the plots; for two are needed to deliver Sue into the hands of Phillotson. The first of these is the Sue–Jude–Arabella triangle, a familiar fictional pattern Hardy has already worked out in *Tess*. The second is the Sue–Jude–Phillotson triangle, which looks more and more like a Freudian family romance. Standing in for his father and namesake Jude, Little Father Time—both child and father, in a parodically un-Wordsworthian way—acts out the child's desire to block the union between Mother and Father, as well as his suspicion that such opposition is suicidal, that Father is going to win in the end. He has advised against the marriage of his parents, and goes on to break up their relationship. But he dies in the process, and succeeds only in delivering his 'mother' over to the original 'father', and to the patriarchal order with which that father has recently renewed his connection.

[40] See Hardy (1928), 19–20, and the poem 'Childhood among the Ferns'.

For Phillotson has suddenly lined up with Gillingham. Indeed, Phillotson's 'character' shifts according to the needs of the plot and the symbolic structure. Callously tactless when Jude attempts to renew acquaintance with him, smoothly courteous to Arabella in the same situation (382); articulately sensitive to Jude and Sue's Shelleyan oneness while obtuse and even vulgar in his emotional intercourse with his wife; gallant, even heroic in giving Sue up in the first place; finely independent of Gillingham then, cravenly suggestible in the end—Phillotson is not really the consistent figure invented by Lawrence.[41] Rather, he seems to be a counter manipulated by a text in pursuit of certain patterns of meaning, his character necessarily sacrificed to his multiple functions. Although himself excluded from Christminster, Phillotson now becomes, when he possesses Sue, one of the excluders. The unworthy world of men who love women defeats Jude in the end.

Yet while he robs Jude, Phillotson also acts for Jude. The text has spoken of revenge upon Sue—revenge which it now takes. The text, through little Jude, hands Sue over to a father who will torment her. Sue, like her own mother, has abused her 'husband'. Jude, unlike his real father, has never retaliated. But he has played father—taken Phillotson's part in the wedding rehearsal Sue sadistically insisted he enact. And he has, like Sue's student lover, warned her that she could play her 'game' once too often (313). It is easy to see Sue's fate as retribution for the way she has acted to Jude—retribution which Jude himself cannot be allowed to think of taking. The way the text dwells on her shrinking white body has, however, a certain sadistic relish. Jude had spoken of the 'utter contempt' a man might feel for a tease after she was dead and gone (313). That after Jude himself is dead and gone Phillotson remains to enact his revenge is an irony the text cannot openly acknowledge.

Instead, it must end with the assertion that Jude, even in death, remains the object of both women's desire. In the last line of the novel Arabella suddenly speaks for Sue, in heightened language which recalls Marty South's envoi to *The Woodlanders*:

'She may swear that [she's found peace] on her knees to the holy cross upon her necklace till she's hoarse, but it won't be true . . . She's

41 Lawrence (1961), 501–2.

never found peace since she left his arms, and never will again till she's as he is now!' (494)

Arabella's words seem validated by their portentous placement. But her sudden elevation into choric commentator is as disconcerting as her assertion is implausible: Sue was never very consistent in her desire to be in Jude's arms, and if she has suddenly become so, it is less, one might feel, because he is the only man for her than because she has finally lost him. But Arabella's rhetoric does not seem intended to leave the reader with any such cynical reflection.[42]

What gives Arabella the authority to speak for Sue? Why do women suddenly unite like this in Hardy? The unexpected ending seems to express once again Hardy's intuition that women are somehow united in a way men cannot understand. Something more is going on in this particular novel, however, where Arabella's words always acquire a peculiar authority (and an attractiveness for certain critics) whenever she is testifying to Jude's desirability.[43] If the text has blamed women for denying Jude wholeness, it has also implied that a man can get wholeness through a woman. Whatever Jude lacks in his own eyes or in the eyes of the reader, he must not lack in the eyes of Woman; however disparate the natures and needs of Sue and Arabella, they must agree in their desire for him. Arabella's sudden oracular status owes less to her 'character' than to the needs of the text. The magical power of the word is lent to the woman so that it can be borrowed back by Hardy to confirm his male protagonist.

Arabella indeed has the last word. With her resonant conclusion to *Jude the Obscure*, Hardy's career as a novelist also comes to an end.[44] The hostile reception of *Jude* gave Hardy the reason—or the excuse—he needed to return to what he had always considered his first vocation, the writing of poetry. While the poetry is beyond the scope of this study, it seems to me that its

---

[42] Arabella's choric role invites commentary: see Millgate (1971*b*), 324; Gregor (1974), 232; Bayley (1978), 212–13; Boumelha (1982), 150.

[43] See Alvarez (1963), 118; Pickrel (1988), 249.

[44] In effect, although *The Well-Beloved*, which had been serialized under the title *The Pursuit of the Well-Beloved* in 1892, appeared, radically revised, in volume form in 1897.

complexity is of a rather different kind from that of the novels I have been discussing.

It is interesting, when looking at the few poems which are generated by and linked to the fiction—poems like 'The Pine Planters' and 'In a Wood' which derive from *The Woodlanders*, 'The Moth-Signal' which takes off from an episode in *The Return of the Native*, and 'Tess's Lament'—to discover that they quite lack the intensity and the doubleness found in the corresponding passages in the fiction. While it is perhaps scarcely fair to Hardy to single out by title only these poems, which are not his most powerful, their very blandness may nevertheless serve to suggest something about the 'poetic' moments in the novels.

Hardy's anxiety needs space in which to repress itself. In a novel, the deep concerns which are disguised by the moral shape of the main plot will return—obliquely, and as it were under pressure—in figurative ways. The peculiar intensity of Hardy's vision in the novel seems to me to depend on the text's at least partial blindness to its sources, and to require as well, for its full expression, a genre which is more thoroughly dialogic than the lyric poem.[45]

Not all of Hardy's fiction is equally amenable to the kind of analysis I have attempted. However, it seems arguable that works in which these anxieties and images are wholly lacking tend to be lifeless: *The Trumpet Major*, for example, is simply dull, in a way in which *Desperate Remedies*, for all its incoherence, is not. On the other hand, a fiction like 'Barbara of the House of Grebe', in which obsessive interest in bodily dissolution is directly expressed in the plot and imagery, tends to disturb and offend readers. To recognize that the novels which a reading public with realist preconceptions has agreed to call 'major' are those in which strong and easily recognized moral and generic patterns get marked and skewed by private myth is also to suggest that there may be nothing particularly private about the anxieties and fantasies that myth expresses.

45 Bakhtin (1981).

References

Works of Thomas Hardy

Desperate Remedies, London: Macmillan, 1912; Wessex Edition, vol. xv.

Far from the Madding Crowd, London: Macmillan, 1912; Wessex Edition, vol. ii.

A Group of Noble Dames, London: Macmillan, 1912; Wessex Edition, vol. xiv.

Jude the Obscure, London: Macmillan, 1912; Wessex Edition, vol. iii.

The Mayor of Casterbridge, London: Macmillan, 1912; Wessex Edition, vol. v.

A Pair of Blue Eyes, London: Macmillan, 1912; Wessex Edition, vol. x.

The Return of the Native, London: Macmillan, 1912; Wessex Edition, vol. iv.

Tess of the d'Urbervilles, ed. Juliet Grindle and Simon Gatrell, Oxford: Oxford University Press, 1983.

Under the Greenwood Tree, London: Macmillan, 1912; Wessex Edition, vol. vii.

The Woodlanders, ed. Dale Kramer, Oxford: Oxford University Press, 1981.

Critical Works

ABERCROMBIE, LASCELLES (1912), *Thomas Hardy: A Critical Study*, London: Secker, 1912; repr. New York: Russell & Russell, 1964.

ALVAREZ, A. (1963), 'Afterword', in Thomas Hardy, *Jude the Obscure*, New York: New American Library, 1961; repr. in Guerard (1963), 113–22.

ANDERSON, WAYNE C. (1985), 'The Rhetoric of Silence in Hardy's Fiction', *Studies in the Novel*, 17, 53–68.

ANZIEU, DIDIER (1989), *The Skin Ego: A Psychoanalytic Approach to the Self*, trans. Chris Turner, New Haven, Conn., and London: Yale University Press.

AUERBACH, NINA (1980), 'The Rise of the Fallen Woman', *Nineteenth-Century Fiction*, 35, 29–52.

BAILEY, JAMES O. (1946), 'Hardy's "Mephistophelian Visitants"', *PMLA* 61, 1147–50.

BAIR, JUDITH (1977), '*The Mayor of Casterbridge*: "Some Grand Feat of Stagery"', *South Atlantic Bulletin*, 42/2, 11–22.

BAKHTIN, M. M. (1981), *The Dialogic Imagination: Four Essays*, ed. Michael Holquist, trans. Caryl Emerson and Michael Holquist, Austin, Tex.: University of Texas Press.

BARRELL, JOHN (1982), 'Geographies of Hardy's Wessex', *Journal of Historical Geography*, 8, 347–61.

BAYLEY, JOHN (1978), *An Essay on Hardy*, Cambridge, New York: Cambridge University Press.

BEACH, JOSEPH WARREN (1922), *The Technique of Thomas Hardy*, Chicago, Ill.: University of Chicago Press, 1922; repr. New York: Russell & Russell, 1962.

BEEGEL, SUSAN (1987), 'Bathsheba's Lovers: Male Sexuality in *Far from the Madding Crowd*', in Cox (1984), 108–27; repr. in Bloom (1987*a*), 207–26.

BEER, GILLIAN (1983), *Darwin's Plots: Evolutionary Narrative in Darwin, George Eliot and Nineteenth-Century Fiction*, London: Routledge & Kegan Paul.

BENVENUTO, BICE, and KENNEDY, ROGER (1986), *The Works of Jacques Lacan: An Introduction*, London: Free Association Books.

BENVENUTO, RICHARD (1970), 'Another Look at the Other Eustacia', *Novel*, 4, 77–9.

—— (1971), '*The Return of the Native* as a Tragedy in Six Books', *Nineteenth-Century Fiction*, 26, 83–93.

BJÖRK, LENNART A. (ed.) (1985), *The Literary Notebooks of Thomas Hardy*, 2 vols., London and Basingstoke: Macmillan.

BLAKE, KATHLEEN (1978), 'Sue Bridehead, "The Woman of the Feminist Movement"', *Studies in English Literature*, 18, 703–26; repr. in Bloom (1987*b*), 81–102.

BLOOM, HAROLD (ed.) (1987*a*), *Thomas Hardy*, Modern Critical Views, New York: Chelsea House.

—— (1987*b*), *Thomas Hardy's Jude the Obscure*, Modern Critical Interpretations, New York: Chelsea House.

—— (1987*c*), *Thomas Hardy's The Return of the Native*, Modern Critical Interpretations, New York: Chelsea House.

—— (1988), *Thomas Hardy's The Mayor of Casterbridge*, Modern Critical Interpretations, New York: Chelsea House.

BOUMELHA, PENNY (1982), *Thomas Hardy and Women: Sexual Ideology and Narrative Form*, Brighton: Harvester; Totowa, NJ: Barnes and Noble.

BRADY, KRISTIN (1986), 'Tess and Alec: Rape or Seduction?', in Page (1986), 127–47.

BROOKS, JEAN R. (1971), *Thomas Hardy: The Poetic Structure*, London: Elek.

BROWN, DOUGLAS (1961), *Thomas Hardy*, London: Longman, 1954; rev. edn. 1961.

—— (1962), *Thomas Hardy: The Mayor of Casterbridge*, London: Edward Arnold.

BULLEN, J. B. (1986), *The Expressive Eye: Fiction and Perception in the Work of Thomas Hardy*, Oxford and New York: Oxford University Press.

BUTLER, LANCE ST JOHN (1978), *Thomas Hardy*, Cambridge: Cambridge University Press.

CARPENTER, RICHARD (1960), 'Hardy's "Gurgoyles"', *Modern Fiction Studies*, 6, 223–32.

—— (1963–4), 'The Mirror and the Sword: Imagery in *Far from the Madding Crowd*', *Nineteenth-Century Fiction*, 18, 331–45.

—— (1964), *Thomas Hardy*, New York: Twayne.

CASAGRANDE, PETER J. (1971), 'The Shifted "Centre of Altruism" in *The Woodlanders*: Thomas Hardy's Third "Return of a Native"', *ELH* 38, 104–25.

—— (1977), 'Hardy's Wordsworth: A Record and a Commentary', *English Literature in Transition*, 20, 210–37.

—— (1979), 'A New View of Bathsheba Everdene', in Kramer (1979), 50–73.

—— and LOCK, CHARLES (1978), 'The Name "Henchard"', *Thomas Hardy Society Review*, 1, 115–18.

CHASE, MARY ELLEN (1964), *Thomas Hardy from Serial to Novel*, New York: Russell & Russell.

CHILDERS, MARY (1981), 'Thomas Hardy: The Man Who "Liked" Women', *Criticism*, 23, 317–34.

CLARIDGE, LAURA (1986), 'Tess: A Less than Pure Woman Ambivalently Presented', *Texas Studies in Literature and Language*, 28, 324–38.

CLARK, ANNA (1986), 'The Politics of Seduction in English Culture', in Radford (1986), 47–70.

CLARKE, ROBERT W. (1970), 'Hardy's Farmer Boldwood: Shadow of a Magnitude', *West Virginia University Philological Papers*, 17, 45–56.

COLLINS, PHILIP (1980), 'Hardy and Education', in Page (1980), 41–75.

COX, DON RICHARD (ed.) (1984), *Sexuality and Victorian Literature*, Knoxville, Tenn.: University of Tennessee Press.

CULLER, JONATHAN (1982), *On Deconstruction: Theory and Criticism after Structuralism*, Ithaca, NY: Cornell University Press.

CUNNINGHAM, A. R. (1973), 'The "New Woman Fiction" of the 1890s', *Victorian Studies*, 17, 177–86.

DALESKI, H. M. (1980), '*Tess of the d'Urbervilles*: Mastery and Abandon', *Essays in Criticism*, 30, 326–45.

DANBY, JOHN F. (1959), '*Under the Greenwood Tree*', *Critical Quarterly*, 1, 5–13.

DAVIDSON, DONALD (1940), 'The Traditional Basis of Thomas Hardy's Fiction', *Southern Review*, 6, 162–78; repr. in Davidson (1957), 43–61, and in Guerard (1963), 10–23.

—— (1957), *Still Rebels, Still Yankees*, Baton Rouge, La.: Louisiana State University Press.

DELEUZE, GILLES, and PARNET, CLAIRE (1977), *Dialogues*, Paris: Flammarion.

DELLAMORA, RICHARD (1989), *A Study of Masculine Desire*, Chapel Hill: University of North Carolina Press.

DIKE, D. A. (1952), 'A Modern Oedipus: *The Mayor of Casterbridge*', *Essays in Criticism*, 2, 169–79.

DRAFFAN, ROBERT A. (1973), 'Hardy's *Under the Greenwood Tree*', *English*, 22, 55–60.

DRAKE, ROBERT Y., jun. (1960), '"The Woodlanders" as Traditional Pastoral', *Modern Fiction Studies*, 6, 251–7.

DUFFIN, HENRY CHARLES (1937), *Thomas Hardy: A Study of the Wessex Novels, the Poems, and The Dynasts*, 1st edn. 1969; 2nd edn. rev. and enlarged, 1921; 3rd edn. with further revisions and additions, Manchester University Press, 1937; repr. Barnes and Noble, 1962, 1964, 1967.

EAGLETON, TERRY (1971), 'Thomas Hardy: Nature as Language', *Critical Quarterly*, 13, 155–62.

—— (1978), *Criticism and Ideology: A Study in Marxist Literary Theory*, London: NLB, 1976; London: Verso, 1978.

—— (1987), Introduction to the New Wessex Edition of *Jude the Obscure*, London: Macmillan, 1974, 13–23; repr. in Bloom (1987*b*), 61–71.

EASTMAN, DONALD (1978), 'Time and Propriety in *Far from the Madding Crowd*', *Interpretations*, 10, 20–33.

EBBATSON, J. R. (1975), 'The Darwinian View of Tess: A Reply', *Southern Review* (Adelaide), 8, 247–53.

—— (1982), *The Evolutionary Self: Hardy, Forster, Lawrence*, Brighton: Harvester; Totowa, NJ: Barnes and Noble.

EDWARDS, DUANE D. (1972), '*The Mayor of Casterbridge* as Aeschylean Tragedy', *Studies in the Novel*, 4, 608–18.

EGGENSCHWILER, DAVID (1970–1), 'Eustacia Vye, Queen of Night and Courtly Pretender', *Nineteenth-Century Fiction*, 25, 444–54.

ELLIOTT, RALPH W. V. (1984), *Thomas Hardy's English*, Oxford: Basil Blackwell.

ENSTICE, ANDREW, (1979), *Thomas Hardy: Landscapes of the Mind*, London: Macmillan.

ESCURET, ANNIE (1980), '*Tess des D'Urberville*: Le Corps et le signe', *Cahiers victoriens et édouardiens*, 12, 85–136.

EVANS, ROBERT (1968), 'The Other Eustacia', *Novel*, 1, 251–9.

FISCHLER, A. (1981), 'An Affinity for Birds: Kindness in Hardy's *Jude the Obscure*', *Studies in the Novel*, 13, 250–65.

—— (1984), 'Gins and Spirits: The Letter's Edge in *Jude the Obscure*', *Studies in the Novel*, 16, 1–19.

FLEISHMAN, AVROM (1987), 'The Buried Giant of Egdon Heath', in *Fiction and the Ways of Knowing: Essays on British Novels*, Austin, Tex.: University of Texas Press, 1978, 110–22; repr. in Bloom (1987*c*), 95–109.

FLETCHER, IAN (ed.) (1979), *Decadence and the 1890's*, London: Edward Arnold.

FREEMAN, JANET (1982), 'Ways of Looking at Tess', *Studies in Philology*, 79, 311–23.

FRYE, NORTHROP (1957), *Anatomy of Criticism: Four Essays*, Princeton, NJ: Princeton University Press.

—— (1968), *A Study of English Romanticism*, New York: Random House.

FUSSELL, D. H. (1979), 'The Maladroit Delay: The Changing Times in Thomas Hardy's *The Mayor of Casterbridge*', *Critical Quarterly*, 21/3, 17–30.

GALLOP, JANE (1982), *Feminism and Psychoanalysis: The Daughter's Seduction*, London: Macmillan.

GATRELL, SIMON (1979), 'Hardy the Creator: *Far from the Madding Crowd*', in Kramer (1979), 74–98.

GIORDANO, FRANK R., jun. (1978), 'Farmer Boldwood: Hardy's Portrait of a Suicide', *English Literature in Transition*, 21, 244–53.

—— (1984), '*I'd Have My Life Unbe*': *Thomas Hardy's Self-Destructive Characters*, University, Ala.: University of Alabama Press.

GITTINGS, ROBERT (1975), *Young Thomas Hardy*, London: Heinemann.

GOETZ, W. R. (1983), 'The Felicity and Infelicity of Marriage in *Jude the Obscure*', *Nineteenth-Century Fiction*, 38, 189–213.

GOODE, JOHN (1979*a*), 'The Decadent Writer as Producer', in Fletcher (1979), 109–30.

—— (1979*b*), 'Sue Bridehead and the New Woman', in Jacobus (1979*b*), 100–13.

—— (1988), *Thomas Hardy: The Offensive Truth*, Oxford: Basil Blackwell.

GORDON, JAN B. (1987), 'Origins, History, and the Reconstitution of Family: Tess's Journey', *ELH* 43 (1976), 366–88; repr. in Bloom (1987*a*), 115–35.

GREGOR, IAN (1974), *The Great Web: The Form of Hardy's Major Fiction*, London: Faber & Faber.

GRINDLE, JULIET (1979), 'Compulsion and Choice in *The Mayor of Casterbridge*', in Smith (1979), 91–106.

—— and GATRELL, SIMON (1983), General Introduction and Editorial Introduction to *Tess* (1983), *1–103* (page numbers in italic type refer to these introductions; those in roman type to variant readings collected by these editors).

GUERARD, ALBERT J. (1949), *Thomas Hardy: The Novels and Stories*, Cambridge, Mass.: Harvard University Press.

—— (ed.) (1963), *Hardy: A Collection of Critical Essays*, Englewood Cliffs, NJ: Prentice-Hall.

HAGAN, JOHN (1961–2), 'A Note on the Significance of Diggory Venn', *Nineteenth-Century Fiction*, 16, 147–55.

HARDY, FLORENCE EMILY (1928), *The Early Life of Thomas Hardy 1840–1891*, London: Macmillan.

—— (1930), *The Later Years of Thomas Hardy 1892–1928*, London: Macmillan.

HARMON, WILLIAM (1988), 'Only a Man: Notes on Thomas Hardy', *Parnassus*, 14/2, 287–309.

HARPER, CHARLES G. (1911), *The Hardy Country*, 2nd edn., London: Adam and Charles Black.

HARTVEIT, LARS (1977), 'Thomas Hardy, *The Mayor of Casterbridge*: The Persuasive Function of Character', in *The Art of Persuasion: A Study of Six Novels*, Oslo: Universitatsforlaget, 50–70.

HASSETT, MICHAEL E. (1971), 'Compromised Romanticism in *Jude the Obscure*', *Nineteenth-Century Fiction*, 25, 432–43.

HEILMAN, ROBERT B. (1966), 'Hardy's Sue Bridehead', *Nineteenth-Century Fiction*, 20, 307–23.

—— (1970), 'Gulliver and Hardy's Tess: Houhnhnms, Yahoos, and Ambiguities', *Southern Review*, NS 6, 277–301.

—— (1979), '*The Return*: Centennial Observations', in Smith (1979), 58–90.

HOWE, IRVING (1967), *Thomas Hardy*, New York: Macmillan.

INGHAM, PATRICIA (1976), 'The Evolution of *Jude the Obscure*', *Review of English Studies*, 27, 27–37 and 159–69.

IRIGARAY, LUCE (1985), *This Sex Which Is Not One*, trans. Catherine Porter and Carolyn Burke, Ithaca, NY: Cornell University Press.

JACOBUS, MARY (1975), 'Sue the Obscure', *Essays in Criticism*, 25, 304–28.

—— (1976*a*), 'Truthfulness and Taboo', *TLS* 3864 (2 Apr.), 403.

JACOBUS, MARY (1976*b*), 'Tess's Purity', *Essays in Criticism*, 26, 318–38.

—— (1979*a*), 'Tree and Machine: *The Woodlanders*', in Kramer (1979), 116–34.

—— (ed.) (1979*b*), *Women Writing and Writing about Women*, London: Croom Helm, in association with Oxford University Women's Studies Committee; Totowa, NJ: Barnes & Noble.

—— (1982), 'Hardy's Magian Retrospect', *Essays in Criticism*, 32, 258–79.

JAMESON, FREDRIC (1981), *The Political Unconscious: Narrative as a Socially Symbolic Act*, Ithaca, NY: Cornell University Press.

JOHNSON, BRUCE (1983), *True Correspondence: A Phenomenology of Thomas Hardy's Novels*, Tallahassee, Fla.: University Presses of Florida.

JOHNSON, LIONEL (1894), *The Art of Thomas Hardy*, 1894; rev. edn., New York: Dodd, Mead, 1923; repr. 1965.

JONES, LAWRENCE O. (1975), 'Imitation and Expression in Thomas Hardy's Theory of Fiction', *Studies in the Novel*, 7, 507–25.

—— (1978), ' "A Good Hand at a Serial": Thomas Hardy and the Serialization of *Far from the Madding Crowd*', *Studies in the Novel*, 10, 320–34.

JORDAN, MARY ELLEN (1982), 'Thomas Hardy's *The Return of the Native*: Clym Yeobright and Melancholia', *American Imago*, 39, 101–18.

KARL, FREDERICK R. (1975), '*The Mayor of Casterbridge*: A New Fiction Defined—1960, 1975', *Modern Fiction Studies*, 21, 405–28.

KAY-ROBINSON, DENYS (1972), *Hardy's Wessex Reappraised*, Newton Abbot: David & Charles.

KRAMER, DALE (1975), *Thomas Hardy: The Forms of Tragedy*, Detroit, Mich.: Wayne State University Press.

—— (ed.) (1979), *Critical Approaches to the Fiction of Thomas Hardy*, London: Macmillan.

—— (ed.) (1981), *The Woodlanders*, Oxford: Oxford University Press.

LACAN, JACQUES (1977*a*), *Écrits: A Selection*, trans. Alan Sheridan, London: Tavistock Publications.

—— (1977*b*), *The Four Fundamental Concepts of Psychoanalysis*, ed. Jacques-Alain Miller, trans. Alan Sheridan, London: Hogarth.

—— (1982), *Feminine Sexuality: Jacques Lacan and the École freudienne*, ed. Juliet Mitchell and Jacqueline Rose, trans. Jacqueline Rose, New York: Norton.

LAIRD, JOHN TUDOR (1975), *The Shaping of Tess of the d'Urbervilles*, Oxford: Oxford University Press.

—— (1980), 'New Light on the Evolution of *Tess of the d'Urbervilles*', *Review of English Studies*, NS 31, 414–35.

LANGLAND, ELIZABETH (1980), 'A Perspective of One's Own: Thomas Hardy and the Elusive Sue Bridehead', *Studies in the Novel*, 12, 12–28.

LAWRENCE, D. H. (1961), 'Study of Thomas Hardy', in *Phoenix: The Posthumous Papers of D. H. Lawrence*, ed. E. D. McDonald, New York: Viking, 1936; repr. London: Heinemann, 1961, 398–516.

LEA, HERMANN (1969), *Thomas Hardy's Wessex*, 1st edn., London: Macmillan, 1913; 2nd edn., London: Macmillan, 1925; 3rd edn., St Peter Port: Toucan Press, 1969.

LERNER, LAURENCE (1975), *Thomas Hardy's The Mayor of Casterbridge: Tragedy or Social History*, London: Sussex University Press.

LEVINE, GEORGE (1981), 'Thomas Hardy's *The Mayor of Casterbridge*: Reversing the Real', in *The Realistic Imagination: English Fiction from Frankenstein to Lady Chatterley*, Chicago, Ill.: University of Chicago Press, 1981, 229–51; repr. in Bloom (1988), 69–94.

LODGE, DAVID (1966), 'Tess, Nature and the Voices of Hardy', in *Language of Fiction: Essays in Criticism and Verbal Analysis of the English Novel*, London: Routledge & Kegan Paul; NY: Columbia University Press.

—— (1974*a*), Introduction to the New Wessex Edition of *The Woodlanders*, London: Macmillan.

—— (1974*b*), 'Thomas Hardy and Cinematographic Form', *Novel*, 7, 246–54.

—— (1979), '*Jude the Obscure*: Pessimism and Fictional Form', in Kramer (1979), 193–201.

MCCANN, ELEANOR (1961), 'Blind Will or Blind Hero: Philosophy and Myth in Hardy's "The Return of the Native"', *Criticism*, 3, 140–57.

MACCANNELL, JULIET FLOWER (1986), *Figuring Lacan: Criticism and the Cultural Unconscious*, London: Croom Helm; Lincoln, Nebr.: University of Nebraska Press.

MARTIN, BRUCE K. (1972), 'Whatever Happened to Eustacia Vye?', *Studies in the Novel*, 4, 619–27.

MAY, CHARLES E. (1974), '*Far from the Madding Crowd* and *The Woodlanders*: Hardy's Grotesque Pastorals', *English Literature in Transition*, 17, 147–58.

MEISEL, PERRY (1972), *Thomas Hardy: The Return of the Repressed*, New Haven, Conn., and London: Yale University Press.

MEREDITH, GEORGE (1970), *The Letters of George Meredith*, ed. C. L. Cline, Oxford: Oxford University Press.

MILLER, J. HILLIS (1970), *Thomas Hardy: Distance and Desire*, Cambridge, Mass.: Harvard University Press.

—— (1982), '*Tess of the d'Urbervilles*: Repetition as Immanent

Design', in *Fiction and Repetition: Seven English Novels*, Cambridge, Mass.: Harvard University Press, 116–46.

MILLGATE, MICHAEL (1971*a*), 'Hardy's Fiction: Some Comments on the Present State of Criticism', *English Literature in Transition*, 14, 230–8.

—— (1971*b*), *Thomas Hardy: His Career as a Novelist*, London: Bodley Head; New York: Random House.

—— (1982), *Thomas Hardy: A Biography*, New York: Random House.

MOI, TORIL (1985), *Sexual/Textual Politics: Feminist Literary Theory*, London: Methuen.

MORGAN, ROSEMARIE (1988), *Women and Sexuality in the Novels of Thomas Hardy*, London: Routledge & Kegan Paul.

MORGAN, WILLIAM (1986), 'The Novel as Risk and Compromise, Poetry as Safe Haven: Hardy and the Victorian Reading Public', *Victorian Newsletter*, 69, 1–3.

MORRELL, ROY (1965), *Thomas Hardy: The Will and the Way*, Kuala Lumpur: University of Malaya Press.

MORTON, PETER B. (1974), 'Tess of the d'Urbervilles: A Neo-Darwinian Reading', *Southern Review* (Adelaide), 7, 38–50.

—— (1975), '*Tess* and August Weismann: Unholy Alliance', *Southern Review* (Adelaide), 8, 254–6.

MULLER, J. P., and RICHARDSON, W. J. (1978), *Lacan and Language: A Reader's Guide to 'Écrits'*, New York: International Universities Press.

OLIPHANT, MARGARET (1896), 'The Anti-Marriage League', *Blackwood's Magazine*, 159, 135–49.

OREL, HAROLD (ed.) (1966), *Thomas Hardy's Personal Writings: Prefaces, Literary Opinions, Reminiscences*, Wichita, Kan.: University of Kansas Press.

OSBORNE, L. MacKENZIE (1972), 'The "Chronological Frontier" in Thomas Hardy's Novels', *Studies in the Novel*, 4, 543–55.

PAGE, NORMAN (1977), *Thomas Hardy*, London, Boston, Mass.: Routledge & Kegan Paul.

—— (ed.) (1980), *Thomas Hardy: The Writer and His Background*, London: Bell & Hyman.

—— (ed.) (1985), *Thomas Hardy Annual No. 3*, Houndmills, Basingstoke: Macmillan.

—— (ed.) (1986), *Thomas Hardy Annual No. 4*, Houndmills, Basingstoke: Macmillan.

PARIS, BERNARD J. (1969), 'A Confusion of Many Standards: Conflicting Value Systems in *Tess of the d'Urbervilles*', *Nineteenth-Century Fiction*, 24, 57–79.

PARTRIDGE, ERIC (1984), *A Dictionary of Slang and Unconventional*

English, 8th edn., ed. Paul Beale, London: Routledge & Kegan Paul.

PATERSON, JOHN (1959*a*), '*The Mayor of Casterbridge* as Tragedy', *Victorian Studies*, 3, 151–72; repr. in Guerard (1963), 91–112.

—— (1959*b*), '*The Return of the Native* as an Antichristian Document', *Nineteenth-Century Fiction*, 14, 111–27.

—— (1960*a*), 'The Genesis of *Jude the Obscure*', *Studies in Philology*, 57, 87–98.

—— (1960*b*), *The Making of 'The Return of the Native'*, Berkeley, Calif.: University of California Press.

PAULIN, TOM (1975), *Thomas Hardy: The Poetry of Perception*, London: Macmillan.

PECK, JOHN (1981*a*), 'Hardy and Joyce: A Basis for Comparison', *Ariel*, 12, 71–85.

—— (1981*b*), 'Hardy's *The Woodlanders*: The Too Transparent Web', *English Literature in Transition*, 24, 147–54.

PICKREL, PAUL (1988), '*Jude the Obscure* and the Fall of Phaeton', *Hudson Review*, 39, 231–50.

PINION, F. B. (ed.) (1976), *Budmouth Essays on Thomas Hardy: Papers Presented at the 1975 Summer School*, Dorchester: Thomas Hardy Society.

POOLE, ADRIAN (1981), ' "Men's Words" and Hardy's Women', *Essays in Criticism*, 31, 328–45.

PROUST, MARCEL (1954), *A la recherche du temps perdu*, ed. Pierre Clarac and André Ferré, Paris; Librairie Gallimard.

RADFORD, JEAN (ed.) (1986), *The Progress of Romance: The Politics of Popular Fiction*, London: Methuen.

ROBINSON, ROGER (1980), 'Hardy and Darwin', in Page (1980), 128–49.

ROGERS, KATHLEEN (1975), 'Women in Thomas Hardy', *Centennial Review*, 19, 249–58.

ROONEY, ELLEN (1983), 'Criticism and the Subject of Sexual Violence', *Modern Language Notes*, 98, 1269–78.

ROSE, JACQUELINE (1982), 'Introduction-II', in Lacan (1982), 27–57.

RUSKIN, JOHN (1904), *The Works of John Ruskin*, ed. E. T. Cook and Alexander Wedderburn, London: George Allen.

SALDIVAR, RAMON (1983), '*Jude the Obscure*: Reading and the Spirit of the Law', *ELH* 50, 607–25; repr. in Bloom (1987*a*), 191–205; Bloom (1987*b*), 103–18.

SCARRY, ELAINE (1983), 'Work and the Body in Hardy and Other Nineteenth-Century Novelists', *Representations*, 1/3, 90–123.

SCHWARZ, DANIEL R. (1979), 'Beginnings and Endings in Hardy's Major Fiction', in Kramer (1979), 17–35.

SCHWEIK, ROBERT C. (1962), 'Moral Perspectives in *Tess of the d'Urbervilles*', *College English*, 24, 14–18.

—— (1968), 'The Early Development of Hardy's *Far from the Madding Crowd*', *Texas Studies in Language and Literature*, 9, 415–28.

SÉNÉCHEL, JANIE (1980), 'Focalisation, regard et désir dans *Far from the Madding Crowd*', *Cahiers victoriens et édouardiens*, 12, 73–83.

SHERREN, WILKINSON (1908), *The Wessex of Romance*, London: Chapman, 1902; repr. London: Griffiths, 1908.

SHOWALTER, ELAINE (1979), 'The Unmanning of the Mayor of Casterbridge', in Kramer (1979), 99–115; repr. in Bloom (1987*a*), 175–89; Bloom (1988), 53–68.

SILVERMAN, KAJA (1984), 'History, Figuration and Female Subjectivity in *Tess of the d'Urbervilles*', *Novel*, 18, 5–28.

SLACK, ROBERT C. (1957), 'The Text of Hardy's *Jude the Obscure*', *Nineteenth-Century Fiction*, 11, 261–75.

SMITH, ANNE (ed.) (1979), *The Novels of Thomas Hardy*, New York: Barnes & Noble; London: Vision Press.

SNELL, K. D. M. (1985), *Annals of the Labouring Poor: Social Change and Agrarian England, 1660–1900*, Cambridge: Cambridge University Press.

SPACKS, PATRICIA MEYER (1985), *Gossip*, New York: Knopf.

SPECTOR, STEPHEN J. (1988), 'Flight of Fancy: Characterization in Hardy's *Under the Greenwood Tree*', *ELH* 55, 469–85.

STARZYK, LAWRENCE J. (1972), 'Hardy's *The Mayor of Casterbridge*: The Antitraditional Basis of Tragedy', *Studies in the Novel*, 4, 592–607.

STEIG, MICHAEL (1968), 'Sue Bridehead', *Novel*, 1, 260–6.

—— (1970–1), 'The Problem of Literary Value in Two Early Hardy Novels', *Texas Studies in Literature and Language*, 12, 55–62.

—— (1975), 'Fantasy and Mimesis in Literary Character: Shelley, Hardy, and Lawrence', *English Studies in Canada*, 1, 160–71.

STEVICK, PHILIP (1970), *The Chapter in Fiction: Theories of Narrative Division*, Syracuse, NY: Syracuse University Press.

STEWART, J. I. M. (1971), *Thomas Hardy: A Critical Biography*, London: Longman.

SULLIVAN, TOM R. (1974), 'The Temporal Leitmotif in *Far from the Madding Crowd*', *Colby Library Quarterly*, series 10/5, 296–303.

SUMNER, ROSEMARY (1985), 'Some Surrealist Elements in Hardy's Prose and Verse', in Page (1985), 39–53.

TANNER, TONY (1968), 'Colour and Movement in Hardy's *Tess of the d'Urbervilles*', *Critical Quarterly*, 10, 219–39.

VAN GHENT, DOROTHY (1953), 'On *Tess of the D'Urbervilles*', in *The English Novel: Form and Function*, New York: Holt, Rinehart and Winston, 195–209.

VIGAR, PENELOPE (1974), *The Novels of Thomas Hardy: Illusion and Reality*, University of London: Athlone Press.

WELSH, ALEXANDER (1975), 'Realism as a Practical and Cosmic Joke', *Novel*, 9, 23–39.

WICKENS, G. GLEN (1983), 'Hardy and the Aesthetic Mythographers: The Myth of Demeter and Persephone in *Tess of the d'Urbervilles*', *University of Toronto Quarterly*, 53, 85–106.

WIDDOWSON, PETER (1989), *Hardy in History: A Study in Literary Sociology*, London: Routledge.

WILLIAMS, MERRYN (1972), *Thomas Hardy and Rural England*, London: Macmillan.

—— and WILLIAMS, RAYMOND (1980), 'Hardy and Social Class', in Page (1980), 29–40.

WILLIAMS, RAYMOND (1973), *The Country and the City*, London: Chatto & Windus.

WINFIELD, CHRISTINE (1973), 'The Manuscript of Hardy's *Mayor of Casterbridge*', *Papers of the Bibliographical Society of America*, 67, 37–58; repr. in the Norton Critical Edition of *The Mayor of Casterbridge*, ed. James K. Robinson, New York: Norton, 1977, 266–87.

WINTER, MICHAEL (1980), 'A Note towards an Historical and Class Analysis of Thomas Hardy's Novels', *Literature and History*, 6, 174–81.

WOTTON, GEORGE (1985), *Thomas Hardy: Towards a Materialist Criticism*, Dublin: Gill & Macmillan; Totowa, NJ: Barnes & Noble.

WRIGHT, ELIZABETH (1984), *Psychoanalytic Criticism: Theory in Practice*, London: Methuen, ch. 7.

Index